Academic Success Strategies for Adolescents with Learning Disabilities and ADHD

Academic Success Strategies for Adolescents with Learning Disabilities and ADHD

by

Esther Minskoff, Ph.D.
James Madison University
Harrisonburg, Virginia

and

David Allsopp, Ph.D.
University of South Florida
Tampa

·PAUL·H·
BROOKES
PUBLISHING CO.®

Baltimore · London · Sydney

Paul H. Brookes Publishing Co.
Post Office Box 10624
Baltimore, Maryland 21285-0624

www.brookespublishing.com

Typeset by A.W. Bennett, Inc., Hartland, Vermont.
Printed in the United States of America by
Versa Press, East Peoria, Illinois.

The chapter opener graphics for Chapters 1, 2, 4, 5, 6, 12, and 13 are from http://dgl.microsoft.com.

The chapter opener graphics for Chapters 3, 7, 8, 9, 10, and 11 are from Discoveryschool.com.

Library of Congress Cataloging-in-Publication Data

Minskoff, Esther H. (Esther Hirsch)
   Academic success strategies for adolescents with learning disabilities and ADHD / by
Esther Minskoff and David Allsopp.
     p.   cm.
   Includes bibliographical references and index.
   ISBN 1-55766-625-3
   1. Learning disabled teenagers–Education–Handbooks, manuals, etc.   2. Attention-deficit-
disordered youth–Education–Handbooks, manuals, etc.   3. Attention-deficit hyperactivity
disorder–Handbooks, manuals, etc.   4. Active learning–Handbooks, manuals, etc.
I. Allsopp, David, Ph.D.   II. Title.
LC4704.74 .M56 2002
371.92'6–dc21

2002026245

British Library Cataloging in Publication data are available from the British Library.

Contents

About the Authors

Esther Minskoff, Ph.D., Professor of Special Education, James Madison University, 800 South Main Street, MSC 1903, Harrisonburg, Virginia 22807

Esther Minskoff has taught graduate and undergraduate courses in learning disabilities at James Madison University since 1975. She has served as Project Director for two federally funded grants—Steppingstones of Technology Innovations and a Model Demonstration Postsecondary Education Project. She has published extensively in journals and is the co-author of the *Phonics Remedial Reading Lessons* (co-authored with S.A. Kirk & W.D. Kirk, Academic Therapy Publications, 1985). Dr. Minskoff served as President of the Division for Learning Disabilities of the Council for Exceptional Children and was a member of the Professional Advisory Board of the Learning Disabilities Association of America.

David Allsopp, Ph.D., Associate Professor, Department of Special Education, University of South Florida, 4202 East Fowler Avenue, EDUC 162, Tampa, Florida 33620

David Allsopp received his doctorate in special education from the University of Florida in 1995. Prior to this, he was a teacher for middle school students with learning disabilities and emotional/behavior problems in Marion County, Florida. Dr. Allsopp's research and writing interests have focused primarily on instructional methods for students with learning and behavior problems. He has authored or co-authored journal articles, has co-developed instructional development web sites and CD-ROMs, has co-authored multiple federal- and state-funded grants, and regularly presents at state and national conferences. Dr. Allsopp is a member of the Learning Disabilities Association of America and Phi Delta Kappa. He continues to be involved in public schools by working collaboratively with schools and school districts to develop effective school–university partnerships.

Preface

We believe that *Academic Success Strategies for Adolescents with Learning Disabilities and ADHD* is unique because it represents a fusion of the past, the present, and the future of special education. Perhaps this is due, in part, to the generation difference of the authors—Dr. Minskoff is one of the pioneers in the field of learning disabilities and Dr. Allsopp is a member of a new breed of advocates of research-based, best educational practices. Our book is historically anchored to the basic philosophy underpinning the field of learning disabilities; it is contemporaneously anchored to the latest research, issues, and trends in education; and it is futuristically anchored to the use of the most current technology.

The past is represented in our book by the diagnostic/prescriptive approach that we embedded in our basic instructional approach, which we have called the Active Learner Approach. Dr. Minskoff's training with Dr. Sam Kirk and Dr. Allsopp's training with Dr. Cecil Mercer laid the foundation for our basic philosophy, which is the essence of individualization (i.e., we need to identify a child's specific learning strengths and weaknesses and design instruction accordingly). The past is also represented by our experiences as teachers and researchers. We know from our classroom experiences, as well as our research findings, that what is presented in this book is representative of instruction that is effective for improving the educational performance of students with learning disabilities and ADHD.

Special education's present is represented in our book by incorporating current research findings regarding the effectiveness of systematic, direct instruction and strategy instruction. The Active Learner Approach reflects the key instructional features that make systematic instruction and strategy instruction effective. In addition, our book is responsive to current educational issues and trends, especially those involving the integration of students with disabilities into general education and their participation in high-stakes testing. We strongly believe that special education must help students with learning disabilities and ADHD and their teachers meet the rigorous academic challenges of today's schools. To this end, we have designed a course-specific approach to strategy instruction. With this approach, strategies are tailored to help students master learning of the specific content of their courses and successfully complete assignments and tests demonstrating such learning mastery.

Special education's future is represented by our integration of technology to deliver the Active Learner Approach. Our book is best used in conjunction with the Learning Toolbox web site, which we developed for students with learning disabilities, their teachers, and their parents. We believe that on-line delivery of instruction can be viable for students with learning disabilities and ADHD *if* their learning strengths and weaknesses are considered. We have designed the Learning Toolbox to take into consideration the issues of accessibility, navigability, and usability in relationship to student characteristics. The Learning Toolbox is responsive to the specific needs of students with learning disabilities and ADHD because it has reduced amounts of text for reading; uses graphics to enhance the meaning of the reading material; provides a consistent structure for gaining access to the various Learning Toolbox sites; and eliminates distracting stimuli such as nonpurposeful animations and sound effects. To get maximum benefit from *Academic Success Strategies for Adolescents with Learning Disabilities and ADHD,* we urge you to use the on-line presentation of the strategies with your students by gaining access to the Learning Toolbox at http://coe.jmu.edu/learningtoolbox.

We believe that your use of the Active Learner Approach and the specific strategies in our book will make a positive difference in the lives of your students. Although the Active Learner Approach and the corresponding strategies provide an excellent foundation for success, even more important is your belief that your students can and will learn more effectively.

Acknowledgments

The instructional approach and specific strategies in this book were developed by the authors with input from colleagues and former graduate students over a number of years. We thank our colleagues, Jerry Minskoff and Maggie Kyger, for their contributions regarding the direction of the book as well as construction of specific strategies. In addition, we thank Lou Hedrick for helping us to understand the challenges faced by college students with disabilities.

A number of the strategies were developed over the 3-year period of our federally funded Model Demonstration Project for College Students with Learning Disabilities and ADHD in conjunction with graduate assistants who worked as tutors on the project. We are most appreciative of the significant contributions to the development of these strategies by the following James Madison University graduate students: Clinton Sower, Noelle Loue, Katy Elmore, Craig Stoll, Stephanie Foss, Holly Williams, Sam Herr, Lynn Pruszkowski, Jason Roberts, Karla Fitchett, Sharon Estock, Micki Edwards, Caryn Jones, Jennifer Sivigny, and Melody Zimmerman. We also thank the many college and high school students who were tutored by these students and who helped us modify the strategies to meet their special needs.

To my husband Jerry, for his never-ending support for our professional and personal partnership based on eternal love and respect; to my children, Nancy, Rob, and Sandy, for teaching me that a mother is the most important teacher a child has (EM)

To Margaret, my wife, whom I love deeply; to my parents, Marilyn and Ed; to my brothers, Eddie and John, without whom I would not be where I am today; to Danelle and Nancy, the two best teachers I have ever known; and lastly, to my former students at Osceola and Fort King Middle Schools, who truly taught me the wonder of living, of loving, and of learning (DA)

Academic Success Strategies for Adolescents with Learning Disabilities and ADHD

Tailoring Your Instruction for Academic Success

1

An Overview of the Active Learner Approach

- What is the purpose of the Active Learner Approach?

- What are the elements of the Active Learner Approach?

- Who are the target populations for the Active Learner Approach?

- What basic assumptions underlie the Active Learner Approach?

- What is the research foundation for the Active Learner Approach?

- How can the Learning Toolbox be used with this manual?

WHAT IS THE PURPOSE
OF THE ACTIVE LEARNER APPROACH?

There are many manuals and guides available for teaching students with *mild disabilities* (defined in this text as students who have been diagnosed with learning disabilities or attention-deficit/hyperactivity disorder [ADHD]). Most of these resources focus *either* on remedial methods for developing basic academic skills to be used in special education settings *or* on accommodations and modifications of the general curriculum to be used in inclusive settings. This manual is different in that it is *designed to assist special educators who work with students with mild disabilities to become more effective learners so that they can better meet the increasingly rigorous academic expectations of inclusive settings.* Our specialized approach, the Active Learner Approach, must be provided by special educators and focus on the inclusive setting to ensure that students are actively using effective learning strategies to meet the academic demands of the general education classroom.

Two pillars provide the foundation for the Active Learner Approach: 1) consideration of the *unique learning characteristics* of students with mild disabilities and 2) analysis of the *educational expectations* of students with mild disabilities in inclusive settings. Many students with mild disabilities possess characteristics that make them ineffective learners, including passive learning style, poor memory, and attention problems. The Active Learner Approach is designed to directly address these ineffective learning characteristics and replace them with more effective learning strategies. In addition, the Active Learner Approach focuses on the specific academic expectations of a student's educational placement (e.g., if students are reading a chapter about the Civil War and taking a multiple-choice test, then the Active Learner Approach will focus on this material and the skills needed for taking a multiple-choice test based on the chapter). For a complete discussion of these two pillars, see Chapter 2.

There is a critical need to use the Active Learner Approach because of changes in federal legislation involving educational practices for students with mild disabilities. The Individuals with Disabilities Education Act (IDEA) Amendments of 1997, PL 105-17, mandate that a student's individualized education program (IEP) goals and objectives be related to the general education curriculum and that students with disabilities participate in all state and local assessments. Students with mild disabilities must meet the rigorous academic expectations of the general education curriculum if they are to be successful in school and in careers after school. These rigorous academic demands have evolved from two educational trends, one involving increasingly difficult requirements for general education diplomas and the other involving mastery of higher level academic content to pass high-stakes tests. These trends are described in Chapter 2.

WHAT ARE THE ELEMENTS OF THE ACTIVE LEARNER APPROACH?

The Active Learner Approach includes three essential elements: individualized evaluation and intervention; cognitive learning strategy instruction; and systematic, explicit instruction. These three elements are derived from well-established best practices in special education.

Individualized Evaluation and Intervention

There must be an in-depth assessment of a student's learning characteristics in relation to the specific demands of his academic courses. The evaluation seeks to identify both a student's strengths and weaknesses. Then, intervention must be designed based on an analysis of the student's course demands and his strengths and weaknesses. Although individualized evaluation and intervention are based on the diagnostic/prescriptive approach (Lerner, 2000)—a key aspect of special education for students with learning disabilities since Sam Kirk started the field in the early 1960s (Minskoff, 1998)—many aspects of the Active Learner Approach are unique. For example, evaluation focuses on a student's learning characteristics in relationship to course-specific needs. With other approaches, evaluation focuses on formal standardized tests. Individualized evaluation is described in Chapter 3.

Cognitive Learning Strategy Instruction

Students are taught to use strategies to more effectively master the school content of their curriculum through cognitive learning strategies. The instruction focuses on the student; the teacher guides the student to master new skills to meet academic course demands. Instruction on cognitive learning strategies is a well-established best practice in special education (Deshler, Ellis, & Lenz, 1996). Some approaches to cognitive learning strategy instruction are general and teach the students strategies, but the students are left to discover how to apply them to the specific demands of their courses (e.g., a 2-week workshop on study skills). The approach taken with the Active Learner Approach involves course-specific strategy instruction. Students are first taught cognitive learning strategies and then taught to apply these to meet the demands of their classes. In addition, the strategy instruction is not time limited (e.g., to 2 weeks) but rather is intense and prolonged. Cognitive learning strategy instruction is fully described in Chapter 4.

Systematic, Explicit Instruction

The focus during systematic, explicit instruction is on the teacher. Students with mild disabilities are hard to teach and may not learn unless they are provided with explicit instruction. The systematic instruction involved in the Active Learner Approach involves one-to-one intervention in which the teacher models the skill, guides the practice of the skill, and, finally, monitors independent practice and application of the skill in conjunction with the general education teacher. Systematic instruction, often called *direct instruction,* is another well-established practice from the field of special education that has been found to be effective in assisting students with disabilities to learn (Carnine, 1999; Swanson, 1999). The role of systematic instruction in the Active Learner Approach is presented in Chapter 4.

WHO ARE THE TARGET POPULATIONS
FOR THE ACTIVE LEARNER APPROACH?

The Active Learner Approach was designed for adolescents and adults with mild disabilities who are being required to master academic content at the middle school, secondary, and postsecondary levels. Most of these students have already mastered the basic skills of reading, writing, and arithmetic. They must now learn how to apply these skills to learn academic content effectively and independently.

Special education teachers at the middle and secondary levels who teach in a resource setting and/or co-teach in the general education setting compose another target population. They should use the Active Learner Approach with their students and monitor student usage of the approach in general education classes. Too often, special educators who work at the middle and secondary levels are merely tutors who reteach content or administer accommodations. The Active Learner Approach is more challenging than a tutorial approach because it requires teachers to master the basic systematic, explicit instructional approach as well as be knowledgeable about a number of different cognitive learning strategies. Chapter 5 describes how to use the Active Learner Approach, and Chapters 6–13 present the cognitive learning strategies for the areas of organization, test taking, study skills, notetaking, reading, writing, math, and advanced thinking.

More students with mild disabilities are entering postsecondary education (Henderson, 1998), so personnel who work with these students must determine whether these students need instruction to become more effective learners. For those students who need this instruction, there must be personnel available who have training in special education. Such personnel may provide services through the Division for Disability Services or resources available to all students (e.g., the writing lab).

WHAT BASIC ASSUMPTIONS
UNDERLIE THE ACTIVE LEARNER APPROACH?

One of the basic assumptions underlying the Active Learner Approach involves the division of labor between general and special educators. General educators have expertise in the specific academic subject matter that they teach. They have the expertise in the "what" of teaching. It is impossible for general or special educators to know how to teach all subject matter areas at all academic levels. Special educators have expertise in modifying the subject matter to make it more learner friendly, and they have expertise in teaching students how to become better learners. They have expertise in the "how" of teaching. The purpose of this manual is to assist special educators to acquire this expertise.

Another assumption underlying the Active Learner Approach is that the nature of special education varies at different instructional levels and for different students depending on their academic, learning, and attitudinal characteristics. The primary emphasis of special education at the elementary level should be on the remediation of academic learning problems. For students who have adequate cognitive and academic functioning for their school placement and who are motivated to succeed academically, the emphasis at the middle and secondary levels should move to an approach that develops independent learning strategies in the students. For students who have low cognitive and academic levels and/or are not motivated to succeed in school, a functional and/or remedial approach may be more appropriate.

The third assumption is that students with mild disabilities can learn new knowledge and skills at any age, even at the secondary and postsecondary levels. Many believe that an approach that advocates accommodations and avoidance of students' disabilities is the best approach, especially for older students. Such a compensatory approach does *not* prepare students to learn the rigorous academic content they need for school success. A remedial approach that seeks to develop new skills and knowledge to enable students with mild disabilities to meet rigorous academic demands will prepare them for school success. The research described in the next section supports this assumption. Even college students who were on academic probation and suspension were able to master the strategies of the Active Learner Approach and significantly improve their grades (Minskoff, Minskoff, & Allsopp, 2001). These findings support the conclusion that educators should never give up trying to teach new skills and knowledge to students with disabilities who are motivated to learn.

WHAT IS THE RESEARCH FOUNDATION FOR THE ACTIVE LEARNER APPROACH?

The approach described in this manual is based on more than 20 years of extensive research with students with mild disabilities at all levels of instruction and with different subject matter areas. Much of the research is based on the experience of Dr. Minskoff, who served on two federally funded grants to train secondary level teachers of students with learning disabilities. Dr. Minskoff has also been involved in three federally funded grants on transition and vocational rehabilitation for adolescents and adults with learning disabilities. Dr. Allsopp has received grants to develop Math Vids, an interactive web site for teaching math to students with math learning disabilities.

In 2001, we completed a study of the elements of the Active Learner Approach with college students with mild disabilities (Minskoff, Minskoff, & Allsopp, 2001). Both qualitative and quantitative analysis of the grades for student performance for semesters before, during, and after intervention with the Active Learner Approach indicated that the students made significant improvement in grades as a result of the Active Learner Approach. They were able to sustain these improvements after intervention. Of the 46 students, 50% significantly improved in their overall grade point average; of the 19 students who were on academic suspension or probation, 47% improved to good standing. Also, students improved in grades for the courses that were the focus of the course-specific instruction, thereby supporting the effectiveness of the course-specific strategy approach. In one instance, a student received an *A* in a course that she had previously failed. Her professor wrote the following on one of her tests: *"Nothing makes teaching more worthwhile than for a student to show the type of progress you show here. Thanks for your persistence and congratulations to you and your tutor."*

HOW CAN THE LEARNING TOOLBOX BE USED WITH THIS MANUAL?

Based on the positive results of the study with college students, we received a federal grant to field test a web site using the Active Learner Approach with high school students, their teachers, and their parents to determine whether the Internet can provide an effective means for delivering instruction to students with learning disabilities and ADHD. This web site, titled the Learning Toolbox, includes the same instructional approach and strategies as presented in this manual and can be found at http://coe.jmu.edu/learningtoolbox. It is recommended that the Learning Toolbox be used in conjunction with this manual. Presenting the strategies using the Learning Toolbox should be used in addition to traditional methods of presentation such as chalkboards, charts, and print versions of the strategies.

Before using the Learning Toolbox with students, be sure you explore all parts of the web site so that you can readily navigate it, and read the teacher directions. There are video clips included in the directions, which present in-depth examples of how a teacher uses the Active Learner Approach with a reading comprehension strategy tailored to the specific classroom needs of a high school student. If you have limited experience with systematic instruction and fitting instruction to meet the unique general education needs of students, then it is strongly recommended that you watch these video clips because they clearly show the various steps in using this instructional approach.

One of the learning strategies that is emphasized in this manual is the use of visualization, in which students are taught to mentally picture graphics that will help them understand and recall information (see Chapter 4). The graphics provided with each of the strategies should be viewed as a visualization strategy. For example, for the test-taking strategy, BRAVE, students are taught to overcome nervousness while taking a test. The first step involves breathing deeply. The graphic corresponding to this step shows a pair of lungs. Students are encouraged to picture this graphic as a cue to breathe deeply when they find that they are experiencing anxiety while taking a test.

Another advantage of using the Learning Toolbox is accessibility when students are in different settings, especially at home. Students should be encouraged to gain access to the strategies they are learning in different settings so that they learn to generalize their use. If parents want to be involved in helping with their children's education, then parent accessibility to the web site should be encouraged as a means of providing additional guided practice.

The Learning Toolbox should be viewed as a way of extending and enriching the Active Learner Approach presented in this manual. This web site provides a means for linking traditional instruction via teacher direction with electronic instruction.

GETTING STARTED

Follow the directions presented in Chapter 3 of this manual for identifying a student's specific needs by using the Active Learner Questionnaires for Students and Teachers (see Appendixes A and B) as well as student responsiveness to general education classroom demands. Once you have identified a student's specific needs, select the corresponding strategies to be taught. Each strategy should be taught to the student using different formats. The first format uses the web site. As you model each step of the strategy, point out the graphics and how they will help the student better understand and recall the steps. A second format for presentation of the strategies uses charts hung around the classroom so that students can gain access to a strategy whenever they need to use it. Be sure to model each step on a chart and relate each step to the step shown on the Learning Toolbox. Finally, have the students keep a strategy notebook with the print versions of the strategies they are learning so that they can gain access to them whenever and wherever they need them. Print versions of the strategies can be found at www.brookespublishing.com/minskoff.

2

Foundation for the
Active Learner
Approach

**Active
Learner
Approach**

- What are the two pillars underlying the Active Learner Approach?

- How are ineffective learner characteristics related to learning advanced academic content?

- What are the academic expectations for students with mild disabilities in general education classes?

WHAT ARE THE TWO PILLARS
UNDERLYING THE ACTIVE LEARNER APPROACH?

The Active Learner Approach is tailored to students with mild disabilities who have been placed in a new educational situation (i.e., the general education classroom). Until the enactment of the Individuals with Disabilities Education Act (IDEA) Amendments of 1997 (PL 105-17), a large number of students with mild disabilities were educated outside the general education classroom and did not have to participate in the general education curriculum or the high-stakes assessment required of students without disabilities. In fact, only 50% of students with disabilities participated in state- and districtwide assessment prior to the 1997 IDEA amendments (Heubert & Hauser, 1999). General education placement rates for students with learning disabilities grew by 151% from 1993 to 1999. This increase has been attributed to more students being identified as having learning disabilities and the movement of students from resource settings to general education classroom settings (McLesky, Henry, & Axelrod, 1999). Hence, the nature of the demands on students with mild disabilities has changed dramatically. Previously, there may have been lower academic expectations of students with mild disabilities in special education settings. One of the reasons underlying the push to place students with mild disabilities in the general education classroom has been to raise academic expectations for them.

In order to meet the rigorous academic demands of the general education curriculum, students must know how to learn. They must know how to use strategies to master different types of content (e.g., historical facts versus math concepts) for different purposes (e.g., writing an essay versus taking a multiple-choice test). By virtue of their disabilities, many students with mild disabilities have ineffective learning characteristics, making it difficult for them to meet these academic demands. There are many characteristics that have been ascribed to students with learning disabilities (Lerner, 2000), but only those that are relevant to learning rigorous academic content are considered here. Characteristics such as motor or phonological awareness problems that are frequently associated with learning disabilities are important but not for mastery of advanced academic content. It is recognized that they are essential for analyzing performance of students with mild disabilities for other purposes (e.g., problems with learning to use cursive writing, problems with learning phonics).

The Active Learner Approach involves individualized evaluation of a student's learning characteristics and analysis of how a student responds to the academic demands of the curriculum (see Chapter 3). The learning characteristics that were used as the basis for designing the Active Learner Approach are presented in Table 2.1 and include:

- Active learner versus passive learner

- Independent learner versus learned helplessness

- Metacognitive strengths versus metacognitive weaknesses

- Strong cognitive processes versus weak cognitive processes

- Memory strengths versus memory weaknesses

- Attention strengths versus attention weaknesses

- Good impulse control versus poor impulse control

- Generalization strengths versus generalization weaknesses

Table 2.1. Learning characteristics of students with mild disabilities and the Active Learner Approach

Effective learner characteristics	Ineffective learner characteristics
Active learner	**Passive learner**
Uses strategies and activates prior knowledge	Does not use strategies or activate prior knowledge
Independent learner	**Learned helplessness**
Approaches learning and studying without teacher prompting and guidance	Needs constant prompting and guidance when learning or studying
Metacognitive strengths	**Metacognitive weaknesses**
Monitors learning and thinking processes	Does not monitor learning and thinking processes
Plans ahead	Does not plan ahead
Strong cognitive processes	**Weak cognitive processes**
Uses higher order processing skills to master complex learning	Does not use higher order processing skills needed for mastery of complex learning
Memory strengths	**Memory weaknesses**
Uses strategies to aid short- and long-term recall of information	Does not use strategies for short- and long-term recall of information
Attention strengths	**Attention weaknesses**
Can sustain attention over long periods and can select relevant from irrelevant information	Cannot sustain attention over long periods and cannot select relevant from irrelevant information
Good impulse control	**Poor impulse control**
Has a reflective style	Does not stop and think
Generalization strengths	**Generalization weaknesses**
Can apply learning to new situations	Does not apply learning to new situations

In the following section, we describe each of these learning characteristics, their relationship to learning rigorous academic content, and how the design of the Active Learner Approach takes these characteristics into consideration. Most of these characteristics are closely interrelated (e.g., passive learner and learned helplessness) but are listed separately because of the uniqueness they contribute to the learning situation.

HOW ARE INEFFECTIVE LEARNER CHARACTERISTICS RELATED TO LEARNING ADVANCED ACADEMIC CONTENT?

Active Learner versus Passive Learner

Research has supported the finding that many students with learning disabilities are passive learners (Torgesen, 1982). Passive learners do not approach learning with a plan, do not self-regulate their learning, and do not make connections between ideas. For example, when students with learning disabilities have to read a chapter for a geography class, they do not first preview the sections of the chapter, nor do they take notes or self-question while reading. They merely read the chapter. This does not enable them to organize the information and relate it to other ideas, nor does it help them study for a test on the information. They do not relate the current information to prior knowledge about the information. They do not seem to be aware that students who are academically successful are good at employing strategies to help them learn. When a college student who was an athlete participating in our research study on the Active Learner Approach was shown how to use a particular study strategy, he said with complete surprise, "I didn't know people did things like this!" At a later study session, he proudly modeled use of the strategy to his fellow teammates. Many students who are passive learners may be mistakenly perceived as having motivational deficits (Mercer & Mercer, 1998). They are perceived as not wanting to learn, instead of not knowing how to learn.

As children progress through the grades, they are expected to take charge of their own learning. By high school, teachers assume that students can learn and study on their own. Therefore, they teach in a manner that expects active learning from their students. Such an expectation is not tenable for many students with learning disabilities who are passive learners.

The Active Learner Approach is designed to help students become more active learners, particularly through the use of instruction on cognitive learning strategies. The students are given the means to become more active in their approach to learning. They are taught how to learn and how to use graphic organizers, self-talk, visualization, and other strategies. The systematic, explicit instructional approach ensures that students learn these strategies by adhering to the procedures of teacher modeling, guided practice, and independent practice.

Independent Learner versus Learned Helplessness

Research supports the finding that some students with learning disabilities exhibit learned helplessness (Bos & Vaughn, 2002; Hallahan, Kauffman, & Lloyd, 1999). This may be related to an external locus of control in which students attribute the outcome of events to luck, chance, fate, and other events outside of their influence. Some students with disabilities feel that there is nothing they can do to improve their school performance, so they give up. Some students have been ineffective learners in the past and because of their failure and frustration, they think that they can't learn. They rely on their teachers and parents to do as much work for them as possible.

It has been our unfortunate experience to observe that some secondary level special education teachers do much of their students' work (e.g., writing a research paper). In some cases, teachers give prompts and cues when giving tests in the special education class resulting in general education teachers denying the special educator a chance to provide any testing. The special educators do not do this because they want to cheat. They do this because they don't want their students to fail. However, the students are learning that they don't have to learn how to learn if they can get others to do their work for them. One college student who was involved in our study of the Active Learner Approach stated that he wished he could have brought his mother to school with him because she did all of his work for him when he was in high school. Another college student stated that she was dropping out of the program because the tutor was making her do all the work, and she wanted the tutor to do the work.

The excessive use of accommodations also may result in learned helplessness. Many IEPs at the secondary level focus exclusively on accommodations (e.g., having students take tests orally rather than in writing, having untimed tests, having more time to complete assignments). These accommodations may be appropriate, but using accommodations excessively may result in the students' inability to learn how to write responses on a test or learn to manage time when taking tests or to complete assignments. Education for students with disabilities should not *just* focus on providing accommodations but should also include remediation of the disability (i.e., raising the students' levels of functioning in their disability areas).

The Active Learner Approach is designed to teach students strategies so that they can learn on their own. The steps in the systematic, explicit instructional approach have the students starting out with guided practice of new strategies they have learned and then moving to independent practice. These steps ensure that the students do the work and the teacher provides modeling and prompting but does not do the work.

Metacognitive Strengths versus Metacognitive Weaknesses

Metacognition, also called *executive functioning,* refers to how individuals manage their learning processes. Metacognition includes two aspects: an individual's awareness of skills and strategies needed to perform a cognitive task and the ability to use self-regulating strategies to monitor one's thinking processes and to undertake fix-up procedures when there is a problem (Bos & Vaughn, 2002). Metacognition has been described as thinking about thinking (Mather & Goldstein, 2001). Students with learning disabilities may have difficulties with various aspects of metacognition, such as metamemory, metalistening, and metacomprehension in reading (Hallahan, Kauffman, & Lloyd, 1999). Many students with metacognitive weaknesses lack organizational skills and do not know how to go about learning and studying (Lerner, 2000). In our study of college students, we found that students with organizational problems had the most severe academic problems. They could not organize their time or lay out and adhere to study plans.

We have all had the experience in which we have been reading and suddenly become aware that we are not paying attention to the meaning of what we read. We immediately return to the point in the reading in which our attention lapsed, and we reread the material. Students with metacognitive weaknesses may take a long time to become aware of their lack of attention while reading; when they do become aware, they do not go back and find the spot where they need to start rereading. They simply keep reading.

The teaching model underlying the Active Learner Approach identifies organization problems as the most severe learning problem and, therefore, the first area to be addressed. Organization skills focus on both time and materials management. In addition, the Active Learner Approach uses self-talk as a major instructional technique. This approach is used for a number of areas, especially in reading, where the students self-question to extract main ideas and details. This helps make the thinking process explicit and visible, which is necessary for the development of metacognitive skills (Beyer, 1997). With self-talk, students can become aware of their thinking processes. Talk-alouds or think-alouds have been recognized as effective means for developing metacognitive skills (Swanson, 1999).

Strong Cognitive Processes versus Weak Cognitive Processes

The content of coursework becomes more abstract as students progress through the grades. At the elementary level, most instruction is focused on mastery of basic academic skills, but at the secondary level, there is a focus on knowledge. To master knowledge, a student must have strong higher order processing skills, specifically in abstract thinking and problem solving (Vaughn, Gersten, & Chard, 2000). Some students with learning disabilities have weak cognitive processing skills (Bos & Vaughn, 2002; Hallahan, Kauffman, & Lloyd, 1999) and need to learn to form categories, compare and contrast, and solve problems. Some high school students can learn facts but cannot manipulate those facts. They do not interrelate new information with previously learned information. They are concrete learners; they do not deal effectively with abstract ideas, especially in abstract content areas such as psychology and economics.

The Active Learner Approach includes strategies for advanced thinking skills. This section helps students apply such advanced thinking skills as problem solving, cause-and-effect relationships, comparing and contrasting, categorizing, and sequencing to different subject matter areas.

Memory Strengths versus Memory Weaknesses

Some students with mild disabilities have problems in short-term, or working, memory and/or long-term memory (Bos & Vaughn, 2002). Research has shown that students with learning disabilities have problems in auditory short-term memory and *working memory,* which is defined as the ability to keep a small amount of information in mind while simultaneously carrying out further cognitive operations (Hallahan, Kauffman, & Lloyd, 1999). Problems in long-term memory are especially significant because in the upper grades it is assumed that students recall information that they learned in earlier grades. Long-term memory for academic content may be a special problem for students with learning disabilities because of processing problems with long-term memory as well as inadequate instruction in academic areas in the earlier grades. Student test performance is especially dependent on memory skills, and those with memory impairments will do poorly on teacher-made and standardized tests. Students with long-term memory problems will have significant difficulties in situations where high-stakes testing involves passing an end-of-course test based on material learned throughout the school year. They may have memorized the material when they learned it in October but do not have recall of it in May. Problems in both working memory and long-term memory may make it difficult for students to activate prior knowledge—an important requirement for effective learning. In addition, many students with memory problems do not use strategies to help them learn. Their passive learning style prevents them from being proactive and trying to organize material to be recalled in meaningful ways using different strategies.

The Active Learner Approach includes training in memory strategies in the section on study skills. Students are taught to use different strategies (e.g., verbalizing, mnemonics, visualization). The requirement of memorizing the steps in the strategies is minimized with the Active Learner Approach. Students are *not* expected to memorize the steps in each strategy, as is done with other approaches. Rather, the students are encouraged to use print versions of the strategies so that they can constantly refer to the steps. The only section that does require students to memorize the steps in strategies is test taking. This is necessary because students cannot take written material into test settings.

Attention Strengths versus Attention Weaknesses

Students with learning disabilities and ADHD frequently have difficulties with attention. They may not be able to work for long periods of time. With block scheduling frequently used in the secondary schools today (Santos & Rettig, 1999), students are often expected to work for periods as long as 90 minutes. Many cannot sustain attention for this lengthy period unless constantly prompted by the teacher. Another aspect of attention involves attending to relevant information and ignoring irrelevant information. This area has been identified as a problem for some students with learning disabilities (Tarver, Hallahan, Kauffman, & Ball, 1976). For example, when students are taught to take notes, they are instructed to pick out the most important ideas. This is difficult for students with problems with selective attention.

Some of the strategies in the Active Learner Approach are directly designed to help students control their attention. One strategy helps students when taking notes in a lecture; another helps when studying. In addition, there is a strategy to help them use self-talk to identify the most important information when trying to keep to the topic when writing. Students are taught to question themselves to determine if each paragraph and sentence is related to the topic of the paper. They are taught to discard unessential information.

Good Impulse Control versus Poor Impulse Control

Impulsivity is a characteristic associated with ADHD as well as with some learning disabilities. Impulse control, along with attention, is one of the foundation building blocks for learning (Mather & Goldstein, 2001). Students lacking in impulse control are not able to master the higher levels of learning. Good impulse control is related to a reflective cognitive style (Bender, 1998). Students with learning disabilities are impulsive, not reflective (Hallahan, Kauffman, & Lloyd, 1999). A reflective cognitive style is especially important for test taking. Students who are impulsive often pick the first or second choice on a multiple-choice test and do not consider all of the options.

The Active Learner Approach addresses impulsivity, especially for test-taking skills. The CRAM strategy is designed to help students systematically analyze the alternatives on a multiple-choice test in order to help them overcome impulsivity.

Generalization Strengths versus Generalization Weaknesses

Generalization involves a student's ability to apply a particular target behavior to other situations (Rivera & Smith, 1997). Studies have shown that many students with learning disabilities have difficulty applying strategies they learn in one situation to other situations (Deshler, Ellis, & Lenz, 1996). They found that students could learn new strategies but only use them when prompted by their teachers. Obviously, this makes it difficult for them to become independent learners.

The Active Learner Approach is designed to facilitate generalization by emphasizing independent practice using the systematic, explicit instructional model. In addition, students are guided in applying the strategies to their different courses and they don't have to work independently until the teacher feels that they are ready.

WHAT ARE THE ACADEMIC EXPECTATIONS FOR STUDENTS WITH MILD DISABILITIES IN GENERAL EDUCATION CLASSES?

Standards-based educational reform in general education has been sweeping the country. States have set higher standards of learning and have used tests to determine if students are meeting these standards. In a report by the American Federation of Teachers (Glidden, 1999), it was stated that the standards-based reform movement was getting stronger in all states. In 1995, 33 states had or were planning assessments aligned with their standards, and in 1998, 49 states had assessment programs (Glidden, 1999). Requirements for graduation in various states have been expanded to include more coursework at more advanced levels. This trend toward reform has been based on the concept of accountability for students, teachers, schools, and school districts. Accountability has been determined by the use of three high-stakes decisions: tracking (assigning students to schools, programs, or classes based on their achievement levels); promoting students to the next level; and allowing students to receive their high school diplomas (Heubert & Hauser, 1999).

Use of test results to determine high school graduation is especially relevant to secondary level students with mild disabilities. The standards-based reform movement has moved into special education with the concept of accountability for educating students with disabilities. This is based on the assumption that challenging academic standards are necessary for students with disabilities to reach their highest potential (McDonnell, McLaughlin, & Morison, 1997). This reform movement has been codified in IDEA '97. Prior to the amendments, the law did not mention the general curriculum and students with disabilities. The IDEA '97 provisions dealing with the IEP and participation in state- and districtwide assessment reflect the influence of the standards-based reform movement of general education on the education of students with disabilities.

Prior to IDEA '97, the law emphasized the special education services that students with disabilities received, but now, IDEA '97 emphasizes general education for all students with disabilities. The IEP is the primary tool for ensuring the student's involvement and progress in the general curriculum. The IEP must include the following:

- A statement of the student's present level of educational performance including how the student's disability affects the student's involvement and progress in the general curriculum

- A statement of measurable annual goals related to meeting the student's disability-related needs in order to enable the student to be involved and progress in the general curriculum

- A statement of program modifications or supports for school personnel that will be provided for the student to advance appropriately toward attaining the annual goals, be involved and progress in the general curriculum, participate in extra-curricular and other nonacademic activities, and to be educated and participate with other students with and without disabilities

A second provision that is new to IDEA '97 is that children with disabilities be included in general state- and districtwide assessment programs with appropriate accommodations and modifications in administration, if necessary. The emphasis of participation in such assessment programs has been on provision of accommodations. Thurlow, Elliott, and Ysseldyke (1998) proposed the following four categories of accommodations: changes in presentation (e.g., taped versions of tests for students with reading disabilities); changes in response mode (e.g., having large bubbles for students to record their responses); changes in timing (e.g., extended time for testing); and changes in setting (e.g., individual administration of tests). A court ruling in Oregon requires that students with learning disabilities be provided with the same accommodations as stated in their IEPs when taking statewide tests (Disabilities Rights Advocates, 2001).

It is imperative to keep the following in mind, however. *All of the accommodations in the world will not help students if they have not learned the content of the general curriculum.* In the report on high-stakes testing submitted to Congress by the National Research Council, it is stated that tests for high-stakes decisions about individuals should only be used after changes have been made in teaching and curriculum to ensure that students have been taught the knowledge and skills that will be tested (Heubert & Hauser, 1999). Mere exposure to the curriculum without appropriate teaching of the content to students with disabilities is not adequate. The rigorous academic demands of standards-based curriculum are difficult for students without disabilities to meet but are more difficult for students with disabilities. The purpose of the Active Learner Approach is to provide specialized teaching of the general curriculum to compensate for the ineffective learning characteristics that make it difficult for students with disabilities to master the general curriculum with traditional teaching methods. Once students have been given specialized instruction using general curriculum content, then and only then is it fair to assess them with appropriate accommodations.

There have been many arguments about the fairness of high-stakes testing for all students (Kohn, 2001; Ohanian, 1999). Concerns regarding high-stakes testing for students with learning disabilities have also been voiced (Manset & Washburn, 2000). Questions have been raised regarding the lack of evidence that including students with learning disabilities in state assessment programs is pedagogically sound and the lack of evidence for the use of norm-referenced tests rather than criterion-referenced tests for measuring specific skill-related goals. Whatever the criticisms and concerns regarding high-stakes testing, it is a reality and educators have no choice but to do all they can to assist students with disabilities to meet the demands that are placed on them in today's schools.

In the National Research Council report on high-stakes testing, the authors proposed that one criterion for assessing whether a test is used appropriately is determining whether student performance on a test reflects knowledge and skills based on *appropriate instruction* or is attributable to *poor instruction, language barriers, or disabilities* (Heubert & Hauser, 1999). It is the responsibility of special educators to ensure that students with disabilities are provided with appropriate instruction that includes specialized teaching methods to enhance the likelihood that they will master general curriculum content.

The individualized evaluation aspect of the Active Learner Approach provides useful information relative to the IDEA '97 requirement that a student's present level of performance include a statement as to how a child's disability affects the child's involvement and progress in the general curriculum. For example, if the results of the Active Learner Student Questionnaire (see Appendix A) indicate that a student has problems with study skills and reading comprehension, then these two areas should be described in relation to the demands for studying and reading comprehension in the student's coursework. Additional information about a student's present level of performance relative to the general curriculum should be compared with a student's academic level and prior knowledge relative to the course content. The use of a specific student's coursework assignments as the basis of the Active Learner Approach is designed to make sure that the student does not just develop general learning strategies but rather specific strategies to apply to the everyday demands of her coursework.

The position statement concerning high-stakes testing presented by the American Educational Research Association (AERA, 2000) included sound recommendations for decision making using such tests for *all* students. The recommendation that when testing is used for individual student certification (e.g., high school diploma), students must have had a meaningful opportunity to learn the tested content and *cognitive processes*. AERA made clear that it is not just the information that the students must learn, but they must also master the cognitive processes for information acquisition. One of the purposes of the Active Learner Approach is to develop cognitive processes. AERA further pointed out that it must be shown that the tested content has been incorporated into the curriculum, materials, and *instruction* with which students are provided before high-stakes consequences are imposed for failure. Another recommendation deals with appropriate attention to students with disabilities. AERA proposed that steps should be taken to ensure that the test score inferences accurately reflect the intended construct rather than any disabilities and their associated characteristics extraneous to the intent of the measurement. Finally, AERA recommended that ongoing evaluation of intended and unintended effects of high-stakes testing be determined. This is especially true concerning drop-out rates, which have been shown to be higher for states with standards-based reform (Heubert & Hauser, 1999). In addition, students with learning disabilities have higher drop-out rates than students without disabilities and students with other types of disabilities. These two factors—high-stakes testing and the presence of learning disabilities—may combine to produce extremely high drop-out rates for such students. The results of the National Longitudinal Transition Study showed that dropping out of school is the culmination of a cluster of school performance problems, with poor grade performance as one of the most significant factors (Wagner, 1991). It would be tragic if the laudable goal of improving the quality of education for students with disabilities results in the unintended consequence of higher drop-out rates for students with learning disabilities and ADHD.

3

Individualized Evaluation

■ What three areas are evaluated with the Active Learner Approach?

■ How are learner needs evaluated?

■ How is student responsiveness to specific academic demands assessed?

■ How is academic achievement assessment used to plan instruction?

INTEGRATING THE EVALUATION

What Three Areas Are Evaluated with the Active Learner Approach?

With the Active Learner Approach, individualized evaluation is used to obtain information so that you can plan instruction for a specific student. Just knowing that a student has been diagnosed with a learning disability or ADHD does not provide you with the tools to plan instruction. It is necessary to go beyond labels and obtain information that helps you to identify what to teach a student and how to do so. To plan effective instruction with the Active Learner Approach, it is necessary to obtain assessment information based on the following three areas:

1. The student's unique learning needs

2. The student's responsiveness to the academic demands of her classes

3. The student's level of academic achievement

The first two areas of information are obtained through informal methods. Learning needs are determined from questionnaires. Student responsiveness to academic demands is determined through analysis of a student's performance on specific course assignments based on portfolios and teacher-directed probes of how a student attempts to meet academic demands using teacher questions as well as observation as a student performs academic tasks. Academic achievement is assessed through

1. Formal norm-referenced testing in which an individual is compared with others of his age or grade placement

2. Criterion-referenced curriculum-based assessment

3. Informal assessment, such as informal reading inventories

It is important to emphasize that there are two purposes for assessing students with disabilities: 1) instructional planning as used with the Active Learner Approach and 2) eligibility purposes. Testing for eligibility requires use of formal norm-referenced testing along with guidelines for interpreting test results based on state regulations concerning special education placement (Mercer, Jordan, Allsopp, & Mercer, 1996) or guidelines such as those of the Association on Higher Education and Disability (AHEAD) for assessing postsecondary students with learning disabilities (AHEAD, 1996). Although testing for eligibility purposes is important for understanding the whole individual, it is not discussed here because the results of such testing are usually of limited usefulness for planning instruction.

How Are Learner Needs Evaluated?

With the Active Learner Approach, learner needs are evaluated by separate questionnaires completed by the students and their teachers. The results of the Active Learner Student Questionnaire (see Appendix A) allow for an analysis of how the student perceives her learning. The results of the Active Learner Teacher Questionnaire (see Appendix B) provide for an analysis of how others perceive the student's learning. The questions on the Student Questionnaire correspond to those on the Teacher Questionnaire so that direct comparisons can be made. The items on both questionnaires correspond to the eight areas of strategies instruction in the Active Learner Approach: organization, test taking, study skills, notetaking, reading, writing, math, and advanced thinking.

Each of the items on the questionnaires corresponds to a specific learning strategy (e.g., both the Student Questionnaire item, "I have difficulty understanding multiple-choice questions," and the Teacher Questionnaire item, "Has difficulty understanding multiple-choice questions," correspond to the CRAM strategy described in Chapter 7). In this way, it is possible to directly link assessment with intervention. Appendix C contains a list of strategies that correspond to each item on the questionnaires so that you can easily link specific problems with related strategies.

What Are the Components of the Active Learner Questionnaires? The Active Learner Student and Teacher Questionnaires are broken down into separate sections for organization, test taking, study skills, notetaking, reading, writing, math, and advanced thinking. Each item on the Active Learner Student Questionnaire is phrased as an "I" statement (e.g., "I have difficulty understanding difficult words that I read."). The student is directed to write a Y for yes if the statement always applies to him or her, an S for sometimes if it applies some of the time, and an N for no if it never applies. The Active Learner Teacher Questionnaire contains the same items; however, the phrasing excludes the word "I" (e.g., "Has difficulty understanding difficult words that he or she reads."). Before making a judgment, the teachers are directed to compare the student being rated with other students with whom they work. They are to write Y for yes if the statement always applies to the student, S for sometimes if it applies some of the time, N for no if it does not apply, and DK for don't know if they cannot rate the student on the item.

How Are the Active Learner Questionnaires Used? The steps for using the questionnaires are presented in Table 3.1. The first step is to photocopy the Student and Teacher Questionnaires so that responses can be directly recorded on them. Have the student complete the Student Questionnaire after fully explaining the purpose (i.e., finding out what problems the student thinks she has). If a student has difficulty understanding the meaning of an item or reading an item, then provide assistance. However, do not prompt the student on how she should respond. If, for example, a student does not believe that she has a problem with taking tests, but you think that she does, do not comment on the student's perceptions at this time. Have all teachers who work with a particular student complete a Teacher Questionnaire. In some cases, several teachers may complete only parts of the questionnaire. For example, a student's algebra teacher may only be able to complete the math section.

Table 3.1. Steps in using the Active Learner Questionnaires

1. Photocopy the Student and Teacher Questionnaires.
2. Have the student complete the Student Questionnaire.
3. Have all teachers who work with the student complete copies of the Teacher Questionnaire.
4. Analyze the ratings all teachers gave to each item and resolve any differences in opinion.
5. Compare student and teacher ratings on the questionnaires.
6. Conference with the student and discuss results of the questionnaires.

After the teachers have completed the questionnaires, compare their ratings for each item. Differences between teachers need to be resolved. For example, if the biology teacher rates a student as always having difficulty understanding the meaning of difficult words that are read but the technology teacher does not, then the difference may be due to the academic content area. The biology curriculum may use more difficult words than the technology curriculum.

Next, compare the student's ratings with the ratings given by you and the other teachers. Identify items that were indicated as problems by the student and the teachers. All items that were rated as always being a problem by all raters should be viewed as accurately reflecting the student's areas of difficulty. Items rated as sometimes being problems should be viewed as content-specific areas of difficulty. Both areas suggest a need for strategy instruction. Identify items that were identified as problems by the student but not by the teachers, or vice versa. Differences may reflect a student's or a teacher's lack of awareness. For example, if all teachers rated a student as having difficulty remembering what was read but the student did not, then the student may not be aware of his problem. Or, if a student rated himself as being extremely nervous when taking tests but the teachers did not, then the teachers may not be aware of the student's test anxiety. Discuss these differences with the student and the other teachers to determine whose perceptions are accurate.

Finally, have a conference with the student and discuss the results of the questionnaires, highlighting both the student's strengths and weaknesses. Explain the Active Learner Approach to the student and obtain her commitment to it. It is critical that you explain the benefits of mastering the strategies to make sure that the student understands that she will have to work hard, but the payoff will be getting better grades. Encourage the student to take responsibility for her own learning. This is especially important for overcoming the learned helplessness that impedes some students from becoming active learners. It is recommended that you and the student sign a contract in which you both agree to be active participants in the Active Learner Approach. A sample of a contract is included in Appendix D. Both you and the student need to sign the contract to demonstrate that success of the Active Learner Approach is dependent on teamwork between you and the student. The Active Learner Approach can only be successful if the student "buys into it" as a willing and active participant.

HOW IS STUDENT RESPONSIVENESS TO SPECIFIC ACADEMIC DEMANDS ASSESSED?

Before designing an instructional intervention plan using the strategies of the Active Learner Approach, you must know how a student is performing on tasks in classes. Determining how well a student is meeting the academic demands of the general curriculum comes from two sources: the student's performance on various tests and assignments in class and teacher-directed probes of student learning of specific academic tasks.

How Is Student Performance Analyzed?

The student's grades on specific assignments need to be examined using a portfolio format. Each student should organize a portfolio of all tests, written assignments, and works in progress that teachers can use to evaluate the student's performance and identify specific areas that need attention. You need to question the student about why he thinks a low or high grade was given on an assignment. For a student who has an external locus of control, low grades on an essay examination may be attributed to time limits, unclear questions, or having a bad day. A good grade may be attributed to luck. It is important to discuss reasons for receiving low or high grades and relate these to student effort and knowledge.

Students should also keep track of all grades on all assignments in their portfolios. Many students are unaware of their status in each of their courses because they do not record grades for tests or assignments that have been returned by the teacher, or they discard tests or assignments after they are returned. A major aspect of the Active Learner Approach involves assisting students to develop awareness of their academic status on each assignment in each class.

It is important to analyze students' portfolios in relation to the Active Learner Student and Teacher Questionnaires. For example, if a student has low grades on essay examinations and also has problems with organizing ideas and keeping to the topic when he writes, as indicated on the questionnaires, then a possible reason for the low grades may be a writing problem in addition to or instead of mastery of the knowledge tested.

What Are Teacher-Directed Probes of Student Responsiveness to Academic Demands?

Teacher-directed probes can identify problems students are experiencing while they are performing specific academic tasks and what, if any, strategies they are using while engaged in learning. This information is obtained through think-alouds, in which a student verbalizes what she is thinking as a task is being performed. Initially, ask open-ended questions to elicit what the student is doing mentally (e.g., "What are you doing to try to figure out the word that you can't read?"). These questions assess the expressive level of understanding, which is the highest level of student response.

Often, students have difficulty doing think-alouds. When students cannot answer open-ended questions, give prompts using objective questions (e.g., "Are you trying to figure out the word that you don't understand by looking at the words around it?"). Objective questions assess the receptive level of understanding, which is an important step toward the eventual achievement of expressive understanding. If a student still cannot identify what he is thinking, then this usually indicates the student's lack of metacognitive awareness of his thinking processes. When a student cannot respond expressively or receptively, model the think-aloud process. Through guided practice, lead the student to analyze his own thinking processes.

For teacher-directed probes of *reading problems,* think-alouds are used to determine if the student is having difficulty with word identification, word comprehension, or different types of passage comprehension. For example, if a student cannot answer a comprehension question about a passage that she has read silently, then ask her to read the question aloud. Then, ask the student what is being requested to determine if she understands the question. If the student does, then ask her where the answer might be in the passage and have her look back to find it. If the student cannot respond to any expressive level task, ask her a multiple-choice question to determine if she can select the correct answer but not retrieve it. Through this analysis, you may be able to identify where in the reading process the student is having difficulties.

For teacher-directed probes of *writing problems,* have the student respond to requests for think-alouds at the different stages of the writing process: planning, drafting, and editing/revising. For example, while a student is planning a paper, ask him to think-aloud as he brainstorms ideas. If a student has difficulty brainstorming ideas, present appropriate and inappropriate ideas, and have him evaluate whether the ideas fit the topic of the paper. While the student writes the first draft, ask him what he is thinking at certain points (e.g., "How are you trying to find words to fit your ideas?"). If a student cannot use think-alouds at the drafting stage, then provide word prompts. At the editing/revising stage, ask the student to describe what type of errors he is searching for. If he cannot generate a type of error, give prompts such as, "Are there any spelling errors in the first paragraph?"

For teacher-directed probes of *math problems,* have the student verbalize what she is doing as a computational problem is being solved. For word problems, have her identify the steps to take to solve the word problem. You can also give cues to solving the problems and then observe whether the student can pick up on these cues. Interview the student to determine the reasons behind her incorrect math responses and to yield information that can be directly linked to remediation of a specific math problem (Liedtke, 1983).

HOW IS ACADEMIC ACHIEVEMENT ASSESSMENT USED TO PLAN INSTRUCTION?

Academic achievement assessment should be based on formal norm-referenced testing, criterion-referenced curriculum-based assessment, and informal assessment using inventories. All three types of assessment serve different purposes, and all are useful.

Formal norm-referenced tests are important for indicating how students compare with other students in the nation who are the same age or in the same grade. However, these tests do not identify how a student is performing with the actual curriculum that he is being required to learn. It is important that the content of the norm-referenced tests be analyzed in relation to the content of a student's curriculum. If a student is being tested on items that are not included in the school curriculum, then the test is not a valid measure of the student's performance.

The most frequently used norm-referenced test of academic achievement is the Woodcock-Johnson Psychoeducational Battery (Woodcock, McGraw, & Mather, 2001). This test includes subtests for assessing reading, math, writing, and content areas such as humanities, social studies, and science. Because this test is designed for students from the age of 5 through adulthood, there are a limited number of items assessing skills at the various age levels, especially the secondary level. A test that is useful for assessing reading at the secondary level is the Nelson-Denny Test of Reading (Brown, Fishco, & Hanna, 1993), which assesses vocabulary, comprehension, and reading rate.

Criterion-referenced curriculum-based assessment is useful because it measures what a student is being taught. Because there are no norms, the results of these tests cannot be used to compare a student with other students. However, in most cases, a cut-off score to determine when a student passes is established by the creators of the test. The results of criterion-referenced curriculum-based tests can be used to determine whether a student is meeting the criteria set forth in the general curriculum. Criterion-referenced curriculum-based testing includes teacher-made tests. Each teacher establishes what is important to learn in her class, constructs items to assess this content, and establishes the cut-off points to determine the grades. Tests of state standards of learning (high-stakes tests) and high school competency tests are especially important to analyze because they determine whether a student will receive a diploma. In-depth analysis of how a student performs on these various criterion-referenced curriculum-based measures is important for planning instruction.

Informal assessment using inventories provides detailed information on a student's performance in all aspects of a particular academic area. It also assesses how a student learns (i.e., the processes the student uses to master learning). Informal assessment includes inventories of reading and math and is usually process oriented, whereas formal tests are product oriented. Product-oriented tests focus on the right answer, whereas process-oriented assessment focuses on the means by which the student arrives at the right answer. The Qualitative Reading Inventory–3 (QRI–3; Leslie & Caldwell, 2001) provides thorough information on word identification and comprehension and the use of look-backs and think-alouds for fully assessing a high school student's comprehension skills.

No one score may represent a student's performance. It is important to recognize that there may *not* be one set of scores that best represents a student's performance in a particular academic area. It is not unusual to approach a new student based on previously administered academic achievement scores, and then after working with the student, to find the scores to be unrepresentative of her performance on school tasks. Because students are required to master diverse types of tasks in all subjects, it is not possible to use norm-referenced tests to fully evaluate these varied tasks.

It is difficult to obtain one or a few overall scores to represent student performance because measures of specific academic areas differ along three dimensions: the nature of the test items, the nature of the student responses, and the comprehensiveness of the test items. How tests differ on the *nature of the tasks* can be illustrated by comparing norm-referenced with criterion-referenced curriculum-based assessment. For example, the Woodcock-Johnson Psychoeducational Battery uses short paragraphs to determine a student's reading comprehension level. However, criterion-referenced curriculum-based assessment might have a student read a chapter from his science book as an authentic measure of his reading comprehension. The student may do better on the Woodcock-Johnson Psychoeducational Battery because of the short paragraphs than on the science text, which is longer and more complex.

The *nature of the student response* also differs from one type of assessment to another. For example, on the Woodcock-Johnson Psychoeducational Battery reading comprehension subtest, a cloze procedure, in which the student orally supplies a missing word to complete the paragraph, is used. With criterion-referenced curriculum-based assessment, the nature of the student response varies. Students may be asked to answer open-ended questions in writing or answer multiple-choice questions orally. These different types of responses involve different cognitive processes (i.e., expressive and receptive understanding) and, therefore, lead to different results.

Another variable accounting for the difference between norm-referenced testing and criterion-referenced curriculum-based assessment involves the *comprehensiveness of the test items*. Formal tests provide a limited sample of behavior, whereas criterion-referenced curriculum-based assessment and informal inventories provide a wider sample of behavior. The more comprehensive the sampling of test items, the greater the chance that the assessment better represents a student's true level of functioning.

INTEGRATING THE EVALUATION

After you have analyzed the student's responsiveness to the academic demands of his classes as well as the results of any academic achievement testing, integrate these with the results of the questionnaire. Identify the strategies corresponding to the questionnaire items indicating problems and lay out an instructional plan using the strategies corresponding to the items. Designing appropriate strategic learning instruction for students with learning disabilities and ADHD is possible only with the type of individualized evaluation described in this chapter. These evaluations are time consuming and require a high level of teacher expertise in obtaining diagnostic information. Information from questionnaires, portfolios, teacher-directed probes, and criterion-referenced curriculum-based assessment can only be obtained by well-trained special educators who understand the needs and characteristics of students with disabilities and how to analyze general education curricular demands. Traditional evaluations by psychologists and other professionals are less time consuming than individualized evaluation by special educators but cannot yield the type of information that is needed to plan instruction.

4

Cognitive Learning Strategies and Systematic, Explicit Instruction

- What are cognitive learning strategies?

- What are different types of learning strategies?

- What different types of learning strategies are used with the Active Learner Approach?

- What is systematic, explicit instruction?

- What are steps of systematic, explicit instruction?

The Active Learner Approach is designed to develop student mastery of cognitive learning strategies in the areas of organization, test taking, study skills, notetaking, reading, writing, math, and advanced thinking. Students can best master these learning strategies when teachers use systematic, explicit instruction. In this chapter, cognitive learning strategies are described first, followed by a description of systematic, explicit instruction.

WHAT ARE COGNITIVE LEARNING STRATEGIES?

The purpose of the Active Learner Approach is to teach students to use cognitive learning strategies to improve their mastery of rigorous academic school content. These strategies enable students with learning disabilities and ADHD to achieve academic success. Two frequently used definitions of a *learning strategy* are

1. An efficient way to acquire, store, and express information and skills (Mercer & Mercer, 1998)

2. How a person thinks and acts when planning, executing, and evaluating performance of a task and its outcomes (Lenz, Ellis, & Scanlon, 1996)

We all use learning strategies without really thinking of them as strategies. For example, you may have a particular way to remember the PIN number for your voice mail, checking account, or e-mail address. Some people associate their PIN numbers with birthdays or special dates, whereas others may remember their PIN numbers because the numbers match the jersey numbers of their favorite sports figures. The particular strategy you use is important only to the extent that it allows you to accomplish important tasks efficiently and successfully.

A misconception some educators have about learning strategies is that they are "crutches" and make students dependent learners–specifically, dependent on the strategy. However, learning strategies that are "written out" and taught are simply formalized versions of "naturally occurring" problem-solving strategies that most students use every day. Although academically successful students use strategies without much instruction or prompting, students with disabilities may need help in developing these strategies.

Learning strategies include thinking and physical actions that are necessary to perform a skill (Lenz, Ellis, & Scanlon, 1996). Whereas the thinking aspect is an essential component of the Active Learner Approach strategies, the physical aspect is important as well because it provides evidence that a student is using a strategy (e.g., writing note cards). The movements associated with many of the Active Learner Approach strategies also provide students with kinesthetic cuing, which can facilitate understanding and memory of strategy steps.

Two important characteristics of any effective learning strategy are 1) students must be able to gain access to the strategy, and 2) the strategy must accurately represent the learning task or skill. With the Active Learner Approach, students are guaranteed access to strategies by using printed materials (student strategy cue sheets that include the written steps of the strategy), thereby avoiding accessibility problems for students with memory problems. The students greatly benefit from the strategy cue sheets because they provide them access to the primary steps of a strategy. Some teachers may mistakenly perceive these strategy cue sheets as "cheating." What they do not realize is that the print versions of the strategies give students who have memory retrieval problems equal access to the same strategies as their classmates without memory problems.

The strategies included in the Active Learner Approach have been reviewed and field-tested for the purpose of ensuring they accurately represent designated concepts and skills. These strategies were used, and in some cases refined, during the 3-year federally funded study we conducted with college students who had been diagnosed with learning disabilities and/or ADHD. Each student in the study was experiencing significant academic difficulties, and the strategies we chose or developed for helping each student met the demands of the specific courses they were taking. In some cases, we selected existing strategies found in the literature. In other cases, we developed new strategies. As students attempted to use the strategies, we enhanced, changed, or amended individual strategy steps based on student feedback and the level of success students had with individual strategies.

Effective learning strategies should not only be accurate representations of target learning tasks but also should represent an efficient process for learning and performing the task. Therefore, a student must be able to use the learning strategy in reasonable amounts of time and with high degrees of accuracy. A general rule of thumb is that the number of steps in any learning strategy should not exceed what a student can remember and perform in a reasonable amount of time. Typically, the number of *primary* steps in a strategy should be no more than six or seven. This does not mean that strategy steps cannot or should not have substeps. On the contrary, it is important that some primary strategy steps contain several *secondary* substeps. Secondary-level concepts and skills represent higher order thinking and, therefore, will naturally involve more complexity than a few steps might entail. For the strategies in this book, the bullets beneath each of the steps in a strategy represent the substeps. It is helpful to think of those "secondary steps" as *learning anchors*. These anchors prompt students to perform whatever skills are required to complete the primary step.

The critical features of well-developed learning strategies are shown in Table 4.1. They should include accurate and efficient procedures for relevant learning tasks. They should be accessible because they are memorable or because they can be accessed through strategy cue sheets. Finally, learning strategies should incorporate student thinking and student actions.

WHAT ARE DIFFERENT TYPES OF LEARNING STRATEGIES?

A number of learning strategies have been used with students in special and general education. In order to present these various strategies in an organized manner, we have classified the strategies that are used with the Active Learner Approach into six groups: mnemonics, visualization, verbalization, graphic organizers, structured steps, and multisensory learning.

Table 4.1.   Critical features of well-developed learning strategies

Learning strategies are *accurate* and *efficient* procedures for learning tasks.
Learning strategies are accessible to students because:
- They are memorable
- Students can access them through strategy cue sheets

Learning strategies incorporate student *thinking* and student *actions*.

1. *Mnemonics:* Mnemonics provide structured ways to aid recall and retrieval of information by creating associations that do not exist naturally in the content (Bos & Vaughn, 2002). Use of mnemonics requires that the student organize the information in personally meaningful ways. Mnemonic techniques help students convert abstract language and number content to concrete associations. Associations that use humor and different senses (e.g., sounds, images, smells, tastes, touch, movements, feelings) are especially effective in aiding memory retrieval.

    Three major types of mnemonic techniques are used with the Active Learner Approach: the keyword method, the pegword method, and letter strategies. The keyword method is used to strengthen the relationship between a new word and associated information. The student may associate a keyword with the word to be recalled by imagining an interaction between the two words. The keyword method is good for memorization of tasks such as words for English vocabulary, foreign language, and scientific terms. The pegword method involves rhyming words for numbers and ordered information. This strategy is useful for tasks such as recall of the order of U.S. presidents and multiplication tables.

    Letter strategies are probably the most frequently used type of mnemonic strategy. There are two types of letter strategies: acronyms and acrostics. With the acronym approach, a word is formed based on the first letters of the information to be recalled. The HOMES strategy for recalling the five great lakes—Huron, Ontario, Michigan, Erie, and Superior—and the FACE strategy, for recalling the names of the spaces on the musical staff, are examples of acronyms. Acrostics are sentences constructed using the first letter of each word to represent the information to be recalled. Many of us learned the Order of Operation rule in math through the acrostic, "Please Excuse My Dear Aunt Sally," for parentheses, exponents, multiplication/division, and addition/subtraction. Sometimes acrostics are more memorable than acronyms because they have more meaning.

2. *Visualization:* There are two types of visualization strategies: imagining visual images seen in the past and creating visual images corresponding to information to be recalled or understood. An example of imagining visual images from the past is studying spelling words and shutting your eyes to picture the letters in the words. An example of a strategy in which a person creates a visual image of information is when he pictures Lincoln as a

soldier in the Civil War as a way of remembering the major event of his presidency.

3. *Verbalization:* There are two types of verbalization strategies: verbal rehearsal of information to be learned and use of think-alouds or talk-alouds in which a person uses language to guide her behavior and deepen her understanding of a concept, problem-solving process, or other learning task. Think-alouds and talk-alouds have long been recognized as effective strategies for enhancing learning, especially for strategy steps (Bos & Vaughn, 2002). An example of verbal rehearsal is when a person says history facts aloud when studying as a way of adding to the visual input of reading note cards. An example of a think-aloud is when a person periodically checks his attention when studying by asking himself what he is doing every 10 minutes. Another example of a think-aloud is when a student says her thinking aloud as she performs a learning task such as solving algebra equations. Think-alouds and talk-alouds are especially useful for students learning to monitor their thinking and developing metacognitive awareness (i.e., monitoring and evaluating one's own thinking).

4. *Graphic organizers:* These are excellent means for visually showing relationships between ideas to be learned and have been shown to be effective in assisting students with disabilities to improve their learning (Bos & Vaughn, 2002). Graphic organizers include semantic or concept maps and organizational charts. Semantic and concept maps show the relationship between ideas, concepts, facts, and other information specific to particular content areas. For example, a concept map can be used to help students visualize the animal kingdom and how it is organized (e.g., kingdom, phylum, order, genus, species). Graphic organizers can be presented to students to help them learn (e.g., use of a timeline), or students can generate their own graphic organizers (e.g., creation of a chart to compare different forms of governments while studying).

5. *Structured steps:* With this strategy, a series of steps is identified for the student to follow. This is one of the common features of cognitive strategy instruction (Bos & Vaughn, 2002). The student learns the steps in the order in which they are presented as a way of organizing information. For example, when writing papers, students are taught to always follow three steps: prewriting, drafting, and revising/editing. Mnemonics are often used in conjunction with structured steps to help students remember the steps and complete the steps in the correct order.

6. *Multisensory learning:* With this strategy, students are taught to use their visual, auditory, kinesthetic, and tactile (VAKT) senses to enhance their learning. Whenever a student looks at, labels, traces, and writes information, a multisensory approach is used. This has been a basic strategy underlying special education methodology for many years.

WHAT DIFFERENT TYPES OF LEARNING STRATEGIES ARE USED WITH THE ACTIVE LEARNER APPROACH?

The six cognitive learning strategies of mnemonics, visualization, verbalization, graphic organizers, structured steps, and multisensory instruction have provided the underlying structure for the development of new strategies or selection of existing specific strategies presented in this manual. We have incorporated as many of the six cognitive learning strategies as possible when constructing new strategies. For example, BREAK, the study skills strategy designed to help students remember information for tests, uses mnemonics, visualization, and verbalization. We also made sure that every strategy contains the three critical features of well-designed strategies: accurate and efficient procedures for learning a task, accessibility for students, and incorporating student thinking and student actions. Following are some examples of how the six cognitive learning strategies have been woven into the eight areas for improving student mastery:

1. *Mnemonics:* The study strategies in the Active Learner Approach use mnemonics as a key to learning. One of the steps of the BREAK strategy has the students establish mnemonics using acronyms and acrostics, and another step has the students use keywords to recall information. IF IT FITS (King-Sears, Mercer, & Sindelar, 1992) is a reading strategy that uses the keyword approach to help students remember new vocabulary.

2. *Visualization:* The Active Learner Approach strategies that are presented via the Learning Toolbox (http://coe.jmu.edu/learningtoolbox) have visual cues for each of the steps in a strategy. The purpose of the graphics is to explain the text version of the step and help recall the step. For example, the Learning Toolbox version of the test-taking strategy BRAVE, which is designed to have students overcome nervousness and text anxiety, uses a graphic cue of lungs as the first step—directing the student to breathe deeply. A picture of a beach scene is used for the second step—directing the student to relax. The graphics are designed to aid the students to better understand what the words in each strategy step mean and to recall these steps when they find that they are nervous during a test.

   BREAK, the study skills strategy designed to help students remember information for tests, has a step in which the students are trained to picture information in their mind's eye. The math strategies of the Active Learner Approach make maximal use of visual cues. For example, the visual aid for recalling the steps in long division is the face strategy (see Chapter 12). The eyes are represented by two division signs, the nose by the multiplication sign, the mouth by the subtraction sign, and a beard (goatee) represents bringing down the numeral after the subtraction step. For SPIES, a strategy to help students determine greater than and less than, a graphic of an alligator or a shark's mouth is used to visually aid in understanding the underlying concepts.

3. *Verbalization:* Many of the Active Learner Approach strategies use verbal rehearsal, especially when using note cards for studying. BREAK, the study skills strategy designed to help students remember information for tests, has a step in which the students recite the information aloud. Self-talk is used with PATS, a study skills strategy to help students avoid distractions when studying. The last step in this strategy includes self-talk to control internal distractions. Students are directed to talk to themselves when they become aware that they are being distracted internally (e.g., hunger pangs).

4. *Graphic organizers:* All strategies in the advanced thinking section rely heavily on the use of graphic organizers. For example, with the strategy STOP, which is designed to help students organize information sequentially, timelines are used to help recall time sequences, and visual maps are used for recall of spatial sequences. For the strategy LID, which is designed to help students compare and contrast ideas, a Venn diagram is used. Story maps are used for the reading strategy SPORE, which is used to help students understand narrative text. Story maps using this same strategy are applied to teaching story writing.

5. *Structured steps:* Following explicit steps is used in a number of strategies across the eight areas in the Active Learner Approach. It is used in POWER, a strategy designed to help students write papers in which they must first plan, organize, write, and edit/revise (Englert, Raphael, Anderson, Anthony, & Stevens, 1991). Steps are also used to help students proofread papers for errors in mechanics. With SCOPE, they must first proofread for spelling errors, then go back one at a time and proof for errors in capitalization, order of words, punctuation, and expressing thoughts. Use of a sequential set of steps is also found in BCDE, a reading strategy to help students get the overall ideas of what they read. They are instructed to use a step-by-step approach in which they survey the material before they (B) begin reading, (C) create questions to ask themselves, (D) during reading answer the questions, and at the (E) end of the reading summarize.

6. *Multisensory learning:* Most Active Learner Approach strategies include some motor involvement, especially writing note cards. The math strategies use more multisensory learning than the other areas. The strategy DRAW, designed to help students with whole number and fraction computation as well as solving one-variable algebra equations, has the students answer the response to a problem aloud (auditory), draw it (visual), and write the answer (motor).

WHAT IS SYSTEMATIC, EXPLICIT INSTRUCTION?

Systematic, explicit instruction is carefully planned teaching that includes several essential instructional components that specifically meet the learning needs of students with learning disabilities and ADHD. Systematic, explicit instruction has considerable research support as to its effectiveness with students with learning disabilities (Carnine, 1999; Swanson, 1999; Vaughn, Gersten, & Chard, 2000). Students without disabilities may learn with or without systematic, explicit instruction. Students with disabilities need such instruction because it incorporates specific instructional features that account for and positively impact their ineffective learning characteristics. Analysis of the terminology *systematic* and *explicit* reveals what is special about this approach. *Systematic* refers to the sequential use of instructional components that specify teacher behaviors directly linked to student learning. *Explicit* means that the student doesn't learn through discovery; rather, everything that the student learns is overtly presented. The teacher uses a variety of instructional methods to make concepts accessible to the students. Multisensory teaching modeling (i.e., the use of multiple sensory inputs—auditory, visual, tactile, kinesthetic) is emphasized.

Learning strategies are effective for students with learning disabilities and ADHD when they are taught using systematic, explicit instruction. A potential misconception about learning strategies is that they, in and of themselves, overcome learning problems. This perception may lead some teachers to simply supply students with copies of a strategy without directly teaching the strategy. When the students don't use the strategy or don't use it appropriately, the teacher may conclude that the teaching strategy is not helpful. It is important to remember that learning strategies are like any skills we want students to learn—they need to be taught!

WHAT ARE THE STEPS OF SYSTEMATIC, EXPLICIT INSTRUCTION?

The five steps involved in systematic, explicit instruction are presented in Table 4.2. The first step provides an introduction of the strategy to be learned. This is followed by the teacher modeling the strategy. Then, the student is provided guided practice; this is followed by independent practice. The final stage teaches for generalization. These steps are similar to the stages of acquisition and generalization in the instructional model for teaching strategies advocated by Deshler, Ellis, and Lenz (1996). In addition, these steps incorporate the procedural steps involved in strategy instruction described by Meichenbaum and Biemiller (1998) and the results of analysis of intervention research with students with learning disabilities (Swanson, 1999; Vaughn, Gersten, & Chard, 2000).

Step 1: Introduction

At this advanced organizer stage, you provide an overview of what you will be teaching. Use the LIP strategy: L is for linking the strategy to prior strategies

Table 4.2. Steps of systematic, explicit instruction

1. Introduction of strategy—advanced organizers including linking the strategy to previous learning, identifying the purpose of the strategy, and providing rationale for the learning strategy
2. Modeling of strategy—teacher models steps of strategy and then models it in the context of specific student assignments
3. Guided practice—teacher gradually requires student to start applying strategy to assignments while providing support
4. Independent practice—teacher provides opportunities for student to apply strategy to assignments with little or no support
5. Generalization—teacher provides opportunities for student to apply strategy to other subjects and other settings

learned, I is for clearly identifying the strategy to be learned, and P is for providing a rationale for learning the strategy. The purpose of LIP is to help the student develop meaningful connections between what he already knows and the strategy to be learned. LIP also clearly identifies what the student will learn and why it might be important to him. This step lays the foundation for the student acquiring an initial understanding of the strategy.

A very important aspect of this stage is a clear teacher presentation of the rationale for teaching a particular strategy. The rationale should be based on the results of the individualized evaluation, including the results of the questionnaires and the analysis of the student's responsiveness to the academic demands of the general curriculum. This stage should involve teacher–student discussions leading to self-understanding. You need to clearly point out the benefits of using the strategy. For example, if analysis of the questionnaires indicates that the student has difficulty taking multiple-choice tests and if analysis of her grades on multiple-choice tests in her history and biology classes indicates that she does poorly on such tests, then the teacher should provide the rationale that the student needs instruction in CRAM, a strategy designed to improve a student's ability to take multiple-choice tests. Through these discussions, the student should commit to putting in the effort needed to learn and use the strategy. Without student commitment to learning a strategy, it is not possible for the student to achieve mastery.

Step 2: Modeling

At this stage you clearly model the strategy's purpose and each step in the strategy. First, introduce the purpose of the strategy and explicitly relate the purpose to the preceding discussion on the rationale for using the strategy. Fully read and explain each step in the strategy. At this stage you are making instruction visible and explicit, which is an essential feature of effective intervention for students with learning disabilities (Vaughn, Gersten, & Chard, 2000). As you describe each step, model how to do each step using multisensory teaching methods. Then, you model applying the strategy to the student's specific course assignments. The steps must be applied to the student's assignments so that the student can "see" how the strategy is put into operation. This step is important for explaining what strategies are being used and why they will be helpful. This is difficult for teachers to do because they must know the strategy well and they must know the nature of the academic demands on the student, which requires the teacher to do advanced planning. For example, if you are teaching the study strategy BREAK, you would model how to create mnemonics and explain why this is an effective way to study. You would provide a lot of cueing and demonstration of examples and nonexamples. When a strategy is modeled within the context of the student's course, he can develop a clear perspective of how the strategy works. This makes the strategy more meaningful than if the strategy is simply taught out of context. It also assists students to develop a plan of action to guide their learning, which has been identified as an effective instructional practice for children with learning disabilities (Vaughn, Gersten, & Chard, 2000). If you were modeling the CRAM strategy, then you would use previous multiple-choice tests on which the student did poorly to demonstrate how to apply the strategy. Then, you would construct potential multiple-choice questions for an upcoming biology test that the student is studying for and model applying the strategy to these potential questions.

Step 3: Guided Practice

This step begins the student's transition to independent use of a strategy. As the teacher, you gradually release your direction, and the student gradually assumes more responsibility for demonstrating her understanding of the strategy and ability to use it appropriately. At the early stages you use a great deal of support and cueing, and as the student demonstrates mastery, your support and cueing fade. At this step you would start with opportunities at the easy level and progress to more difficult levels. Controlling the task difficulty at this stage is a critical factor in effective instruction (Vaughn, Gersten, & Chard, 2000). *Scaffolding* is another term for fading and indicates the need to provide a high level of teacher support initially and then gradually remove the support. This allows the teacher to provide the student with a supported transition from initial acquisition of the strategy (gained during explicit teacher modeling) to beginning proficiency of the strategy to a high level of proficiency with teacher guidance. Scaffolded instruction is adjustable and temporary and can be removed when no longer necessary.

At the early stages of guided practice, have the student practice using examples that you used for modeling, and then provide new examples. Have the students make sure that they are using each step in the strategy by following the print version of the strategy.

Monitor student use of strategies by using visual representations of the student's progress in mastering the strategy (e.g., charts, graphs). Charting the number of steps your student accurately implements is one way to do this. Then, as the student begins to apply the strategy in a targeted course, have the student keep a record of all grades obtained on assignments and tests in which she used the strategy. Give positive reinforcement for using the strategy (effort) and for improving grades (performance). Students with learning problems greatly benefit from seeing their progress, and a visual representation of the learning progress also provides them with positive reinforcement. It is important to remember that learning new skills is perceived to be a risky proposition by some students with learning disabilities. Helping students see their learning through a chart or graph and providing positive reinforcement will go a long way in helping students believe that they can learn and overcome learned helplessness.

Step 4: Independent Practice

Once the student has demonstrated mastery of all steps and substeps of the strategy, she is ready to apply the strategy to assignments without the aid of the teacher. This transition to independence is difficult for some students who will resist teacher attempts to move to this stage because of their learned helplessness. After the student applies a strategy independently, have her work on samples so that you can monitor if she is successfully applying the strategy. For example, if the student has a multiple-choice examination in English and applied the CRAM strategy independently, then have her bring in the examination. Have the student demonstrate how she used CRAM, and evaluate whether she was successful.

Students benefit from multiple practice opportunities to master use of a learning strategy. Simply remembering a learning strategy and its steps is not sufficient for success for students with ineffective learning characteristics; neither is their ability to demonstrate accurate use of the learning strategy one time. Students with learning disabilities need multiple opportunities to practice applying a learned strategy to appropriate tasks within the content of the courses with which they are having difficulty. It is important to monitor the student's performance to determine if he uses the strategy without being asked or cued to do so and if he matches the appropriate strategy to the task.

Step 5: Generalization

After the student demonstrates mastery of a strategy at the independent practice level, determine whether she is able to generalize the use of the strategy to different situations, settings, teachers, and materials. You need to determine if the student continues to use the strategy after direct instruction of the strategy has stopped. For example, if she is taking the norm-referenced SAT for college entry, review with her whether she used CRAM for the multiple-choice sections.

Use of maintenance activities will allow students to retain mastery of strategies and facilitate generalization. You can have a 5-minute maintenance activity at the beginning of the class once or twice a week in which you feature the "Strategy of the Day." A strategy can be chosen and students are asked to recall the steps involved and describe how they used the strategy in the past week.

By implementing the five components of systematic, explicit instruction (introduction to teaching the strategy, teacher modeling, guided practice, independent practice, and generalization), you can help your students become more active, independent, and effective learners. You can be confident that you are providing your students with the kind of instruction that gives them the best opportunity for academic success. The next chapter provides detailed directions for how to apply this systematic, explicit teaching approach to develop learning strategies using the Active Learner Approach.

5

Implementing the Active Learner Approach

What is the purpose of this chapter?

- Purpose
- Introduction of case study

How do you implement the Active Learner Approach?

- Component 1: Individualized evaluation of student learning characteristics in relation to specific course demands
- Component 2: Development and implementation of a systematic strategy instructional plan
- Component 3: Evaluation of student success/make strategy instruction decisions
- Active Learner Approach Implementation Guide/Checklist

WHAT IS THE PURPOSE OF THIS CHAPTER?

Now that you have a basic understanding of the Active Learner Approach and its individual components, it is time to learn how the Active Learner Approach components can be implemented in a coordinated and continuous process to teach students with learning disabilities and ADHD important content-specific academic skills. The implementation of the Active Learner Approach is described according to three major components: 1) individualized evaluation of student learning characteristics in relation to specific course demands, 2) development and implementation of a systematic strategy instructional plan, and 3) evaluation of student success/make strategy instruction decisions (see Table 5.1). Descriptions of critical instructional features are provided for each component and the steps within each component. In conjunction with a description of each component and how each component can be implemented, a vignette involving a secondary-level student and her special education teacher is presented. Throughout the chapter you will follow how special education teacher Mr. Johnston and his student Jennifer implement each component. We hope that this will provide you with an organized and meaningful context within which to visualize how *you* can implement the Active Learner Approach with your students.

Meeting Jennifer

Jennifer is a tenth-grade student who has an identified learning disability that significantly affects her ability to read and gain meaning from class texts. She was identified and began receiving special education services in third grade. Although she has made significant progress in word recognition skills and reading fluency, Jennifer still struggles with reading comprehension. Jennifer also experiences some difficulty with taking tests. In particular, she has difficulty performing well on objective tests that involve multiple-choice questions. Memory retrieval is an area of difficulty for Jennifer, and this affects her reading comprehension and her test-taking skills. Her academic strengths include mathematics and music. Jennifer plays several instruments, including the guitar and the trumpet, and she is a member of her high school marching band. Although Jennifer does have friends, she is quite shy and is unsure of her academic abilities. Sometimes, her lack of confidence makes it difficult for her to ask questions in class or to advocate for herself in terms of appropriate accommodations. Jennifer is currently taking algebra II, American history, band II, biology I, physical education, and psychology with general education teachers. She also spends one period a day with Mr. Johnston, her special education resource teacher. Jennifer is working toward earning a standard diploma and has aspirations of going to college.

Meeting Mr. Johnston

Mr. Johnston is in his seventh year of teaching, and he has been a special education resource teacher since the beginning of his teaching career. He spent 4 years at the local middle school and is now in his third year at Paladin High School. He teaches students with mild disabilities including students with learning disabilities, ADHD, behavior disorders, and mild mental retardation. Mr. Johnston enjoys his students but is growing more and more disgruntled with

Table 5.1. Three major components of the Active Learner Approach

1. Individualized evaluation of student learning characteristics in relation to specific course demands
2. Development and implementation of a systematic strategy instructional plan
3. Evaluation of student success/make strategy instruction decisions

the many "extra" duties and assignments he has been given, not to mention the ever-increasing levels of required paperwork. There are days when Mr. Johnston wonders how he will ever get everything done! He gets frustrated when he can't focus on what he believes is important, most notably providing his students with the kind of instruction he knows they truly need. One of his many duties is to "follow" the progress of his 26 students in each of their general education classes. All total, that comes to 104 different classes that he is supposed to monitor. Given this caseload, Mr. Johnston still loves what he does and wants to make a difference for his students. Mr. Johnston has developed strong collaborative relationships with several general education teachers and has found these relationships very beneficial.

Jennifer's Current Academic Difficulties

Jennifer is doing adequately in most of her classes, but she is really struggling in American history and is also having difficulty in biology I. Jennifer is especially concerned about her American history class because this is a required course for graduation and is one of the courses covered by the state assessment. Mr. Johnston has seen Jennifer continually struggle with courses that require a lot of reading. He has managed to help Jennifer complete assignments in these classes but is fearful that this "tutorial" approach will not continue to be effective. He also wonders about the long-term effects of this kind of stopgap approach on Jennifer because she is not learning any strategies that will really help her in the future. Mr. Johnston has an idea about how to approach Jennifer's situation differently and wants to speak with Jennifer about it.

HOW DO YOU IMPLEMENT THE ACTIVE LEARNER APPROACH?

Component 1: Individualized Evaluation of Student Learning Characteristics in Relation to Specific Course Demands

Step 1: Introduce the Active Learner Approach An essential aspect of the Active Learner Approach is to encourage students to take an active role in their education. Students cannot be treated as passive participants during instruction if this is to occur. For students to really buy into becoming active participants in their learning, they must not be only equipped with the necessary skills but also be equipped with an understanding of how and why a particular instructional process can be successful. Therefore, it is important that students have the opportunity to understand how the Active Learner Approach can assist them. To this end, it is important that you communicate to students the purpose of the Active Learner Approach and relate it to something important or meaningful to them (e.g., passing high-stakes tests, achieving a standard diploma, going to college). Also, it is important to help students understand the nature of learning strategies. One way to help students with learning disabilities and ADHD understand the Active Learner Approach is by using concrete examples that help them better understand strategies and their purposes.

MR. JOHNSTON INTRODUCES THE
ACTIVE LEARNER APPROACH TO JENNIFER

Mr. Johnston introduces the Active Learner Approach to Jennifer by explaining that an alternative approach to the difficulties she is having in her classes might be helpful. He explains to Jennifer that the Active Learner Approach will equip her with strategies that will allow her to be more successful in her present classes and that the strategies she learns in one class will be helpful for her in other classes as well. Jennifer is not certain what Mr. Johnston means by the term *strategies*. Mr. Johnston explains to her that strategies are like tools in a tool chest or like a road map. Pulling out a small hammer and road map from his desk, Mr. Johnston explains:

> Tools, like hammers or screwdrivers, allow us to build things or fix things that are broken. Road maps help us get from one place to another when we don't know the way. Screwdrivers, hammers, and road maps all help us do different kinds of things. Once we learn how to use them, we can accomplish similar tasks in the future using the same tools or maps. Strategies are just like tools in a toolbox or a road map for a particular city or state. Instead of helping us build things or find our way when driving, they help us accomplish things we want to do in school, such as reading textbooks in a way that we understand what we are reading, taking multiple-choice tests so we can show what we really know, or taking notes in a way that helps us remember what was covered in class. When you learn a strategy for a particular skill such as reading your American history textbook for meaning, then you can use it for reading textbooks in other classes as well.

With this explanation, Jennifer asks how she can learn strategies.

   Step 2: Evaluate Your Student's Current Academic Performance by Examining Grades in All Courses   In order to determine how to help your students achieve their learning goals, it is important to find out where they are currently struggling academically. Certainly, it is helpful to use any previous evaluation information to assist you (e.g., achievement tests, cognitive tests). Even more important, though, is determining in what courses your students are having the most difficulty and what particular types of assignments they seem to struggle with the most. Doing this provides you with a picture of your students' immediate learning needs and provides you with a place to start to make instructional decisions. A simple form can be used to write down their current overall grade in a course as well as grades on specific assignments (see Figure 5.1). After collecting this information for each relevant course, you can easily summarize your students' performance in a way that clearly shows what course(s) and

Course:	
Teacher:	
Assignment	Grade
1.	
2.	
3.	
4.	
5.	
6.	
7.	
8.	
9.	
10.	
Overall course grade to date:	

Figure 5.1. Individual course grade summary sheet to be completed by student and course-specific teachers.

Overall summary		
Course	Overall grade to date	Assignments of concern by type of assignment and grade
Algebra II	A-	None
Biology I	C-	Vocabulary quizzes: D Tests: C-
P.E.	B	None
Psychology	B	None
American history	D-	Tests: F
Band II	A	None
Course/assignments for possible strategy intervention		
Courses/teachers		Types of assignments
American history/Ms. Campbell		Tests: F
Biology I/Mr. Rodriguez		Vocabulary quizzes: D Tests: C-

Figure 5.2.   Overall grade record sheet completed by the special education teacher.

what corresponding assignments your students are doing well with and which ones they are struggling with (see Figure 5.2).

MR. JOHNSTON EVALUATES JENNIFER'S CURRENT ACADEMIC PERFORMANCE BY EXAMINING HER COURSE GRADES

Mr. Johnston has a general idea of how Jennifer is doing in her courses, but he does not have a clear picture of how she is doing with particular assignments that require specific academic/learning skills (e.g., reading, writing, mathematics, study skills). He could meet with each teacher himself, but he wants to encourage Jennifer to take an active part in her learning and in improving her academic performance. Mr. Johnston believes that an important aspect of active learning for students is their ability to effectively communicate with their teachers. Therefore, he believes it is important that Jennifer learn to effectively communicate with her teachers about her school performance. He prepares a simple grade report sheet that Jennifer can fill out (see Figure 5.1).

Mr. Johnston discusses the purpose of the grade sheet with Jennifer and also reviews the appropriate ways to ask her teachers for her grades. Mr. Johnston and Jennifer role play how she might approach Mr. Jones without being too apprehensive. Jennifer's lack of confidence results from her anxiety about what teachers and students might think about her. This is a barrier for Jennifer in terms of communicating with teachers, and Mr. Johnston wants to ensure that Jennifer learn ways to deal with her anxiety. Before Jennifer gets her grades from her teachers, Mr. Johnston communicates with each one to let them know what Jennifer will be doing and why she is doing it.

Mr. Johnston reviews the grade sheets completed by Jennifer and her teachers and summarizes them using the form illustrated in Figure 5.2. Based on Jennifer's current grades, Mr. Johnston has a much better "picture" of Jennifer's present academic performance. In particular, Mr. Johnston clearly sees that Jennifer is having difficulty in two courses: American history and biology I. He also has a clear perspective regarding the types of assignments Jennifer is struggling with in those courses. Mr. Johnston believes this information will help as he works with Jennifer using the Active Learner Approach.

Step 3: Evaluate Your Student's Individual Learning Needs as They Relate to Specific Courses   Once you have a clear picture of how your student is performing in her classes, then you can determine how your student's particular learning needs may affect her success in particular courses. To do this, you must know what particular learning skills your student does or doesn't possess and the degree to which she uses them effectively. The Active Learner Questionnaires in Appendixes A and B can provide you with this knowledge. First, make copies of the questionnaires and have your student and her teachers complete them. You also will complete one. Next, review the questionnaires and evaluate the responses. Look for particular learning areas where your student seems to have the most difficulty (e.g., organization, test taking, reading, writing). Those areas in which the majority of questions indicate difficulties for your student (a high rate of Y responses, which indicates the student always has difficulty with a particular skill) should be areas that are targeted for strategy instruction. As you evaluate the questionnaire responses, also consider the specific courses in which the majority of Y responses occur for a particular learning area. For example, your student may have a high number of Y responses in the learning area of test taking from your student's chemistry and algebra teachers but N or S responses (meaning your student has no difficulty or sometimes has difficulty with a particular skill) from the other teachers. This indicates that there is something unique about the course and content for chemistry and algebra that make performing particular test taking skill(s) difficult for your student. Comparing your student's responses with her teachers' responses provides you with insight regarding how accurately your student perceives her own learning abilities. Because you typically will have a more global view of your student's learning strengths and learning needs (compared with your student's content teachers who work with her only in one content area), comparing your ratings with other teachers' ratings helps you better visualize how your student functions in specific content areas. After you have reviewed the questionnaires, you need to discuss the results with your student. Including your student at this point is important because it maintains her active involvement in evaluating her own learning. In addition, she can provide you with valuable feedback about her own perceptions of her learning difficulties as they relate to specific courses. With your direction, you and your student can determine which specific skills and corresponding strategies you will work on as well as what specific courses you will target for strategy instruction. The following steps provide you with a structure for evaluating your student's needs as they relate to specific courses:

1. Copy and complete the Active Learner Questionnaires in Appendixes A and B.

2. Evaluate the completed Active Learner Questionnaires.

3. Discuss the questionnaire results with your student.

4. Determine which skills and corresponding strategy(ies) to teach.

MR. JOHNSTON EVALUATES JENNIFER'S LEARNING NEEDS AS THEY RELATE TO SPECIFIC COURSES

Copy and Complete the Active Learner Questionnaires in Appendixes A and B

Mr. Johnston makes a copy of the Active Learner Student Questionnaire (see Appendix A), and he makes several copies of the Active Learner Teacher Questionnaire (see Appendix B). He explains to Jennifer that before she can begin learning strategies, they first need to decide what skills she needs the most help with and on what courses they should focus. Mr. Johnston shows Jennifer the Active Learner Student Questionnaire and describes its purpose and format. He decides to assist Jennifer as she responds to the first few items on the questionnaire. He wants to be sure that she understands what to do but is careful to not influence how she responds to the questionnaire. When he is confident that Jennifer understands how to complete the questionnaire correctly, he explains to her that he will fill out a questionnaire as well. He also tells Jennifer that he is going to ask several of her teachers to complete the questionnaire. Once everyone has completed the questionnaire, Jennifer and Mr. Johnston will compare the responses and use the questionnaires to help them decide what skills and course to focus on first.

That afternoon, Mr. Johnston asks Ms. Campbell and Mr. Rodriguez, Jennifer's American history and biology I teachers, to complete the questionnaire. Mr. Johnston believes it is important to determine what skills Ms. Campbell and Mr. Rodriguez believe Jennifer is having difficulty with because American history and biology I are the courses in which she is struggling the most. Mr. Johnston also asks Jennifer's algebra II teacher, Ms. Bartell, to fill out the questionnaire because he is interested to see how she "sees" Jennifer's skills in the context of a class she does well in. Mr. Johnston also takes a few minutes to share with them what he hopes to do with the information. Figure 5.3 illustrates the results from the completed reading section of the questionnaire for Jennifer by Mr. Johnston, Ms. Campbell, Mr. Rodriguez, and Ms. Bartell.

Evaluate the Completed Active Learner Questionnaires

As you can see from Figure 5.3, there are several items in which there is substantial agreement and other items in which there are discrepancies. Mr. Johnston reviews the results of the questionnaires and notes those items in which Y (meaning Jennifer always has difficulty with the skill) was recorded by everyone or nearly everyone (see Figure 5.4). He reasons that these skills truly must be skills Jennifer has trouble with in most, if not all, of her courses.

As Mr. Johnston examines the ratings for these items, he notices that Ms. Bartell's ratings are discrepant from everyone else's ratings. Mr. Johnston concludes that there must be something different about how these skills are used or emphasized in Jennifer's algebra II course; perhaps less reading from a textbook is required. In addition, mathematics has always been a relative strength area for Jennifer. Mr. Johnston reasons that Ms. Bartell's ratings reflect both differing course demands in terms of reading in algebra II and that mathematics is a strength for Jennifer. In contrast to this situation, the reading demands in both American history and biology I are greater, and this could certainly explain the ratings of Ms. Campbell and Mr. Rodriguez. Mr. Johnston also thinks about his rating, and he admits to himself that most of the reading he has worked on with Jennifer has been related to the humanities and history. He certainly has observed her struggle with reading in these areas. Given that Jennifer also rates these items as skills she always has difficulty with, Mr. Johnston surmises that these are specific skills in need of attention across all courses in which reading from the text is emphasized.

Reading	Jennifer's rating	Mr. Johnston's rating (special education resource teacher)	Ms. Campbell's rating (American history teacher)	Mr. Rodriguez's rating (biology I teacher)	Ms. Bartell's rating (algebra II teacher)
Vocabulary					
1. I have difficulty understanding difficult words that I read.	Y	Y	Y	Y	S
2. I forget vocabulary words I learn.	Y	Y	Y	Y	N
Comprehension					
1. I have difficulty getting the overall ideas when I read material for my classes.	Y	Y	Y	Y	N
2. I have difficulty understanding the main idea when I read.	Y	Y	Y	Y	N
3. I have difficulty understanding the details when I read.	N	Y	Y	S	N
4. I have difficulty understanding stories that I read.	N	S	Y	N	N
5. I read slowly.	Y	Y	Y	S	S
6. I have difficulty understanding what I read from the computer screen.	N	S	N	N	N
7. I don't usually use aids to help me read.	N	Y	Y	S	N

Figure 5.3. Results from the reading section of the Learning Questionnaires. Y means the statement is always true, S means the statement is sometimes true, N means the statement is not true. *Note:* Items in the left column are written in the first person as reflected in the Active Learner Student Questionnaire. Actual items in the Active Learner Teacher Questionnaire are worded in the third person.

Next, Mr. Johnston notes items in which only one or two teachers recorded Y (always has difficulty) and the others recorded S (sometimes has difficulty) or N (never has difficulty; see Figure 5.5). Mr. Johnston reasons that these items may represent skills of difficulty related to the particular content and demands of the course taught by the teacher who recorded Y.

As Mr. Johnston examines these responses more closely, he notices that Ms. Campbell, Jennifer's American history teacher, responded that Jennifer *always* has difficulty with these skills. In contrast, Mr. Rodriguez, Jennifer's biology I teacher, responded that Jennifer *sometimes* has difficulty or *never* has difficulty with these skills. Mr. Johnston responded with a Y to three of the four items. Looking back at Jennifer's grades in biology I and civics from last year, he sees that Jennifer made a

B- in biology I but a *C-* in civics. Mr. Johnston reasons that there must be something significant regarding how the reading skills represented by these items are used in history/social studies-type courses compared with science-related courses. Perhaps the skills represented by these items need to be considered primarily in context of Jennifer's American history course.

Reading	Jennifer's rating	Mr. Johnston's rating (special education resource teacher)	Ms. Campbell's rating (American history teacher)	Mr. Rodriguez's rating (biology I teacher)	Ms. Bartell's rating (algebra II teacher)
Vocabulary					
1. I have difficulty understanding difficult words that I read.	Y	Y	Y	Y	S
2. I forget vocabulary words I learn.	Y	Y	Y	Y	N
Comprehension					
1. I have difficulty getting the overall ideas when I read material for my classes.	Y	Y	Y	Y	N
2. I have difficulty understanding the main idea when I read.	Y	Y	Y	Y	N

Figure 5.4. Questionnaire items of high concern (all or nearly all teachers recorded Y).

Reading	Jennifer's rating	Mr. Johnston's rating (special education resource teacher)	Ms. Campbell's rating (American history teacher)	Mr. Rodriguez's rating (biology I teacher)	Ms. Bartell's rating (algebra II teacher)
Comprehension					
3. I have difficulty understanding the details when I read.	N	Y	Y	S	N
4. I have difficulty understanding stories that I read.	N	S	Y	N	N
5. I read slowly.	Y	Y	Y	S	S
7. I don't usually use aids to help me read.	N	Y	Y	S	N

Figure 5.5. Questionnaire items of moderate concern (one or two teachers recorded Y).

Last, Mr. Johnston examines Jennifer's responses in comparison to his responses. Because he has a more global view of how Jennifer deals with academic
demands compared with her content-specific teachers (e.g., Ms. Campbell, Mr.
Rodriguez, Ms. Bartell), he thinks this comparison will help him better visualize how
Jennifer perceives her own learning abilities. Figure 5.6 depicts the ratings of Jennifer and Mr. Johnston.

In particular, Mr. Johnston is interested in those skills in which he rated Jennifer
as always having difficulty with (Y) but in which Jennifer rated herself as not having
difficulty (N). These items are shaded in Figure 5.6. Item numbers 3 and 7 under
"Comprehension" represent skills where this is true. It is interesting to Mr. Johnston
that Jennifer doesn't perceive these skills as ones with which she has difficulty. Mr.

Reading	Jennifer's rating	Mr. Johnston's rating (special education resource teacher)
Vocabulary		
1. I have difficulty understanding difficult words that I read.	Y	Y
2. I forget vocabulary words I learn.	Y	Y
Comprehension		
1. I have difficulty getting the overall ideas when I read material for my classes.	Y	Y
2. I have difficulty understanding the main idea when I read.	Y	Y
3. I have difficulty understanding the details when I read.	N	Y
4. I have difficulty understanding stories that I read.	N	S
5. I read slowly.	Y	Y
6. I have difficulty understanding what I read from the computer screen.	N	S
7. I don't usually use aids to help me read.	N	Y

Figure 5.6.   Results from the reading section of Learning Questionnaires (Jennifer and Mr. Johnston).

Johnston recalls a number of times when working with Jennifer in a tutorial situation that she did not independently use information such as tables, headings in bold print, and highlighted text to answer questions or complete assignments (skills related to item 7). Because these are certainly important kinds of skills for gaining meaning from textbooks, Mr. Johnston notes this as something he and Jennifer need to examine more closely in the future. He is intrigued to know that Jennifer may perceive some of her learning abilities differently from him. He decides he might need to be more explicit in terms of what skills she may need to focus on instead of assuming she is independently aware of them.

Discuss the Questionnaire Results with Your Student

The next day, Mr. Johnston and Jennifer discuss the results of the Active Learner Questionnaires. Mr. Johnston first asks Jennifer to discuss her thoughts regarding the responses she gave. As he listens, Mr. Johnston notes insights that result from Jennifer's comments.

Then, Mr. Johnston shares with Jennifer a summary of her teachers' responses as well as his own. Mr. Johnston emphasizes those items that she and the majority of her teachers agree on. First, he emphasizes those areas that Jennifer *never* has trouble with (relative strengths). Mr. Johnston points out to Jennifer that these items represent areas of strength. He explains to Jennifer that she can use these skills to assist her as she develops other skills.

Next, Mr. Johnston points out those items in which Jennifer *always* has trouble. He explains that these are the skills she most likely needs to develop using strategies. Mr. Johnston also explains that because nearly everyone responded *always* to these items, it is probable that Jennifer needs to work on developing these skills in all content/course areas.

Then, Mr. Johnston points out those items in which *one or a few* of the teachers responded with *always*. He explains to Jennifer that these items represent skills that she needs to develop for only one or a few content/course areas. He asks Jennifer if she notices a difference between performing these skills in courses in which teachers do not have a concern and those courses in which teachers do have a concern. He points to item 7 for reading comprehension, "I don't usually use aids to help me read," and asks Jennifer to think how she might (or might not) have to use this skill in Ms. Campbell's American history class compared with Ms. Bartell's algebra II class. As they discuss this issue, Jennifer and Mr. Johnston determine that there are unique differences between the two courses. Reading the text is not an essential part of Ms. Bartell's class, whereas reading is a large part of Ms. Campbell's class. Also, Jennifer notes that her algebra II text has many examples involving numbers and math symbols that she comprehends, whereas her American history text has a lot of charts and tables that contain mostly words. Many times she struggles with the meaning of the terms or phrases used in these charts and tables. With this discussion, Jennifer and Mr. Johnston determine that it is likely Jennifer can perform these skills well in some courses because the need for the skill is less or the characteristics of the course/content area "fit" how she learns best. In contrast, the specific demands of another course/content area make using the skill more difficult because it is required to a greater extent or the characteristics of the course/content do not "fit" how Jennifer learns best.

Determine Which Skill(s) and Corresponding Strategy(ies) to Teach

After reviewing the results of the Active Learner Questionnaires, Mr. Johnston believes he has a much clearer picture of how he can help Jennifer. He also believes Jennifer gained some insight into how she learns, why she is able or unable to do well in certain courses, and what particular skills she needs to develop. Mr. Johnston is pleased that Jennifer saw "physical" evidence (in the form of the questionnaires) that teachers perceived her as having learning strengths instead of only having learning difficulties.

As Mr. Johnston examines his summary of the questionnaire responses, he prioritizes those skills that would have the most impact for Jennifer given her current academic difficulties. Mr. Johnston also wants to attend to Jennifer's particular concerns about her American history and biology I courses and the fact that these courses are linked to state assessments and obtaining a regular diploma. Mr. Johnston knows he and Jennifer cannot possibly work on every skill and skill area Jennifer needs help with relative to these courses, so he decides to focus on one area for now. Based on his prior experience with Jennifer, the documentation in her cumulative folder, and now the ratings on the questionnaires, Mr. Johnston believes that they should focus on reading. Although the assignments Jennifer has performed poorly on in American history and biology I are quizzes and tests, the teachers agree that her test-taking skills are not the primary issue because their tests primarily consist of short-answer questions rather than multiple-choice items (the kind of test-taking items Jennifer traditionally has difficulty with). In contrast to objective tests, the teachers' tests rely heavily on understanding concepts presented in the texts. Given this reality, Mr. Johnston believes that they should focus on how Jennifer applies reading to content courses in the hope that by improving her understanding from reading text, Jennifer will perform better on tests and quizzes.

He uses the results of the Active Learner Questionnaires to list those skills that are of highest priority, namely those reading skills the majority of teachers, in particular Jennifer's American history and biology I teachers, rated as skills with which Jennifer always has difficulty. In addition, Mr. Johnston recognizes that Jennifer is having the most difficulty with American history, so he adds to the list those skills Ms. Campbell rated as Jennifer *always* having difficulty with but which the other teachers did not. Table 5.2 depicts the questionnaire items Mr. Johnston listed as high priority skills and the courses to which they pertain.

Mr. Johnston shares this list with both Ms. Campbell and Mr. Rodriguez as well as with Jennifer. As he does this, he asks for their opinions about which skills they think are most important for Jennifer to learn. Each person picks the four skills he or she believes are the most important. There is agreement regarding two items, but there are differing opinions regarding the other two. Table 5.3 illustrates the four skills each person rated as most important.

Table 5.2. Reading questionnaire items/skills of high priority

American history and biology I

Item 1 (Vocabulary):	I have difficulty understanding difficult words that I read.
Item 2 (Vocabulary):	I forget vocabulary words I learn.
Item 1 (Comprehension):	I have difficulty getting the overall ideas when I read materials for my classes.
Item 2 (Comprehension):	I have difficulty understanding the main idea when I read.

American history only

Item 3 (Comprehension):	I have difficulty understanding the details when I read.
Item 4 (Comprehension):	I have difficulty understanding stories that I read.
Item 5 (Comprehension):	I read slowly.
Item 7 (Comprehension):	I don't usually use aids to help me read.

Based on this information, it is clear to Mr. Johnston that reading comprehension questionnaire items 1, "I have difficulty getting the overall ideas when I read material for my classes," and 2, "I have difficulty understanding the main idea when I read," reflect skills Jennifer needs to develop in order to be successful in both American history and biology I because everyone included this skill in their list. Mr. Johnston notices that he and Ms. Campbell agree that item 3, "I have difficulty understanding the details when I read," is an important skill. He also notices that Jennifer did not list that item. He recalls that this was a skill Jennifer rated as *never* having difficulty with. Mr. Johnston decides this should be a skill Jennifer develops because Jennifer is apparently unaware that it is one she has difficulty with and because it is a skill he and Ms. Campbell think is important.

Mr. Johnston sees that Jennifer and Ms. Campbell included item 5 under reading comprehension, "I read slowly," on their lists. Although reading rate is certainly important, this is a reading skill that requires a long period of time to develop. He believes more benefit can be gained from focusing on other skills at this point. Mr. Johnston also sees that Jennifer and Mr. Rodriguez included item 1 under reading vocabulary, "I have difficulty understanding difficult words that I read." Although Mr. Johnston did not list this item, he can understand why Mr. Rodriguez believes this is important given the nature of the vocabulary in biology. The fact that Jennifer sees this as important is meaningful to Mr. Johnston as well. He wants to be sure Jennifer sees the value in the skills she learns. He knows that unless she values them, then it is unlikely she will learn to use them successfully. Mr. Johnston decides this skill should also be a skill of focus. Mr. Johnston shares with Jennifer the four skills he believes will be most helpful for her at this point and explains his reasoning for choosing each one. Mr. Johnston asks for Jennifer's input about his choices. Jennifer appreciates the fact that Mr. Johnston asks for her opinion. She also feels good that her responses to the questionnaire were included and taken seriously by Mr. Johnston. Mr. Johnston's explanations regarding the reasons he thought these four skills would be most helpful made sense to Jennifer, and this helped her better understand why they are the ones she will learn. With his explanations and respect for her thoughts, Jennifer agrees that these four skills seem like good ones on which to

Table 5.3. Four reading skills rated most important by person

Jennifer	Mr. Johnston	Ms. Campbell	Mr. Rodriguez
Item 1 (Comprehension): I have difficulty getting the overall ideas when I read materials for my classes.	Item 1 (Comprehension): I have difficulty getting the overall ideas when I read materials for my classes.	Item 1 (Comprehension): I have difficulty getting the overall ideas when I read materials for my classes.	Item 1 (Comprehension): I have difficulty getting the overall ideas when I read materials for my classes.
Item 2 (Comprehension): I have difficulty understanding the main idea when I read.	Item 2 (Comprehension): I have difficulty understanding the main idea when I read.	Item 2 (Comprehension): I have difficulty understanding the main idea when I read.	Item 2 (Comprehension): I have difficulty understanding the main idea when I read.
Item 5 (Comprehension): I read slowly.	Item 3 (Comprehension): I have difficulty understanding the details when I read.	Item 3 (Comprehension): I have difficulty understanding the details when I read.	Item 1 (Vocabulary): I have difficulty understanding difficult words that I read.
Item 1 (Vocabulary): I have difficulty understanding difficult words that I read.	Item 7 (Comprehension): I don't usually use aids to help me read.	Item 5 (Comprehension): I read slowly.	Item 2 (Vocabulary): I forget vocabulary words I learn.

focus. The next day, Mr. Johnston discusses with Ms. Campbell and Mr. Rodriguez the four skills they will work on with Jennifer. Ms. Campbell and Mr. Rodriguez are appreciative of Mr. Johnston's efforts to include them in helping Jennifer and also like the fact that the skills chosen will be taught in relation to the specific courses they teach. They confess that they find it difficult to meet all the needs of their students, particularly students with disabilities, and are thankful that someone has a logical plan for helping them to do this for Jennifer. Table 5.4 shows the questionnaire items and the corresponding strategies Mr. Johnston, Jennifer, Ms. Campbell, and Mr. Rodriguez agree to work on *together*.

Component 2: Development and Implementation of a Systematic Strategy Instructional Plan

Step 1: Develop a Plan to Teach the Selected Strategies   You need to develop an organized plan to implement systematic strategy instruction effectively. First, you and your student need to determine which strategy should be learned first and in which course(s) your student will use the strategy. Second, you need to identify those individuals (e.g., general education teacher, parents, other school personnel) who are best suited to provide you and your student instructional support as your student learns the strategy and how to use it effectively in his class(es). Third, you need to plan where and how the strategy instruction will be provided (i.e., resource room by special education teacher, general education classroom by content teacher).

Table 5.4. Targeted questionnaire items/skills

Questionnaire item/skill	Strategy
Item 1 (Vocabulary): I have difficulty understanding difficult words that I read.	So We Go C
Item 1 (Comprehension): I have difficulty getting the overall ideas when I read material for my class.	BCDE
Item 2 (Comprehension): I have difficulty understanding the main idea when I read.	RAP-Q
Item 3 (Comprehension): I have difficulty understanding the details when I read.	Ask 5 W's & 1 H & Answer

MR. JOHNSTON DEVELOPS A PLAN TO TEACH JENNIFER THE BCDE STRATEGY

Decide Which Strategy Should Be Taught First

Although all four of the skills and corresponding strategies are important, Mr. Johnston knows that he cannot expect Jennifer to learn them all at once. Therefore, he examines each skill as well as the relative importance each has to Jennifer's immediate success. He knows that it is important that Jennifer experience success early on as they begin implementing the Active Learner Approach. Jennifer presently lacks confidence in her academic abilities, and Mr. Johnston believes that success with her first strategy is very important. Jennifer's concern about American history, in particular, is also something Mr. Johnston thinks is important to consider. He reasons that if Jennifer experiences success in a class that she sees as difficult, yet also sees as important, then her experience will compel her to want to learn additional strategies for that course as well as others. Mr. Johnston decides that the first skill he and Jennifer will focus on is understanding the overall ideas from assigned readings (Item 1, Comprehension). The strategy that corresponds to this skill is BCDE. The BCDE strategy includes four steps for gaining meaning from text and emphasizes prereading activities to help the student survey major topics in a passage. Also, it emphasizes self-questioning techniques during reading to help students actively engage themselves with the text. Last, the strategy emphasizes postreading techniques for helping students summarize in their own words what they learned from reading:

Before reading—survey
Create questions to ask yourself
During reading—answer questions
End of reading—summarize

Identify a Strategy Instruction Support "Team"

General Education Teacher   Mr. Johnson realizes that although he will be responsible for the primary teaching of the BCDE strategy, Jennifer will need support from Ms. Campbell because it is in her American history class that Jennifer will be applying the BCDE strategy. Mr. Johnston also realizes that Jennifer will be completing much of her class readings at home and decides that her parents could also provide helpful support to Jennifer.

First, Mr. Johnston discusses his ideas with Ms. Campbell. He knows that Ms. Campbell is already swamped with work, trying to prepare her students to pass the American history state assessment test. Therefore, he wants to ensure that she does not see her participation on Jennifer's strategy support team as burdensome.

As they discuss Jennifer's situation, Mr. Johnston explains that Ms. Campbell's primary responsibility will be to monitor Jennifer's use of the BCDE strategy in her class after Mr. Johnston has taught her the strategy and provided her opportunities to practice it in his resource class. This includes reminding Jennifer to use it when reading assignments are given, to periodically check with Jennifer to see if she used the BCDE strategy for particular reading assignments, and to communicate with Jennifer and Mr. Johnston about Jennifer's academic performance in those assignments that require use of the BCDE strategy. Mr. Johnston explains that Ms. Campbell's role will be to support Jennifer as she independently uses the BCDE strategy in her class. He tells Ms. Campbell that he will provide Jennifer direct instruction for the strategy as well as a variety of practice activities to help her become proficient with it before she begins to apply it independently. He asks Ms. Campbell for a spare copy of the text so that he can use it as a context for both teaching the strategy and providing Jennifer practice.

Mr. Johnston then shares with Ms. Campbell particular learning characteristics that are barriers to Jennifer's *automatically* using strategies she has learned—in particular, Jennifer's problems with memory retrieval. Mr. Johnston describes how providing support initially and then fading that support over time (i.e., scaffolding) helps students successfully deal with learning barriers such as memory retrieval problems. All of this sounds reasonable to Ms. Campbell, and she appreciates Mr. Johnston describing how Jennifer's particular learning characteristics play a role in her learning because she never had that connection presented to her before.

Last, Mr. Johnston shares with Ms. Campbell a copy of the BCDE strategy cue sheet and describes each step and how it is used. He also asks her if it would be permissible for Jennifer to keep a copy of the strategy cue sheet (a sheet that contains each step of the strategy) in her American history notebook so she can refer to it as needed. Ms. Campbell is surprised to find out that a student wouldn't already know that the steps in the BCDE strategy were good ones to use when reading for understanding. She confesses that she assumed that all students knew how to do these things. She wonders whether there might be other students in her class who could benefit from this strategy. She decides it might be a good idea to present the strategy to her entire class and show her students how they can use it with their American history textbook. She even thinks it would be a good idea to put up a poster-board size display of the BCDE strategy on a classroom wall as a way to remind students to use the strategy when reading. Mr. Johnston is glad that Ms. Campbell sees the value in the strategy and knows that her interest in presenting it to her whole class will provide extra exposure and reinforcement to Jennifer. He also likes the idea that Jennifer will not be the only one using the strategy in Ms. Campbell's class. Mr. Johnston knows this situation will be good for boosting Jennifer's self-confidence.

Parents   Mr. Johnston knows that Jennifer's parents, particularly her mother, have taken a keen interest in assisting their daughter with her learning. He'd like to include Jennifer's mother as a member of the instructional support team but also wants to be sure Jennifer has a say in how that might occur. Mr. Johnston discusses with Jennifer his idea of making her parents aware of what they will be doing. He suggests that Jennifer discuss with them what she is doing and asks her how she thinks they could be most helpful.

At first, Jennifer is hesitant because she does not want a lot of added pressure from her parents. In the past, Jennifer has felt her parents expected too much too soon, and this makes things more difficult for her. Mr. Johnston says he understands her concerns. Mr. Johnston and Jennifer brainstorm ways her parents could help that would not be too stressful for Jennifer. After several suggestions, they settle on some ideas. Jennifer says she first wants to be comfortable with the strategy *before* discussing it with her parents. She tells Mr. Johnston that once she understands the strategy, then she will be more comfortable sharing it with her parents because she will already understand it and understand how to use it. Mr. Johnston adds that Jennifer can bring the strategy cue sheet home and use it to help her describe to her parents what she is doing. Jennifer likes that idea because it will give her something concrete to refer to as she talks with her parents. Jennifer adds that she can also show her parents her American history textbook to explain that this will be the book with which she will use the strategy. Mr. Johnston suggests to Jennifer that at that point he can talk with her mother or father over the telephone to answer any questions they may have. Jennifer says that would be okay with her.

Jennifer likes the idea of Mr. Johnston calling and answering questions she may not be able to answer. It also makes her feel the two of them are on a team. Jennifer likes having some independence with this but also likes having the support Mr. Johnston will provide. Mr. Johnston likes the fact that Jennifer is willing to take an active role in including her parents.

Plan Instruction

Now that Mr. Johnston knows that Ms. Campbell will assist Jennifer as she uses the BCDE strategy and how Jennifer's mom will be included, he thinks about how he can plan instruction that will be the most beneficial to Jennifer. He views his role as providing primary instruction, modeling the strategy and how to use it, ensuring that Jennifer has plenty of opportunities to "try out" using the strategy, providing Jennifer with feedback as she begins learning how to apply the strategy, and monitoring her performance. He has Jennifer in his class once a day for approximately 45 minutes. He decides to block out 20 minutes during that period for the next 5 days to provide Jennifer explicit, systematic instruction. Once Jennifer demonstrates an understanding of the strategy and how to use it, then he will discuss with Ms. Campbell how Jennifer will use the BCDE strategy in her class.

Step 2: Teach the Strategy Using Systematic, Explicit Instruction   This section shows how to teach a strategy using systematic, explicit instruction according to four stages: 1) introduce the strategy and build meaningful student connections, 2) provide explicit teacher modeling, 3) provide guided practice/scaffold instruction, and 4) provide independent practice and generalization of strategy to target course(s). Please note that stage 4 incorporates the last two steps of systematic, explicit instruction (independent practice and generalization) described in Chapter 2. The purpose of this format is to help you understand the essential features of systematic, explicit strategy instruction. Although each stage represents a specific component of systematic, explicit strategy instruction, this teaching approach should be conceptualized as a continuous process rather than as a truncated, piece-by-piece approach to teaching. A summary of its purpose and essential elements is presented for each stage.

Introduce the Strategy and Build Meaningful Student Connections   Once you have a clear idea about what strategy you are going to teach, then you can begin teaching. An important part of systematic, explicit instruction is to help your students find something meaningful about what they are going to learn. Students with learning problems often do not make meaningful connections between what they already know and what they are currently learning. This important learning skill is often "automatic" for efficient and successful learners. Sometimes we assume that all students do this independently. Unfortunately, this is typically not the case for students with learning disabilities and ADHD. However, students with learning disabilities and ADHD *can make meaningful connections* when their teacher encourages connection building by emphasizing it during instruction.

There are three simple things that you can do before you begin to model the skill that will assist your students to make meaningful connections. These three elements can be easily remembered using the mnemonic LIP: link, identify, and provide meaning/rationale (Mercer & Mercer, 1998). One thing you can do is to *link* the skill that your students will learn to their prior experiences and knowledge. It is important that you think about what knowledge or experiences your students have that relates to the strategy and corresponding skill you are teaching. For example, Jennifer has difficulty understanding overall ideas from what she reads in her American history textbook. Perhaps you have students who have similar difficulties. Maybe your students like to read popular magazines such as *Sports Illustrated.* You could link the skill, "comprehending overall ideas from text," to what your students do when they read an article in their favorite magazine. They probably read the table of contents to decide what article they are going to read. When they turn to that page, they probably read the title of the article, which signals to them what the article is going to be about. This is where your link to the strategy can be made. The skill your students use when they read their favorite magazine is the same skill you'd like for them to apply to reading textbooks.

A second thing you can do to help your students build meaningful connections is to clearly *identify* what it is they will be learning. Doing this in a visual as well as auditory way is important. This can be done simply by writing the learning objective on a note card or piece of paper (in words that make sense to your student) and saying the learning objective aloud as the student reads it. It is also helpful to have the student tell you *in her own words* what she is going to learn. This simple technique is important because many students with learning problems do not actively think about the skill they are going to learn. They may go through an entire lesson or teaching session without recognizing the actual skill they are learning. This happens due to possible attention problems, metacognitive deficits, and other passive learning characteristics that are a part of their disabilities. Seeing the learning objective, hearing it, and repeating it in their own words provides the students with multiple "sensory inputs." Combined with the fact that you emphasize what the students will learn, the multiple modes of input make it more likely that the students will know and remember what skill it is they are learning.

A third teaching technique that helps students make meaningful connections is to *provide* a rationale/meaning for learning a strategy. This can be done in a number of ways, but whatever way it is done it must be carried out in a way that is meaningful to your students. Providing meaning to teenagers requires knowing what teenagers are interested in and what they experience. By relating a concept or skill to something relevant in their lives, you subtly help them see how the concept or skill can be important to them. This is essential for many students with learning problems. They often do not see the relevance of academics in their lives. Even if the relevance of a academic concept or skill is readily apparent to most students, the relevance will likely not be apparent to students with learning problems due to their passive learning characteristics, metacognitive deficits, and memory problems.

MR. JOHNSTON HELPS JENNIFER BUILD MEANINGFUL CONNECTIONS

Knowing that he needs to help Jennifer value the strategy she is going to learn, Mr. Johnston knows he also needs to try and connect the skill of "understanding main ideas from assigned readings" to something Jennifer values and has previous experience with. He also wants to be sure Jennifer clearly understands what it is she is going to be learning. Mr. Johnston thinks about Jennifer and her interests and comes up with an idea. Mr. Johnston knows that Jennifer likes music and that she likes to keep up-to-date on what is going on in the music world by reading several popular magazines.

Link

Mr. Johnston lays several magazines out on a table and asks Jennifer if she recognizes any of them. Jennifer immediately rattles off the names of each magazine. Mr. Johnston asks Jennifer how she knows the names of the magazines. Jennifer laughs and replies that the titles are right there on the front cover of each magazine. Next, Mr. Johnston asks Jennifer what kinds of topics each magazine covers. Jennifer describes some topics in general terms. Mr. Johnston asks Jennifer which magazine has the best information about music. Jennifer quickly points to one and says that it has the best coverage of what is happening in the music world. Mr. Johnston asks

Jennifer how she knows that. Quickly, Jennifer turns to the table of contents in the magazine and points to a section titled *Music Today*. Jennifer describes what topics the section covered in that issue. She is especially intrigued by the article on one of her favorite musicians who had a injury that might hamper his ability to play his instrument.

Mr. Johnston asks Jennifer to think about what she did as she responded to his questions about the magazines. Jennifer realizes that she did some specific things, such as reading the titles and examining the table of contents. Mr. Johnston asks Jennifer if doing these things helped her read and understand what was in her favorite magazines. Jennifer thinks about it (something she had never done before) and replies that doing those things did help her.

Identify

At this point, Mr. Johnston introduces the BCDE strategy by showing Jennifer the BCDE strategy cue sheet. He also points to the skill the BCDE strategy helped with, which is written on the BCDE strategy cue sheet. He reads the skill aloud and asks Jennifer to read it as well. Mr. Johnston tells Jennifer that this is the skill they are going to work on and that the BCDE strategy is going to help her learn to understand main ideas from her textbooks. He reminds Jennifer of the conversation that they had a few days ago about strategies and what they were. Mr. Johnston explains that the strategy will teach her how to do particular things that will help her better comprehend what she reads in her textbook, much like the things she already does when reading her favorite magazines (e.g., focusing on titles, using the table of contents).

Provide Rationale/Meaning

Mr. Johnston asks Jennifer if she is worried about passing the American history part of the state assessment test and her American history class. Jennifer says that she is worried. Mr. Johnston explains that learning to use the BCDE strategy will help her pass her American history class as well as help her better understand those concepts that will be included on the state assessment test.

Provide Explicit Teacher Modeling Once you have helped your students build meaningful connections between their prior experiences and the strategy through LIP, then you are ready to help your students initially acquire a beginning understanding of the strategy and the skill it represents. The most helpful tool for students with learning problems is you, their teacher! You are the learning bridge across which the students can find understanding of any concept or skill. There are several key elements that make explicit modeling by a teacher a highly effective instructional strategy:

- Clearly describe the strategy, its purpose, and each step.

- Clearly model/demonstrate how to implement each step of the strategy in a meaningful context (i.e., the content/material the student will be applying it to).

- Use multisensory methods (e.g., visual, auditory, tactile, kinesthetic) to ensure the strategy and its elements are accessible to the student.

- Model both examples and nonexamples of accurate uses of the strategy and its steps.

- *Think aloud* by saying what you are thinking as you perform the strategy.

- Engage the students as you model by asking questions and prompting their thinking at certain points.

By consciously including each of these instructional elements as you explicitly model the strategy, you greatly increase the odds that your students will acquire a beginning understanding of the strategy and how to use it. However, it is important to remember that, at this point, students have only a *beginning* understanding of the strategy. Expecting students with learning disabilities and ADHD to move directly to successful implementation of the strategy without further instruction will likely result in failure.

MR. JOHNSTON EXPLICITLY MODELS THE BCDE STRATEGY FOR JENNIFER

Mr. Johnston Clearly Describes the Strategy

Provide a Visual Display of the Strategy   Mr. Johnston knows he needs to first describe the BCDE strategy, its purpose, and its steps before he begins showing Jennifer how to implement it. He likens this to the time he first learned to snow ski. He remembers how thankful he was when the ski instructor described to him each piece of skiing equipment and the purpose for each piece. He remembers thinking how foolish he would have looked had he tried to "guess" what each piece of equipment was for and/or tried to guess what part of his body the piece of equipment was supposed to be attached to! Mr. Johnston decides that a good way to describe the BCDE strategy to Jennifer is to have a visual display of the strategy, including a statement about its purpose. He also thinks it's a good idea to describe the strategy in the context of Jennifer's American history textbook.

> "Okay, I have a reading assignment in my American history textbook. I need to read pages 45–65. Now, I could simply read the 20 pages and then move on to something else. However, if I did that, I may not really understand what I read very well. So, I'm going to use a strategy that will help me better understand what I read. A strategy is like a map that will help guide me. The name of the strategy I'm going to use is BCDE. I have a visual representation of the BCDE strategy here." (See p. 66.)

BCDE STRATEGY:
TO HELP ME GET THE OVERALL IDEA WHEN I READ

> **B**efore reading—survey
> **C**reate questions to ask yourself
> **D**uring reading—answer the questions
> **E**nd of reading—summarize

Before reading, survey the material to be read.

- Always look over the pages you have to read before you actually start reading.

- If you are reading a textbook, read the title, side headings, paragraph headings, pictures, graphics, bold-face words, and study questions. Think of how this chapter is related to previous chapters.

- If you are reading a story, look back at the previous section you read and predict what you think will happen in this section. Skim the paragraphs to get some ideas of what might be in the section you will be reading. Make predictions about the characters and the actions that you think will take place.

Create questions to ask yourself while you read the material.

- For textbooks, create questions about the material based on the title, side headings, paragraph headings, pictures, graphics, bold-face words, and study questions. Write these on the front of note cards.

- For stories, write questions based on the predictions that you made. Make predictions about the characters and actions.

During reading of the material, answer the questions you wrote on the note cards.

- As you read the material, keep the questions that you wrote in mind.

- When you find the answers to the questions, write them on the backs of the cards.

End of reading—summarize.

- After you have finished reading, look over all the questions you wrote. If you did not find an answer to a question, then go back and try to find it.

- Ask yourself the questions and try to answer them.

- Say aloud to yourself a summary of the main ideas of what you just read.

- Ask yourself how the material you just read is related to material that you read before this.

- Predict how the material you just read will be related to the material that you will read next.

Describe the Purpose of the Strategy   After showing Jennifer a visual display of the BCDE strategy, Mr. Johnston decides that he needs to describe the strategy's purpose.

> "It says here that the purpose of the BCDE strategy is to help me to get the overall idea when I read." Mr. Johnston points to the statement that says what the BCDE strategy is for. He asks Jennifer, "What will the BCDE strategy help me to do?" Jennifer responds by saying it will help Mr. Johnston get the overall idea when he reads. Mr. Johnston then asks Jennifer how getting the overall idea when reading her American history text would help her. After thinking, Jennifer tells Mr. Johnston that if she is able to understand the overall ideas presented in her American history text, she could do better on the tests. She says that Ms. Campbell includes a lot of test questions that come from the reading assignments.

Describe Each Step of the Strategy   At this point, Mr. Johnston begins to describe each step of the BCDE strategy. He knows that before he can expect Jennifer to use the BCDE strategy, she must first understand what each step represents.

> "The BCDE strategy has four primary steps. Each step is represented by the letters B, C, D, and E. These letters are written in darker print and let me know that this is a major step of the strategy. (Mr. Johnston points to each letter as he says this.) The first step, or the B step, of the BCDE strategy is, "Before reading, survey the material to be read." What is the B step? (Jennifer repeats the step.) What does it mean to survey?" (Jennifer says she kind of knows but is not totally sure. Mr. Johnston knows that Jennifer typically has difficulty recalling the meaning of vocabulary words, even though she may actually know them. With this in mind, he brought a set of binoculars that he uses when he goes on bird watching trips. He and Jennifer go to the window of the room and use the binoculars to survey the school grounds for a bird. Mr. Johnston uses this example to help Jennifer remember what the word *survey* means.) "Now, to help us understand how to survey something we are reading, we can use the bulleted items written below the step. (Mr. Johnston points to the bullets below the B step.) These bullets will help us complete the B step." (Jennifer and Mr. Johnston read the bullets and discuss what they mean. As they discuss the B step, Mr. Johnston uses a copy of Jennifer's American history text to show examples of titles, side headings, and so forth. Mr. Johnston and Jennifer continue this process for the remaining steps of the BCDE strategy.)

By clearly describing the BCDE strategy, Mr. Johnston has helped Jennifer begin to acquire an initial understanding of the strategy. He also has provided Jennifer with a foundation for understanding the format and structure of the strategy. This will serve Jennifer well in the future as she learns additional strategies. Mr. Johnston also provided Jennifer instruction using multiple modes of input: visual (e.g., display of the BCDE strategy, use of American history text), auditory (e.g., verbal directions and prompts), and tactile/kinesthetic (e.g., pointing to features of the strategy and textbook, using binoculars). In addition, Mr. Johnston actively involved Jennifer as he described the strategy. All of these instructional features provided Jennifer a much richer and more productive learning experience.

Mr. Johnston Clearly Models How to Implement the Strategy

Now that Jennifer has an initial understanding of the strategy and its purpose, Mr. Johnston thinks she is ready to learn how the strategy and its steps can be implemented. To accomplish this, Mr. Johnston decides to model each step of the strategy using Jennifer's American history text. As he models the BCDE strategy, Mr. Johnston makes a point of using a variety of sensory inputs (e.g., visual, auditory, tactile, kinesthetic), provides examples and nonexamples of steps, and engages Jennifer with questions and other prompts and cueing. Mr. Johnston also decides to model the strategy in the context of an actual reading assignment Jennifer had in American history. Before modeling the strategy, Mr. Johnston reviews the reading selection and notes those particular features of the text he wants to emphasize.

"Okay, I have my American history textbook here. Let me check the page numbers that were assigned for this reading. Hmm, where did I write the page numbers down? Oh, yeah, I wrote them down in my American history notebook. (Mr. Johnston takes out Jennifer's notebook and points to where the page numbers are written down.) Here are the page numbers. Let me see, I need to read pages 45–65. I'll take a piece of paper to mark the last page I need to read. (Mr. Johnston places a piece of paper or sticky note on page 65.) Why do you think I did this? (Jennifer responds by saying the paper will let him know when to stop reading.) That's right, I may get so interested in what I'm reading that I may read all the way to the end of the book!" (Jennifer's lips turn upwards into a slight grin, appreciating the fact that Mr. Johnston made an attempt at a joke.)

"Now that I know the pages I have assigned, I can use the BCDE strategy to help me. What will the BCDE strategy help me to do? (Jennifer responds by reading the purpose of the strategy from the BCDE strategy cue sheet.) That's correct. The BCDE strategy will help me get the overall idea when I read. Okay, the first step in the BCDE strategy is B, which stands for *before reading, survey the material to be read.* (Mr. Johnston points to the B step as he says this.) What does B stand for? (Jennifer responds by saying the step.) Hmm, I can't remember what the word *survey* means. What does survey mean? (Jennifer says that it's like what they did with the binoculars, looking over something for a specific thing or things.) Great! Because surveying what I'm going to read about isn't something I usually do, I wonder why it might be helpful? Well, I guess if I have some idea about what I'm going to read, it can help me connect what I am reading to something I've already thought about. I guess that makes sense. It's kind of like seeing scenes from a new movie before you see the movie. Seeing the preview lets me know what the movie is about. When I go to see the movie, I follow the movie better because I know what to expect. Can you think of another situation where you might preview parts of something before you watch it or buy it?" (Jennifer thinks for a little bit and then says it's similar to what she does when she goes to the music store to buy a CD. By listening to parts of the CD at the listening station, she knows better what the songs on the CD are like. Then, she can decide whether she wants to buy the CD.) Mr. Johnston is impressed by her response. He had not thought of that before! In fact, he never knew it was possible to listen to CDs before you bought them!

"Okay, to survey what I'm going to read, I guess I need to look at different parts of the text that I've been assigned, kind of like looking at the previews of a movie or hearing clips of songs from a CD I might want to buy. Some parts of the reading assignment that will help me do this are the title, headings, pictures, tables, and other things. The title is usually at the beginning of the reading so I'll read it first. (Mr. Johnston points to the title and reads it aloud, "Five Causes of the Revolutionary War.") So, this section must be about five reasons the Revolutionary War occurred. What does the title tell me the reading is about? (Jennifer says that it's about five causes of the Revolutionary War.) Good. Because there are five causes, there probably should be five different headings for each cause. Let me find them. One way to do this is skimming the pages with my eyes and finger looking for words in bold print or for headings. (Mr. Johnston skims through the pages and picks out the headings that represent the five causes.) Oh, here's a heading: *Taxation Without Representation Causes Colonies To Unite.* (Mr. Johnston points to the heading.) How would I know if this heading has to do with a section about one of the causes of the Revolutionary War? (Jennifer responds by saying the word *causes* is in the title.) Good thinking. The word *causes* is a good cue. The heading says that taxation without representation caused the colonies to unite. This tells me that taxation without representation was an important issue to people. This certainly could be a reason the colonies went to war. Let's look for another heading that represents a cause for the Revolutionary War." (Mr. Johnston continues the same process. As they do this, Mr. Johnston points out at least one heading that doesn't represent one of the five causes and asks Jennifer to describe why it wouldn't be a cause.)

"Well, this chapter must be about the five causes of the Revolutionary War. I also know it has additional information in it because some of the headings didn't have to do with causes. There are also some other things in the text that can help me when I survey. Pictures, graphs, bold-face words, and questions at the end can all help me better understand what I am going to read about as well." (Mr. Johnston models how to use several of these other textbook features to survey.)

"Now, another way I could have begun doing my readings is to just open the book and start reading at page 45. I'll do that now." (Mr. Johnston finds page 45 and begins reading.) After reading several paragraphs he asks Jennifer, "Is this a very good way to survey the reading selection? Why not? Is this an example of the B step? (Jennifer and Mr. Johnston discuss why this is not very helpful.) Mr. Johnston continues this process as he models the remaining steps of the BCDE strategy.

By explicitly modeling each step of the BCDE strategy *within the context* of Jennifer's American history textbook, Mr. Johnston has helped Jennifer begin to understand what the BCDE strategy *looks* like and *sounds* like when being implemented in the kind of text with which she will be expected to use the strategy. He has made the BCDE strategy accessible to Jennifer because he integrated a number of important instructional features as he modeled the strategy. He provided Jennifer with a variety of sensory inputs (e.g., visual—using the strategy cue sheet, Jennifer's actual textbook; auditory—verbal think-alouds that made Mr. Johnston's thoughts audible to Jennifer; tactile/kinesthetic—pointing to and having Jennifer point to textbook features such as headings, pictures, and bold-face words). Mr. Johnston also demonstrated examples and nonexamples of the strategy steps. By doing this, Jennifer can better discriminate the features of a particular step by experiencing what it looks and sounds like and what it does not look and sound like. Mr. Johnston also engaged Jennifer as he modeled asking her questions and prompting her to think about why he did what he did.

Provide Guided Practice/Scaffold Instruction   Once a student has acquired an initial understanding of a strategy through systematic, explicit teacher modeling, guided practice/instructional scaffolding provides students with learning disabilities and ADHD a supported way to cognitively solidify their understanding of the strategy. Guided practice, in particular, helps students develop their ability to independently use a strategy. The learning characteristics of students with learning disabilities and ADHD make it difficult for them to transfer their initial understanding of a strategy to using the strategy independently. However, if students are provided a supported way to "try out" their initial understanding, then with feedback and positive reinforcement, they can successfully learn to perform the skill independently. Guided practice/scaffold instruction is characterized by several instructional features:

- Occurs after explicit modeling of the strategy

- Incorporates use of actual course materials

- Teacher direction/support is faded based on individual student needs

- Can be conceptualized as occurring at three levels of support:

  - *High*–teacher directs/models most of the strategy steps; prompts student thinking with questions; student models one step or a part of a step(s)

  - *Medium*–teacher directs/models about half of the steps and student directs/models half of the steps; teacher prompts student's thinking with questions

  - *Low*–student models all of the strategy steps with little or no teacher direction

- Teacher provides specific corrective feedback as needed

- Teacher provides a lot of positive reinforcement for both accuracy and effort

- Provides the teacher a clear way to evaluate student understanding of the strategy

Mr. Johnston Provides Guided Practice/Scaffold Instruction of the BCDE Strategy for Jennifer

Based on Jennifer's responses to his questions and prompts as he previously modeled the BCDE strategy, Mr. Johnston believes Jennifer has acquired a basic conceptual understanding of each strategy step. Now he wants to support Jennifer as she begins applying the strategy steps. If he stops his instruction at this point, he knows it is likely that Jennifer will not be successful in applying the strategy on her own. Jennifer is certainly capable of learning to apply the strategy, but her reading problems and memory retrieval problems will make this difficult without more direction and support.

To help Jennifer achieve learning success, Mr. Johnston knows he needs to gradually fade his direction and modeling rather than just expect Jennifer to now successfully apply the BCDE strategy on her own. He decides to do this in three stages. First, he and Jennifer will go through each step with her American history text while Mr. Johnston provides a high level of direction and support. Next, they will move through the steps again with Mr. Johnston providing some direction and support but less than before. Finally, Jennifer will go through the steps herself with little direction or support from Mr. Johnston. Mr. Johnston will closely monitor Jennifer's ability to assume these graduated levels of self-direction and independence. If Jennifer demonstrates nonunderstanding at any point, then Mr. Johnston will revise how swiftly he fades his direction and support. Together, Mr. Johnston's scaffolded support and the additional practice experiences Jennifer receives make it more likely that Jennifer's reading and memory problems will not interfere with her ability to learn the BCDE strategy and apply it independently.

High Level of Support   At first, Mr. Johnston replicates what he and Jennifer did when he explicitly modeled the BCDE strategy, except he asks a few more questions at critical points. For example, Mr. Johnston decides to ask Jennifer to tell him how to skim for headings that reflect a reading selection's title while they go through the B step. Jennifer is able to answer his questions and show him how to do one or two subskills of the B and C steps. With this knowledge, Mr. Johnston is comfortable with fading more of his direction with the next example.

Medium Level of Support   Using a different reading selection in Jennifer's American history text, Mr. Johnston decides to ask Jennifer to take the lead with the B and C steps while he leads the D and E steps. As Jennifer states and then implements the B and C steps, Mr. Johnston observes that Jennifer is already able to skim using the title and headings to survey. He also notices that Jennifer doesn't pay too much attention to the pictures or graphs. He prompts Jennifer to look at several pictures in the reading selection and asks her if they match any of the topics suggested by the headings she found by skimming. She says the picture of Independence Hall matches one of the headings that reads *Colonists Vote for Independence.* Mr. Johnston asks Jennifer why she didn't mention the pictures as she was modeling the B step. Jennifer says that she was concentrating so much on the words that she totally forgot about the pictures. This made sense to Mr. Johnston because reading requires a high level of cognitive energy for Jennifer due to her reading difficulties. During the medium level of guided practice/scaffold instruction, both Mr. Johnston and Jennifer learned something. Mr. Johnston had a clearer picture of how Jennifer's reading difficulties affected her attention to other textbook features that could help with her comprehension. Jennifer learned, and was happy to know, that textbook pictures and the words in headings often emphasize the same ideas. Mr. Johnston and Jennifer agree this is something they will continue to emphasize as they work on the BCDE strategy.

Low Level of Support   The last level of guided practice/scaffold instruction consists of Jennifer modeling all of the strategy steps with a different reading passage while Mr. Johnston watches, listens, and responds to Jennifer's questions to him about various features of the BCDE strategy. Every once in a while, Mr. Johnston answers a question from Jennifer inaccurately to check Jennifer's metacognition (thinking ability) related to the strategy. At one point, during the E step, Jennifer asks Mr. Johnston to predict what might come next in the chapter subsequent to the one they are reading. Mr. Johnston, with a very straight face, gives a response that is not logical based on the current reading selection. Jennifer quickly picks up on Mr. Johnston's intentional mistake and describes why that cannot be possible given what they had just read. All in all, Mr. Johnston is very pleased by Jennifer's ability to implement each step of the strategy with a fairly high rate of accuracy. Jennifer likes how Mr. Johnston gradually fades his direction and lets her take on more responsibility for performing the strategy. She feels challenged but also supported because she isn't expected to just remember the strategy and how to use it automatically. Jennifer also notices that she is feeling less and less anxious about being able to use the BCDE strategy.

Provide Independent Practice and Generalization of Strategy to Target Courses(s) Through explicit teacher modeling and guided practice/instructional scaffolding, students with learning disabilities and ADHD are provided a way to initially acquire an understanding of a strategy and to strengthen their understanding and ability to implement the strategy with materials from their classes. At this stage, students need to become *proficient* at using the strategy. They need to have multiple experiences "trying it out" on their own and then sharing what they have done with their teacher to receive feedback and additional instruction. Additionally, it is important to work closely with the general education teacher in whose class the strategy is being implemented.

There are two phases to independent practice/generalization as it relates to the Active Learner Approach. In the first phase, students implement the strategy with relevant class materials as part of their resource class and the special education teacher monitors their work. In the second phase, the students apply the strategy to current course assignments *in the natural setting* (i.e., wherever the students would typically implement the strategy for the target course). This generalization phase requires students to use strategies in a relevant setting and context. This is a crucial stage of learning for students with learning disabilities and ADHD and must not be overlooked. Effective collaboration with the general education teacher is essential for generalization of strategies to occur! Some critical instructional elements of independent practice/generalization include

- Occurs after explicit teacher modeling and guided practice/instructional scaffolding

- Uses materials/activities from the course(s) the strategy will be applied to

- Provides student with multiple practice opportunities

- Benefits students through independent practice at two levels of understanding:

  - *Receptive* (students can *recognize* elements of the strategy after prompts and with several choices)

  - *Expressive* (students can *do* each step of the strategy)

- Provides student with corrective feedback and positive reinforcement for both accuracy and effort

- Includes general education teacher

Mr. Johnston Implements Independent Practice for the BCDE Strategy with Jennifer

Mr. Johnston wants Jennifer to practice the BCDE strategy during her resource period before implementing it with Ms. Campbell. Although Mr. Johnston feels good about Jennifer's understanding of the BCDE strategy to this point, he believes that Jennifer's particular learning characteristics could make independent use of the strategy a challenge for her. She demonstrates that she understands each step and that she can implement each step when he is there to provide feedback and prompting. However, he knows that Jennifer's memory retrieval problems can make it difficult for her to recall how to implement one or more steps when she is on her own.

To help Jennifer strengthen her memory for each strategy step (and the procedures within each step) and learn to independently apply each step, Mr. Johnston decides to provide independent practice in two different ways. At the *receptive level* of understanding, he has Jennifer watch him demonstrate various steps and pick out when he is performing the step correctly. At the *expressive level* of understanding, Mr. Johnston gives Jennifer reading assignments of differing lengths from her American history text (readings she had already been assigned during the year), and she has to implement the BCDE strategy using that reading assignment.

An example of Jennifer's receptive level practice involves Mr. Johnston performing examples and nonexamples of the B step and/or specific procedures within the B step and having Jennifer choose which example accurately depicts the B step or specific procedure within the B step. At one point, Mr. Johnston demonstrates three different examples and asks Jennifer to identify which one accurately demonstrates each procedure of the B step. One example includes all three procedures modeled accurately, whereas the other two examples have one procedure missing or one procedure modeled incorrectly. Most important, Mr. Johnston also asks Jennifer to describe why she selected an example (i.e., why it was the accurate one). By doing this, Mr. Johnston is able to evaluate Jennifer's cognitive understanding of the strategy. Mr. Johnston makes a point of providing positive verbal reinforcement to Jennifer for her accuracy and her effort. Mr. Johnston's positive comments encourage Jennifer and also help her *want* to continue learning the strategy even though it isn't easy sometimes.

An example of expressive level practice involves Mr. Johnston giving Jennifer a reading assignment from her American history text and then asking her to implement each step of the BCDE strategy. Mr. Johnston thinks a useful way to do this is to have her take some time to try out the strategy step with the assigned reading and then to meet with him and show him how she implemented it. For example, with the B step, Jennifer takes about 10 minutes to go through the reading assignment and complete each of the three procedures listed on her BCDE strategy cue sheet. As she does this, she highlights headings that indicate major ideas, puts a check by pictures and tables that she thinks are important to the major ideas, and underlines words in bold that she believes are important to understanding the reading. If a school policy prohibits students from writing in textbooks, then sticky notes could be used to mark examples. Mr. Johnston asks her to do these things specifically to see how well she understands how to implement the second bulleted procedure in the B step of the BCDE strategy. Jennifer and Mr. Johnston meet to discuss what Jennifer does as she implements the BCDE strategy. Mr. Johnston checks Jennifer's examples and asks her questions as needed. In particular, Mr. Johnston probes Jennifer about how she implements these steps or parts of a step for which concrete examples are not possible to show (e.g., the procedure in the E step in which Jennifer has to ask herself how the material she reads relates to material that she read before for that class). Mr. Johnston continues to provide positive verbal reinforcement as he and Jennifer work at the expressive level.

Based on Jennifer's performance of independently applying the BCDE strategy during her resource period, Mr. Johnston believes she is ready to begin implementing it with current assignments in her American history class. Mr. Johnston knows that Ms. Campbell will be an important part of this portion of independent practice/generalization. He speaks with Ms. Campbell and updates her on Jennifer's progress. Ms. Campbell is happy to hear that Jennifer is ready to "try out" the BCDE strategy with her class. Mr. Johnston reviews the BCDE strategy with Ms. Campbell so that she understands what Jennifer will be doing. He also asks Ms. Campbell to allow Jennifer to use her BCDE strategy cue sheet any time a reading is assigned. Mr. Johnston asks Ms. Campbell to allow Jennifer to make marks (or place sticky notes) in her textbook as part of implementing the strategy (e.g., underlining bold-face words, placing checks beside important pictures and tables, circling important headings). He explains that this could be one way that Ms. Campbell will know whether Jennifer is using the BCDE strategy and how accurately she is using it. Last, Mr. Johnston asks Ms. Campbell to remind Jennifer to use the BCDE strategy when a reading assignment is given and provide her with positive verbal reinforcement when she demonstrates to Ms. Campbell that she used the strategy with an assigned reading.

Mr. Johnston explains to Jennifer that Ms. Campbell knows she will be using the BCDE strategy in her class and that Ms. Campbell will be periodically checking to see whether Jennifer is using it with assigned readings. He encourages Jennifer to speak with Ms. Campbell to explain the strategy to her and talk about how they can best communicate to each other about how the strategy is working. Mr. Johnston and Jennifer role play this conversation as a way to help Jennifer feel more comfortable speaking with her teacher. After her discussion with Ms. Campbell, Jennifer is pleased to know Ms. Campbell is interested in what she is doing and wants to help. Jennifer also feels good about herself because she had the courage to talk to her teacher directly about something that could help her. This was a new experience for Jennifer.

Component 3: Evaluation of Student Success/Make Strategy Instruction Decisions

An important aspect of being an effective teacher for students with learning disabilities and ADHD is to know if your teaching actually results in student learning. An integral component of the Active Learner Approach is using a variety of student performance data sources to inform yourself about your teaching. The central question you want to answer should be, "Does my teaching result in my student learning?" Examples of data sources that can be used with the Active Learner Approach include your student's grades on assignments *that involve the strategy being learned,* observations of the general education teacher in whose class your student is using the strategy, and periodic learning probes that assess your student's receptive and expressive understanding of the strategy. Evaluation should be done continuously throughout the instructional process and should be done frequently.

Another important result of continuously evaluating/monitoring your students' performance can be that it helps them visualize their learning. By simply charting your students' performance, you can provide them a picture of their learning. Due to metacognitive deficits, students with learning disabilities and ADHD often are not aware of whether they are learning. Simple charts, such as those illustrated in the next few pages, can make this metacognitive process more concrete for these students. It is motivational for students with learning disabilities and ADHD to see their learning progress. Several important elements that make continuous evaluation/monitoring of student performance effective include:

- Evaluation is done frequently.

- Evaluation is done throughout the teaching of a strategy (rather than giving one test after all instruction is completed).

- The evaluation method is both consistent with a student's level of understanding (e.g., receptive versus expressive) and consistent with the context for which he or she is receiving instruction (e.g., in supported resource room environment versus independent use in a general education classroom).

- Student performance can be depicted in a format that is easy to visualize (e.g., chart, table, picture).

- The evaluation method can be done quickly (requires minimal amounts of time).

- Data are used to inform teaching.

MR. JOHNSTON USES
CONTINUOUS MONITORING WITH JENNIFER

Mr. Johnston knows that he has to make the most of his time with Jennifer, particularly when the stakes are so high. He knows that if Jennifer begins failing courses necessary for graduation or if she does not pass state assessments necessary for graduation in tenth grade, then her chances for success in courses and assessments in eleventh and twelfth grade are going to be slim. He knows Jennifer and her parents want her to achieve a standard diploma. With this in mind, Mr. Johnston believes he first needs to know as quickly as possible the extent to which Jennifer is learning the BCDE strategy. Second, he needs to know as quickly as possible the extent to which using the BCDE strategy in American history is helping Jennifer improve her academic performance.

Monitoring Jennifer's Learning
Performance During Resource Instruction

To measure Jennifer's understanding of the BCDE strategy, Mr. Johnston incorporates the use of simple learning probes that Jennifer responds to after each period of instruction and/or practice with him. During the beginning phase of instruction

Table 5.5.   Example of receptive level items

1. When skimming a paragraph in a reading assignment during the B step of
    the BCDE strategy, what should be your main focus?
    a. Getting some ideas of what might be in the section you will be reading
    b. Highlighting every important sentence
    c. Reading every word
    d. Thinking about what you are going to have for lunch
2. When writing questions on note cards during the C step of the BCDE strat-
    egy, write or say what this will help you do.

and practice in which Jennifer is working on her receptive (recognition) level of
understanding, Mr. Johnston develops a simple learning probe that requires Jennifer
to either choose examples of different strategy steps/procedures or write/say the
purpose of strategy steps or procedures. Mr. Johnston wants to give Jennifer the
option of either writing or telling him her answer because sometimes she has trouble writing what she means. The probe consists of 10 questions or prompts, and Jennifer simply circles the correct choice or writes/says the answer. Table 5.5 illustrates
several items from Mr. Johnston's receptive level learning probe. Mr. Johnston
includes both recognition items as well as recall items. Mr. Johnston does not want
to focus on Jennifer's memorization of the steps. Instead, he wants to evaluate Jennifer's conceptual understanding of particular strategy steps, including the purpose
of specific procedures within steps. Mr. Johnston records the number of items Jennifer gets correct and incorrect. He and Jennifer then plot her scores on a simple
chart (see Figure 5.7).

Mr. Johnston makes up a different probe each day based on the steps Jennifer
has received instruction for up to that point. By Thursday, they have covered all four
steps. Based on Jennifer's performance, both Mr. Johnston and Jennifer can easily
see that Jennifer is increasing her understanding of the BCDE strategy at the receptive level of understanding. Mr. Johnston has evidence that his teaching method is
effective, and Jennifer is encouraged to actually see her progress in a visual format.

Based on Jennifer's improving performance as indicated on Figure 5.7, Mr.
Johnston believes Jennifer is ready to begin working at the expressive level of understanding, where she will show him how to implement the steps of the BCDE strategy. As he provides explicit modeling, guided practice, and independent practice
opportunities for Jennifer, Mr. Johnston also evaluates her performance through a
simple expressive level learning probe. Instead of having Jennifer respond to written
questions, Mr. Johnston asks Jennifer to show him how she will implement one or
more steps of the BCDE strategy. Each time he evaluates Jennifer, Mr. Johnston evaluates her ability to implement those steps that have been emphasized during
instruction up to that point. Mr. Johnston uses a copy of the BCDE strategy cue sheet
to record Jennifer's performance. He places a check beside the steps (or specific procedures within a step) that Jennifer is able to perform accurately. He places an X
beside those steps/procedures Jennifer is not able to perform accurately. He also
writes brief notes beside relevant steps as he observes Jennifer. He uses those notes
as feedback cues for Jennifer.

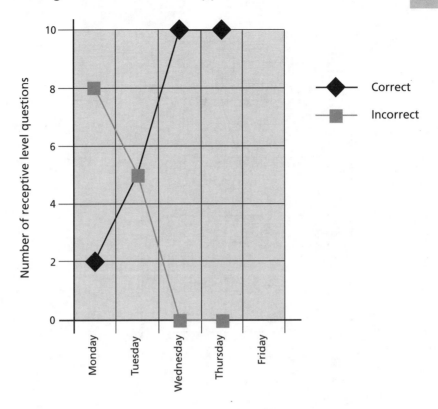

Figure 5.7. Chart showing Jennifer's receptive level understanding of the BCDE strategy.

Mr. Johnston uses *percentage correct* and *percentage incorrect* scores to plot Jennifer's performance on a chart. He chooses a percentage score because each step has varying numbers of procedures, meaning evaluating the number correct or incorrect will not provide comparable scores. The notes Mr. Johnston writes on the strategy cue sheets serve as a second way for him to check Jennifer's progress. By placing the cue sheets in a folder, he is able to review his notes over successive days to see how Jennifer performed with specific aspects of the strategy, something that is difficult to do by only looking at the chart. Figure 5.8 shows Jennifer's expressive level performance chart.

Mr. Johnston sees a dramatic increase in performance between Monday and Tuesday but a drop in percentage correct on Wednesday. He isn't sure why this might have occurred. As Mr. Johnston reviews the strategy cue sheets he uses to record Jennifer's performance, he notices that on Monday and Tuesday, Jennifer modeled the B and C steps. However, on Wednesday, she modeled the B and C steps again but also modeled the D step. He notes that Jennifer performed the B and C steps with nearly 100% accuracy on Wednesday but had trouble with the D step. That explains her decreased performance as shown on the chart. This lets Mr. Johnston know that the D step should be a point of emphasis during instruction on Thursday.

Jennifer's performance on Thursday indicates that Mr. Johnston made an effective instructional decision. Her performance increased to 100% accuracy. Mr. John-

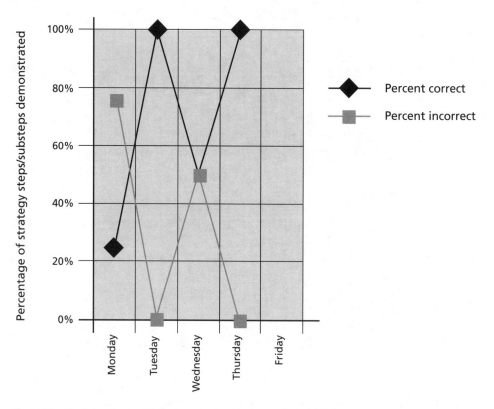

Figure 5.8. Chart showing Jennifer's expressive level understanding of BCDE strategy.

ston decides to note on the chart what steps Jennifer is working on each day so he and Jennifer will have a better understanding of what the chart was actually indicating day to day about Jennifer's performance. He does this by simply writing the letter that represents the steps at the top of the chart directly above each day that data were plotted.

Monitoring Jennifer's Performance Using the BCDE Strategy in Her American History Class

As Jennifer moves to using the BCDE strategy in her American history class, Mr. Johnston uses two methods for monitoring her performance. First, he makes a point to check with Ms. Campbell to see whether Jennifer appears to be using the strategy with her assigned readings. Ms. Campbell mentions she saw Jennifer turn to the BCDE strategy cue sheet she keeps in her notebook both times she had students complete a reading assignment in class that week. Hearing this is encouraging to Mr. Johnston because he is somewhat worried that Jennifer is reticent to use her strategy cue sheet in class.

Second, Mr. Johnston and Ms. Campbell communicate regarding Jennifer's grades on assignments that involve gaining understanding from readings. In particular, Mr. Johnston keeps track of how Jennifer performs on weekly quizzes and unit tests. Earlier, when he examined Jennifer's grades in American history, Mr. Johnston noted that her lowest grades were on Ms. Campbell's quizzes and tests. Ms. Campbell mentions that a significant amount of material on quizzes and tests comes from assigned readings. Mr. Johnston reasons that if the BCDE strategy is going to help Jennifer, then it should be reflected in increased quiz and test grades. Mr. Johnston and Jennifer keep a simple chart that depicts her grades by percentage score on each quiz and test (see Figure 5.9).

Jennifer's grade on the first weekly quiz grade after she begins using the BCDE strategy was a *D*. This is similar to her previous quiz grades. Seeing this, Mr. Johnston asks Ms. Campbell what kinds of concepts Jennifer missed on the quiz. Ms. Campbell reviews Jennifer's quiz and notices that she missed questions that asked her to relate information and ideas from the current week's reading assignments to information and ideas learned previously. For example, the current week's readings discussed the reconstruction of the South after the Civil War. Previous readings discussed the reasons the South seceded from the Union. One quiz question asked students to list several concerns Southerners might have had about how the Union was going to "reconstruct" the South. Students were asked to relate these concerns to reasons the South originally seceded from the Union. Mr. Johnston looks at the BCDE strategy and quickly recognizes that perhaps Jennifer and he need to emphasize the E step during his time with her. Part of the E step, "Ask yourself how the material you just read is related to material that you read before this," pertains specifically to the kind of questions Jennifer missed on the quiz.

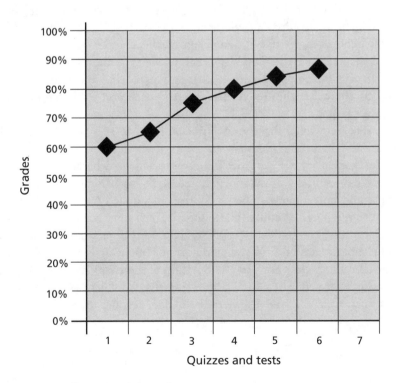

Figure 5.9. Jennifer's quiz and test grades.

By having procedures in place to monitor Jennifer's initial understanding of the BCDE strategy and her ability to implement the strategy in Ms. Campbell's class, Mr. Johnston is able to make effective instructional decisions that benefit Jennifer. Jennifer is able to elevate her first-term grade in American history from a *D* to a *C+*. If Mr. Johnston and Ms. Campbell wait until the end of the term to see Jennifer's final grade, it is likely that Jennifer will not be able to improve. The specific information Mr. Johnston learns about Jennifer's understanding *and* use of the strategy by evaluating her throughout the term enables him to teach Jennifer in a truly individualized and effective way. Mr. Johnston sees the power of continuous monitoring of student performance when it is closely linked to teaching.

This chapter has demonstrated how a special education teacher and student worked together with other teachers to implement the Active Learner Approach. Although teaching certainly is, and should be, a fluid process, the implementation of the Active Learner Approach has been demonstrated according to three major components, which are comprised of several steps. Every component and element described is important and can lead to success for your student. However, as with learning anything new, it is not expected that you will be able to implement every element of the Active Learner Approach described in this chapter after reading it once. You are encouraged to try out those elements of the Active Learner Approach that you see as most beneficial to you and your students, given your individual instructional situation. As you use the Active Learner Approach more and more, refer back to this book and try to incorporate additional elements of the approach until you are completely implementing the Active Learner Approach. The Active Learner Approach Implementation Guide/Checklist is provided at the end of this chapter to help you as you implement the Active Learner Approach. Copy it and use it to help you conceptualize the Active Learner Approach and to monitor your implementation of it.

Also, remember that the case used in this chapter is not intended to be prescriptive in nature. The case is simply meant to illustrate how various aspects of the Active Learner Approach *can be* implemented based on the individual needs of one student. It is hoped that Jennifer's case stimulates ideas about how you could implement the Active Learner Approach with particular students you are teaching. Although your students may have some similarities to Jennifer, most will undoubtedly have different needs, both in terms of their learning characteristics and the demands of the courses they are having difficulty with. But this is the very point and nature of the Active Learner Approach—it provides you with an individually responsive way to help your students become active learners and, therefore, help them become academically successful!

The Active Learner Approach Implementation Guide

Checklist

Individual Course Grade Summary Sheet

Overall Grade Record Sheet

Performance Monitoring Chart (Frequency)

Performance Monitoring Chart (Percentage)

Performance Monitoring Chart (Grades)

Checklist

Component/step	Completed(√)
1. Evaluate your student's learning characteristics in relation to specific demands of the courses he or she is taking.	
A. Introduce the Active Learner Approach to your student.	———
B. Evaluate your student's current academic performance by examining his or her grades in all courses.	———
C. Evaluate your student's individual learning needs as they relate to specific course concerns.	———

C1. Copy and complete the Active Learner Questionnaires.
    C2. Evaluate completed Active Learner Questionnaires.
    C3. Discuss the results of the Active Learner Questionnaires with your student.
    C4. Determine which skills and strategies to teach your student.
    C5. Target course or courses for intervention.	

2. Develop and implement a systematic strategy instruction plan.	
A. Develop a plan to teach selected strategies.	———

A1. Decide which strategy to teach first.
    A2. Identify a strategy instruction support team.
    A3. Plan the instruction.	

B. Teach strategies using explicit systematic instruction.	———

B1. Build meaningful student connections (e.g., LIP).
    B2. Explicitly model the strategy.
    B3. Provide guided practice/scaffold your instruction.
    B4. Provide independent practice and generalization of strategy to target course(s).	

3. Evaluate student success and make instructional decisions. *This component is done in conjunction with Component 2—Develop and implement a systematic strategy instruction plan.*	
A. Continuously monitor and chart student's receptive and/or expressive understanding of the strategy.	———
B. Make instructional decisions based on student performance.	———
C. Continuously monitor and chart student's use and success with the strategy in the target course(s).	———
D. Make instructional decisions based on student performance.	———
Celebrate your student's success (and yours)!!	

Academic Success Strategies for Adolescents with Learning Disabilities and ADHD
by Esther Minskoff and David Allsopp
©2003 Paul H. Brookes Publishing Co.

Course:	
Teacher:	
Assignment	Grade
1.	
2.	
3.	
4.	
5.	
6.	
7.	
8.	
9.	
10.	
Overall course grade to date:	

Academic Success Strategies for Adolescents with Learning Disabilities and ADHD
by Esther Minskoff and David Allsopp
©2003 Paul H. Brookes Publishing Co.

Overall summary		
Course	Overall grade to date	Assignments of concern by type of assignment and grade

Course/assignments for possible strategy intervention	
Courses/teachers	Types of assignments

Academic Success Strategies for Adolescents with Learning Disabilities and ADHD
by Esther Minskoff and David Allsopp
©2003 Paul H. Brookes Publishing Co.

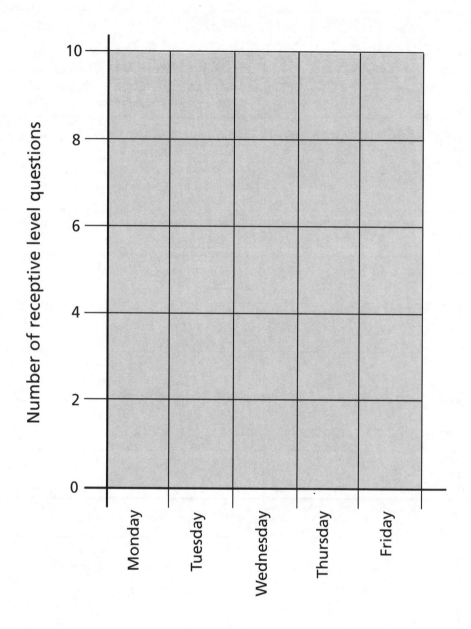

Number of receptive level questions

10 —
8 —
6 —
4 —
2 —
0 —

Monday   Tuesday   Wednesday   Thursday   Friday

 Correct

Incorrect

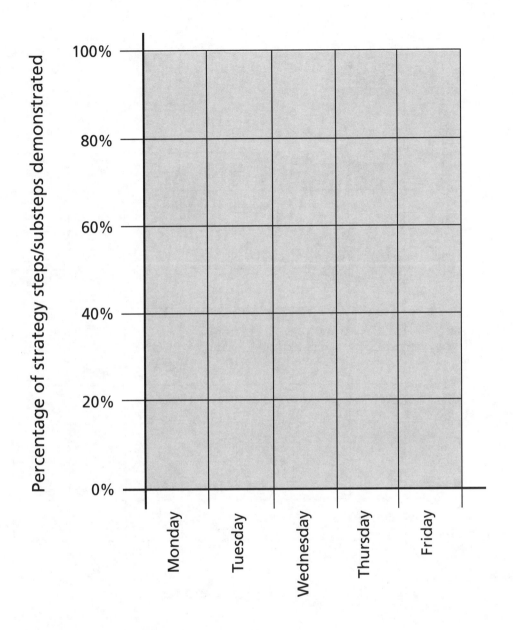

Percentage of strategy steps/substeps demonstrated

100%

80%

60%

40%

20%

0%

Monday Tuesday Wednesday Thursday Friday

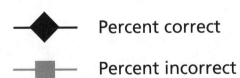

Percent correct

Percent incorrect

Academic Success Strategies for Adolescents with Learning Disabilities and ADHD
by Esther Minskoff and David Allsopp
©2003 Paul H. Brookes Publishing Co.

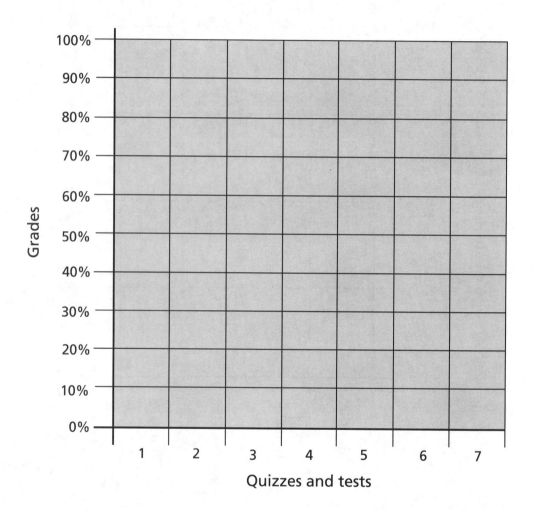

Grades

100%
90%
80%
70%
60%
50%
40%
30%
20%
10%
0%

1   2   3   4   5   6   7

Quizzes and tests

Academic Success Strategies for Adolescents with Learning Disabilities and ADHD
by Esther Minskoff and David Allsopp
©2003 Paul H. Brookes Publishing Co.

Section II

Strategies for Academic Success

6
Organization

- Why do students with learning disabilities and ADHD need to learn organizational skills?

- What are the different subskills of organization?

- What is special about teaching organizational skills?

- What are strategies for using a planner or calendar?

- What are strategies for keeping track of tests and assignments?

- What are strategies for going to class?

- What are strategies for setting goals?

- What are strategies for keeping notebooks?

- What are strategies for remembering items for class?

- What are strategies for remembering items for home?

WHY DO STUDENTS WITH LEARNING DISABILITIES AND ADHD NEED TO LEARN ORGANIZATIONAL SKILLS?

Difficulties with organization are a major obstacle to academic success for many, if not most, students with learning disabilities and ADHD. In our study of college students with mild disabilities, we found that students with deficits in organization had the lowest grades and the most academic difficulty in meeting college demands (Minskoff, Minskoff, & Allsopp, 2001). Organization encompasses management of time and materials. Time management includes using planners and calendars, setting goals based on priorities, attending class, and being punctual. Obviously, if a student does not keep track of tests and assignments, does not prioritize devoting time to school over other activities, and does not go to class, then academic success is impossible. If a student does not devote time to studying, then development of reading, writing, and math strategies is useless. Therefore, training of organization skills must be done before improving other areas of difficulty.

Students with learning disabilities and ADHD have organizational difficulties because of memory problems and limited metacognitive skills for actively managing their learning in relationship to time. It is common for a student to come into a resource class and tell the special education teacher that he has a test the next period and has not studied. When asked why he didn't say anything about this earlier or study earlier, he responds that he didn't think about it until that point in time. It becomes impossible for the teacher to help him pass the test. Absence of an overall plan for given time periods (e.g., a day, a week, a month, a marking period, a semester, a year) is characteristic of these students. Changing a student's cognitive style to become aware of time is a challenging but necessary objective.

In addition to difficulties managing time, many students with learning disabilities and ADHD have difficulties managing materials. They don't keep separate notebooks for their classes, they don't bring items they need to class, and they don't bring materials home that they need for studying or doing homework. Some students keep their lecture notes from different classes in one notebook and have trouble determining which notes go with which classes. Some keep their notes on loose-leaf pages and mix the pages from all of their classes together. They often stuff assignments and materials given out by the teachers into their book bags or pockets and then can't find them. Students may write assignments and tests on sticky notes and put these in their lockers. The students think that they are organized, but the notes are not usable because they're in their lockers and not at home or class. Their lockers often look like they have been hit by tornadoes, as do their desks at home. Many teenagers are messy, but they know where things can be found. This is not true for students with organizational problems. Some have developed learned helplessness because their teachers and parents have always managed their time and materials. For example, they may go to the resource class before each class to get what they need from the special education teacher, or their parents may lay out what they need to bring to school the next day. Because of these students' disorganization and resulting inability to complete school work successfully, their parents and teachers do as much as possible for the students, rather than teach them to become organized.

WHAT ARE THE DIFFERENT SUBSKILLS OF ORGANIZATION?

Organization is divided into time management and materials management. These two areas are related because they represent the metacognitive skill of coordinating time and activities. Time management includes the subskills of using planning aids to keep track of time, planning using time variables, and setting goals. Planning using time variables involves advanced cognitive skills. Classifying activities into school, work, social, and home responsibilities requires the student to use the higher order processing skill of categorization. The student then assigns values to the various categories in terms of personal importance that requires evaluative thinking. The following four subskills of time management (and the corresponding Active Learner Student Questionnaire items found in Appendix A) are taught with the Active Learner Approach.

1. Using planning aids: "I don't use a planner or calendar."

2. Recording tests and assignments in the planning aids: "I don't keep track of tests and assignments."

3. Attending class: "I have trouble getting to class."

4. Setting goals: "I have difficulty setting goals."

Materials management is made up of three subskills: keeping notebooks for each class, bringing items to class, and bringing items home. The following three subskills of materials management (with the corresponding Active Learner Student Questionnaire items found in Appendix A) are taught with the Active Learner Approach.

1. Using notebooks: "I don't keep a separate notebook for each class."

2. Organizing materials for classes: "I forget to bring things I need to class."

3. Organizing materials for home: "I forget to bring home things that I need for studying or for homework."

WHAT IS SPECIAL ABOUT
TEACHING ORGANIZATIONAL SKILLS?

Most strategy instruction approaches include attention to organization (Mastropieri & Scruggs, 2000; Mather & Goldstein, 2001; Strichart, Mangrum, & Iannuzzi, 1998). Use of planners and calendars is a well-accepted best practice for developing time management skills (Bos & Vaughn, 2002).

With the Active Learner Approach, instruction for organizational skills is heavily dependent on the use of the scaffolding approach (i.e., at first you need to provide a great deal of structure and support, but these *must* be removed gradually). It is important not to continue to provide strong support because this leads to learned helplessness. In the initial stages of instruction, you must organize the student's time and materials. For example, initially, you will devote instructional time in the resource class to recording all assignments and tests on a daily basis. After that, you will have the student do this independently at the start of the resource period. After that, require her to do this before coming into the resource class. Gradually, eliminate the amount of cueing that reminds her to do this.

Students with organizational difficulties seem to lose or misplace items frequently. Therefore, it is important to have back-up planners and notebooks. Having students try to recall where they were when they lost an item may help them keep track of their materials and also develop memory skills for thinking back in time to what and where they were when specific events occurred.

Enhancing student awareness of time can be facilitated by making sure that they wear watches and by having them keep schedules in their notebooks. If possible, require them to make lists for what they need for each class and for each day. Give them pads of paper to do this, and have them check off items on the list as they gather them. Some students are resistant to using these aids. They say, "This is not me. I just don't do things like this." It is important for you to show them that they must change themselves if they are to become successful in school. Having them contract with you to use this approach for a limited period of time (e.g., 1 week) and showing them their improved performance may result in the students becoming more motivated to use organizational strategies.

WHAT ARE STRATEGIES FOR USING A PLANNER OR CALENDAR?

Use of a master schedule, weekly schedule, and daily schedule has been found to increase college students' control over their lives, which leaves them feeling more relaxed (Pauk, 1997). Students *must* have planners in order to have organized schedules. If students do not own planners or calendars, then provide them with these, or print the examples in Appendix E. Have students put these planners and calendars in a notebook. Use daily, weekly, and marking period planning so you can demonstrate the interrelationship of the three. Students frequently lose planners or calendars, so keep a supply of these available. Also, try to have the students track down where they lost their planners or calendars to develop self-monitoring skills.

WHAT ARE STRATEGIES FOR KEEPING TRACK OF TESTS AND ASSIGNMENTS?

To demonstrate how to keep track of tests and assignments in calendars, use the 3C strategy. With the first step of this strategy, the students create a calendar for the marking period; with the second step, for a week; and with the third step, for a day. First, start with the marking period calendar. Analyze the assignments and tests that are given in the class syllabus and write them on the semester calendar. If they are not given in the syllabus, then have the students ask their teachers for these dates. As new assignments are given, add these to the marking period calendar. Be sure to include all school activities, especially extra-curricular obligations. For example, if a student is on the basketball team, then record the dates of all the basketball games. This will demonstrate to the student the need to coordinate study plans with extra-curricular obligations. In addition, add any other times that represent regular obligations (e.g., a job).

At the second step of this strategy, the student creates a weekly planner. To show the relationship between the marking period calendar and the weekly calendar, analyze the type of work that has to be done for each assignment and other obligations and how the different work must be allocated over several days. For example, if the student has a term paper due on a particular date, then guide the student in listing all the tasks that he has to do to write the term paper. After he generates this list, have him put the tasks in order. Then, have him estimate the amount of time to accomplish each task and allocate time in the weekly planner accordingly. Have him write each task in this planner while also considering other obligations, such as work. Clearly demonstrate how to divide up the time so that the final assignment is completed on schedule.

The third step of this strategy has the students creating daily lists. Demonstrate how to go from the weekly to daily calendars. Make a list of the items (both academic and nonacademic) that have to be done. Then, have the students use a daily planner to fill in items to be done on an hour-by-hour basis.

Many students fill in daily planners, but they do not consult them on a regular basis. Make sure that the students read their planners every day before school starts and check them again every day at the end of school to see what they have accomplished. Also, have them review their weekly planners on Sunday nights so they know what to expect in the upcoming week.

3C:
TO HELP ME KEEP TRACK OF TESTS AND ASSIGNMENTS

Create a calendar.
Create a weekly planner.
Create daily lists.

Create a calendar for the marking period.

- Lay out all assignments and tests for each course using the syllabus.

- If assignments are not listed in the syllabus, then ask your teachers for them.

- Fill in all school activities, including extra-curricular activities (e.g., basket-ball games, school musicals).

- Fill in after-school activities, such as hours that you work at a job.

- Add new items to the calendar as soon as you become aware of them. Keep your calendar up-to-date.

Create a weekly planner.

- Lay out plans for the week based on the marking period calendar.

- Include all assignments, tests, school activities, and work obligations.

- Lay out study plans over a weekly period to give yourself enough time to study for tests or do everything needed for assignments.

- Review your weekly calendar at the beginning of the week, usually Sunday night or Monday morning, so that you know what to expect.

- As you complete each item on your weekly calendar, check it off. At the end of the week, see which items have not been checked off and decide whether to include them in the next week's planner.

Create daily lists.

- Based on your weekly calendar, make a daily to-do list. If you use a daily planner, then transfer the items on this list to specific times.

- Consult your list at the beginning of the day and at certain times through-out the day.

- Check off each item on the list as you complete it.

- At the end of day, analyze the items you didn't do and decide whether to add them to the next day's to-do list.

WHAT ARE STRATEGIES FOR GOING TO CLASS?

Many students with mild disabilities are tardy or have poor class attendance, and they have to be instructed about the causes and consequences of their actions. In a study in which employers were asked to rate the most important job skills for employing people with disabilities, attendance and punctuality were identified as the most important work behaviors for keeping a job (Min-skoff & DeMoss, 1994). Students with learning disabilities and ADHD must be taught that good attendance and punctuality are essential for success in school and on a job. The LIST strategy is designed to help students reflect on these causes and consequences. First, the students analyze their opinions of the class in order to develop their abstract cognitive skills so that they can reflect on the causative factors for tardiness or poor attendance. They are to analyze why they are late or frequently absent from class and what they are accomplishing if they do not attend the class. Second, the students analyze the consequences of tardiness and poor attendance, which requires them to develop abstract cognitive skills in projecting consequences. Third, students set goals to increase their motivation for attending class. Finally, students talk to their teachers to let them know that they are working on improving their punctuality and attendance. Rehearse with the students what they will say to the teachers in this meeting. Be sure that they do not blame the teacher or the nature of the class for their problems. They must take responsibility for their tardiness or poor attendance.

In order to use this strategy, you will have to guide the students in self-analysis. Many of them will blame the teacher (e.g., she's boring) or the class (e.g., math is boring). This strategy will require that you guide the students in what may be a painful analysis (e.g., not going to class because the work is difficult for them). If students are not motivated to be successful in a class, then LIST will not work. However, the purpose of LIST is for you to give the students reasons to be motivated to succeed in class.

LIST:
TO HELP ME IMPROVE CLASS ATTENDANCE AND PUNCTUALITY

Look at the causes.
Identify the consequences.
Set goals to increase your motivation.
Talk to your teacher.

Look at the causes of your poor attendance and tardiness.

- Analyze why you are late or absent from each class. Look at causes such as
  - I don't care.
  - I don't like the class.
  - I don't like the teacher.
  - I don't understand the material.
  - I'm getting poor grades in the class.
  - I have too many other things to do.

- Analyze what you accomplish by not going to class.
  - Nothing
  - Socialize with my friends
  - Sleep late
  - Get other work done

Identify the consequences of your poor attendance or tardiness.

- Analyze what will happen as a result of your poor attendance or tardiness.
  - Lower final grade
  - Fail the class
  - Have to take the class again
  - Make the teacher think I don't care
  - Unable to participate in sports and clubs
  - Will not be able to graduate

Set goals to increase your motivation to attend class and be punctual.

- Think of the negative consequences of poor attendance. Write these down and look at them every time that you consider being late or absent from class. Try to visualize what will happen (e.g., not being able to graduate and the resulting type of job you will have to get).

- Set up a plan to reward yourself for improved attendance and punctuality. Use rewards such as buying yourself something you want (e.g., a new CD) for going to class for a certain period of time (e.g., an entire week).

Talk to your teacher.

- Make an appointment to talk to your teacher about your plans to improve your attendance and punctuality.

- Clearly present your plans to do everything possible to improve your attendance and punctuality.

- Do not blame the teacher or the nature of the class. Take responsibility.

- Rehearse how you will present your case with your special education teacher, friend, or parent.

WHAT ARE STRATEGIES FOR SETTING GOALS?

Some of the organizational problems of students with mild disabilities result from lack of setting goals and prioritizing what is most important in their lives.

The TAP-D strategy is designed to assist students in selecting goals that are most important for academic success. In this strategy, you lead the students through the steps of identifying activities that they engage in and arranging the activities into categories. This requires students to use the advanced cognitive skill of classification, to evaluate these different categories in relationship to academic success, and to set priorities. At the first step of TAP-D, guide the students in brainstorming all of the things that they *need* to do and all the things that they *want* to do. Have them write these activities in two separate columns. If there are activities that they both need and want to do, then have them write them in both columns. Discuss how these activities will be easiest for them to do. At the next stage, present four types of tasks: school, work, social, and home. Lead the students in classifying the activities they brainstormed in the first step into these four categories.

At the next stage, have them prioritize these categories. Discuss that school must be ranked first if they are to be academically successful. Work and/or home may be ranked second depending on their individual circumstances. Discuss how social activities might be the most fun but may be the least important in terms of meeting responsibilities at school, home, and work.

The discussion regarding prioritizing may involve personal issues that you may want to discuss privately with a particular student, rather than in a group. For example, a student may have a sick parent and need to be home to take care of the parent, or a student must work because her parents are unemployed.

TAP-D:
TO HELP SET GOALS

Think of things you need to do.
Arrange them in categories.
Prioritize.
Do it!

Think of things you need to do.

- First, make a list of things that you *need* to do for a particular day or a particular week.

- Then, make another list of things that you *want* to do for that day or week.

- If there are things that you need to do and also want to do, then list them in both columns.

- Think about why you need to do each of these things and why you want to do each of these things.

Arrange the things you need to do into categories.

- Use the following four categories: school, work, home, and social.
- Go back to the list of things you need to do and sort them into each of these four categories.
- Do the same with the things you want to do.
- Compare the differences between the sorting of categories for things that you want to do and things that you need to do.

Prioritize.

- Prioritize each of these four categories on the basis of what is most important. School must be ranked first if you are to be successful academically. Being successful in school will lead to being successful in the workplace. Work or home may be ranked second depending on your specific situation. Social activities may be least important for your success.
- Now, prioritize each of these four categories on the basis of what is most important to you. Compare your rankings with the rankings necessary to be successful as a teenager and an adult.
- Ask yourself, "Am I willing to prioritize school as number one?" If you are, then you need to go back and look at all the tasks that you have to do that you listed in the school category and do them.
- As a way of helping yourself do tasks that you need to do, use tasks that you want to do as reinforcement for doing tasks that you need to do. For example, you may hate to write term papers, but you know you have to do this if you are to pass your English class. You want to go to the movies. Use going to the movies as reinforcement after you have completed your term paper.

Do it!

- It is difficult to keep these priorities. It is a good idea to make the lists of things you want and need to do on a daily or weekly basis and then sort them into the four categories.
- This will help you stick with priorities that will lead to school success. Your planning is useless if you don't follow your plan.

WHAT ARE STRATEGIES FOR KEEPING NOTEBOOKS?

The first requirement for effectively managing materials is for students to keep separate notebooks for each class. Many students use notebooks with dividers for different subjects. This is not a good idea because they may need more pages than provided in the section, or they may confuse sections and write notes in the wrong place. The BAND strategy is designed to help students keep notebooks so that they can effectively take notes and keep their work organized. The first step in BAND directs students to get a different colored notebook for each class. This will help students readily gain access to their notebooks when needed. The second step instructs the students to divide their notebooks into sections such as notes and homework. The third section directs the students to update their notebooks daily. The final step instructs them to buy a new notebook if they lose one. It is common for students with mild disabilities to lose notebooks. Therefore, they must replace them and get the contents that are lost from the teacher or another student. You may have to work with students on rehearsing conversations they will have with other students or teachers regarding getting materials that were lost.

BAND:
TO HELP ME KEEP A SEPARATE NOTEBOOK FOR EACH CLASS

Buy a different notebook for each class.
Always divide each notebook into sections.
Need to update notebooks daily.
Do buy a new notebook if you lose one.

Buy a different notebook for each class.

- Get notebooks of different colors or with different pictures.

- Try to associate the color or the picture on the notebook with each class to make it easier to find. For example, get a green notebook for science because plants are green, and get a red notebook for math because you hate math and you see red when you think of math. Or, get a notebook with a picture of a beach scene and use that for English because you like to read books when you go to the beach.

- Try to buy notebooks that have pockets in the front and back.

- Write the name of the subject in large letters on the front and back of each notebook.

Always divide each notebook into sections.

- Have a section for notes and another for homework assignments. In the section on assignments, list the materials you will need to bring home.

- Make sure that you get a notebook with pockets so that you can put loose-leaf paper in them and use them to store handouts from the teacher.

Need to update your notebook daily.

- Date all sections every time you write in a notebook.

- As you complete items in the homework section, cross or check them off to show that they are done.

- Go through your pockets daily and clean out any loose-leaf papers or handouts that you no longer need. Make sure to hand in any worksheets that you may have in the pockets of your notebook.

Do buy a new notebook immediately if you lose one.

- If you lose one of your notebooks, buy a new one with the same color or picture as the notebook that you lost.

- Replace the notes that were in the lost notebook by getting them from a friend or asking the teacher for help.

- Replace any worksheets, handouts, or assignments by asking your teacher or friends for copies.

WHAT ARE STRATEGIES FOR REMEMBERING ITEMS FOR CLASS?

Students who are disorganized come unprepared to class. They may forget to bring pencils, books, permission slips, and so forth. In some cases, the students go to their resource class between periods to have the special education teacher remind them what they need. This leads to learned helplessness and must be phased out. The CLASH strategy is designed to help students remember to bring specific items to class. This strategy helps students remember to bring items from home to school and from their lockers to each class. The first step requires them to check their calendars or planners to see what they will need for the next day. With block scheduling, the students have different classes each day. They must be reminded to see what classes are taught the next day. The second step has them list the items they need to bring from home to school. The next two steps are designed to help them put needed materials in their book bags and set them by the door so that they don't forget them. The last step requires them to make lists of materials that they need for each class and put this list on their locker door. They are instructed to look at this list before going to each class. In many high schools today, the lockers are small, and students need to carry most of their materials in their book bags because they may not have time between classes to go to their lockers. In such cases, it is especially important for students to transfer what they need into their book bags at the beginning of the school day.

CLASH:
TO HELP ME REMEMBER TO BRING THINGS TO CLASS

Check your calendar.
List the items you need for the next day.
Always gather the materials from your list.
Set your book bag by the door.
Have a list in your locker of the materials you need.

Check your calendar or planner to see what classes you have the next day.

- Check your calendar or planner to see what classes you have the next day. If you're on block scheduling, remember to check which type of classes you will have the next day.

- Check your planner for any assignments or tests for the next day.

- Check your notebook for each subject to see what materials you need to bring home.

List the items you need for the next day the night before.

- On a piece of paper, list all the things you will need for all your classes the next day.

- Make sure you remember to bring any special forms that have to be signed by your parents.

Always gather the materials from your list and put them in your book bag.

- Gather everything that you need the night before and put the things in your book bag.

- Don't wait until the morning because you may be rushed and forget to check.

Set your book bag by the door so you won't forget it.

- Put your book bag right by the door so that you can't miss it when you walk out the next morning.

Have a list in your locker of what materials you need before each class and look at this list before each class.

- At the beginning of the school day, write a list on a sticky note of what you will need for each class and stick it on the inside of your locker. If you have a dry-erase board on your locker, then use that. Use this method only if you go to your locker between each of your classes.

- As you take the materials for each class, pull off the sticky note or erase the item from the dry-erase board.

WHAT ARE STRATEGIES FOR REMEMBERING ITEMS FOR HOME?

Many students with mild disabilities forget to bring home what they need for homework and studying, which obviously penalizes their academic performance. Many teachers prepare their students' book bags and make sure that they take home what they need. This leads to learned helplessness if it is not followed by instruction by the teacher.

The ADAPT strategy is designed to help students bring items home that they need for studying and homework. It also helps them monitor their needs throughout the school day. The first step of this strategy is for students to make a list of what they need to take home at the end of each class. The second step has them look at the list at the end of the day to see what needs to go home. If they are unclear as to specific assignments or have other questions, then they need to consult with their teachers for clarification. Next, they need to pause before they leave school and ask themselves if they have everything that they need. The last step instructs them to find ways to do assignments and homework if they have forgotten something at school.

ADAPT:
TO HELP ME REMEMBER TO BRING HOME
THINGS THAT I NEED FOR STUDYING AND HOMEWORK

At the end of each class, make a list.
Decide what you need to take home from the list.
Ask your teacher to explain.
Pause, and ask yourself, "Do I have everything I need?"
Try not to give up!

At the end of each class, make a list of what you need to take home.

- In the homework section of your notebook or planner, make a list of what you need to take home for studying and homework for each class.

- Think ahead by including items on your list that you will need to complete an assignment that is due in a few days.

Decide what you need to take home from your list at the end of the day.

- Look at the list and see what work you finished at school and see what needs to be taken home.

- Check off items on the list as you put them in your book bag.

- Check the list to determine if you need to ask your teacher about any specific assignment.

Ask your teacher to answer questions you have about homework or studying.

- After reviewing your list, ask the teacher questions for clarification.

- After the teacher answers the questions, make sure you have the necessary materials to take home.

Pause right before you walk out of school, and ask yourself, "Do I have everything that I need?"

- Even if you checked your list, make sure you check it one more time before leaving school because once you're out of school, you won't be able to get the materials you need.

Try not to give up even if you discover at home that you have forgotten something.

- If you need something, then call a friend to try to borrow the material you need.

- If available, call a homework hot line or check a school homework web site.

- If the teacher approves, then call the teacher for help.

- If you cannot get help from anyone, then complete the assignment the best that you can. Do not leave the assignment undone just because you forgot something. Always try to do the best that you can!

TROY, A STUDENT WITH ORGANIZATIONAL DIFFICULTIES

Troy is a high school freshman whose major difficulties involve time and materials management. Although he has a planner, he does not enter assignments in it. When Mrs. White, Troy's resource teacher, helps him enter assignments, he does not independently refer to it. He forgets to bring needed materials to class and also forgets to bring home materials he needs for studying and homework. Troy has been identified as being gifted and having ADHD. He is in accelerated classes; however, he is doing poorly because he does not get his assignments in on time and does not study for tests because he does not have the appropriate materials at home.

Mrs. White and Troy decide that he would benefit from using the 3C strategy to help him keep track of tests and assignments. He also will be taught to use the CLASH and ADAPT strategies to help him prepare for class and homework.

Mrs. White starts instruction using 3C by having Troy record all due dates for assignments and tests on a marking period calendar that is in his planner. From this, she models how to transfer items from this calendar to his weekly planner. Then, she models how to make daily to-do lists from his weekly calendar. Troy readily uses this approach as long as Mrs. White guides him through the process. However, he has difficulty doing this independently, so they set up a time of day (before classes) and a place (library) where he has to do it on his own. Over the semester he does this and shows mastery of independently maintaining his planner.

He is taught to use CLASH and ADAPT to be prepared in class and at home. Again, he does well as long as he is guided by Mrs. White; however, he does not use these strategies independently. Mrs. White has him use these strategies along with 3C in the library before classes begin.

Over a semester, Troy makes progress in managing time and materials, and his grades in all his classes improves significantly. However, he still has difficulty in independently using these strategies and needs to have support from Mrs. White in using these strategies without prompting over the next semester.

7

Test Taking

- Why do students with learning disabilities and ADHD need to learn test-taking skills?

- What are the different subskills of test taking?

- What is special about teaching test-taking strategies?

- What are strategies to reduce test anxiety?

- What are strategies for time management when taking a test?

- What are strategies for carefully reading test directions and questions?

- What are strategies for taking multiple-choice tests?

- What are strategies for taking true/false tests?

- What are strategies for taking essay tests?

- What are strategies for activating study skill strategies when taking a test?

WHY DO STUDENTS WITH LEARNING DISABILITIES AND ADHD NEED TO LEARN TEST-TAKING SKILLS?

Most students with learning disabilities and ADHD are not test-wise. They have not independently developed metacognitive strategies to cope with the varied testing demands in today's schools. Ironically, students with disabilities are required to take more tests than students without disabilities. They are legally required to take part in all statewide assessment for students without disabilities (Individuals with Disabilities Education Act [IDEA] Amendments of 1997). In addition, students with disabilities who are in general education classes must take all the tests associated with such classes. Finally, they must be assessed for eligibility for special education and for individualized education program (IEP) purposes. This chapter presents strategies to make students with disabilities more test-wise when taking the following types of tests:

- Group standardized academic achievement tests (e.g., Iowa, Stanford 9) that are required as part of statewide assessment for all students

- High-stakes testing that is required for grade promotion and graduation as part of statewide assessment for all students

- Curriculum-based tests (e.g., textbook quizzes) and teacher-made tests

Students with learning disabilities and ADHD may have difficulty with test taking because of *anxiety*. Children with learning disabilities are reported to have higher levels of test anxiety than children without disabilities (Bryan, Sonnefeld, & Grabowski, 1983). Swanson and Howell (1996) found that this test anxiety was due, in part, to poor study skills. This finding points out the importance of ensuring that all students with learning disabilities have good study skills so that test anxiety from this source can be reduced.

Some students have crippling anxiety when faced with a test. This often prevents them from demonstrating what they know. Many students with learning disabilities and ADHD associate tests with failure. They have taken a number of tests to become eligible for special education, and they may feel that these tests "proved" they have disabilities. They generalize and believe that they cannot be successful on any tests. To some students, tests represent their disabilities.

Some anxiety is necessary when taking a test so that students are motivated to do their best; however, achieving the right level of anxiety is problematic for students with disabilities. An "I don't care" attitude is associated with too little anxiety, whereas a crippling "I can't do this" attitude is associated with too much anxiety.

Being test-wise involves knowing how to *manage time effectively* during testing. Students with learning disabilities and ADHD often cannot work under time constraints. They must be taught to work quickly on timed tests and accurately on untimed tests. Being test-wise also involves reading questions and directions carefully. Many students who are impulsive do not have a careful, analytical approach and, therefore, may not read directions or may read them superficially.

Effective test taking involves use of different *strategies to match the format of the test*. Objective tests involving multiple-choice and true/false questions require different strategies from essay tests. Students with learning disabilities must be taught different strategies for different test formats, and they must be taught to apply these strategies as needed. This is difficult for some students with disabilities who are not flexible in their approach to learning.

Many students with learning disabilities and ADHD have *difficulty activating strategies that they used for studying* when they are taking a test. They compartmentalize their thinking and learn strategies related to a specific situation and have difficulty transferring from the study setting to the testing setting. The metacognitive difficulties of some students prevent them from making this transfer; therefore, it is imperative that instruction be directed at developing the important skill of activating study strategies when taking a test.

WHAT ARE THE DIFFERENT SUBSKILLS OF TEST TAKING?

Test taking involves a number of different subskills, ranging from emotional aspects (e.g., anxiety) to reading (e.g., reading directions carefully) to metacognitive skills involving strategy activation and transfer. The following seven subskills of test taking (with the corresponding Active Learner Student Questionnaire items found in Appendix A) are taught with the Active Learner Approach.

1. Test anxiety: "I get extremely nervous when I take a test."

2. Time management: "I have difficulty completing tests on time."

3. Reading questions: "I don't read directions or questions carefully."

4. Test format—multiple-choice tests: "I have difficulty understanding multiple-choice questions."

5. Test format—true/false tests: "I have difficulty with true/false tests."

6. Test format—essay tests: "I have difficulty with essay tests."

7. Activating study skill strategies: "During a test, I have difficulty remembering what I studied."

WHAT IS SPECIAL ABOUT
TEACHING TEST-TAKING STRATEGIES?

For most other areas of strategy instruction, the Active Learner Approach does not require students to memorize the steps in the strategy. Because so many students with learning disabilities have memory problems, it would complicate their mastery of the Active Learner Approach to require memorization of all the steps in all the strategies. Rather, the students are encouraged to keep a notebook with the strategies written down so that they can refer to the steps as they are needed. However, this is not the case with test-taking strategies. The students must memorize the steps in each of the strategies so that they can readily retrieve them while taking tests. Because of this, it is necessary to insert an additional step in the teaching process. After a strategy is modeled by the teacher, there needs to be explicit instruction on memorization. At this stage, the students need to rely on the spelling of the acronym and try to recall any associated graphic cues as aids to recalling each step.

It is best to use students' actual tests that they have taken in the past in order to teach test-taking strategies. It may be necessary to obtain these from the students' general education teachers because many teachers do not allow students to keep past quizzes and tests. Tell the general education teacher that you will return the tests after you demonstrate to the students how test-taking strategies could have been used to improve their performance on the tests.

It is important to teach students with mild disabilities to keep all past quizzes and tests in a separate section of their notebooks where that can be readily accessed. In addition, the students need to keep a record of all their scores on past tests. Many students discard past tests and do not know their academic status in their courses. Some do not want to keep the tests because they received low grades that remind them of how poorly they are doing in school. Have the students devote a section of their notebooks to recording each grade on every assignment in each class so they know their status in each class and so they can see improvement in test scores as a result of applying the strategies of the Active Learner Approach.

Another special aspect of teaching test-taking strategies involves students' advocating for themselves to receive accommodations and modifications while taking tests. As part of an overall self-advocacy program designed to make students with mild disabilities more independent, it is useful to have the students identify any accommodations and modifications that would improve their test performance. Such accommodations and modifications usually fall into one of the following four categories: timing/scheduling, setting, presentation, and response (Thurlow, Elliott, & Ysseldyke, 1998).

For timing/scheduling accommodations, students may request that the time of day of the test be changed. For example, testing might be changed to early in the morning so that anxiety does not build up during the day while waiting for the test. Another accommodation might involve breaks during the testing to practice anxiety reducing techniques, such as those in the BRAVE strategy. Extended time on a test is a frequently used accommodation and usually involves a time-and-a-half relationship to the original time limit (e.g., if a test is 1 hour long, extended time would be 1½ hours). In some cases, no time limits are provided as an accommodation.

Setting accommodations may involve individual or small-group testing as a way of reducing anxiety that arises from the student watching other students perform faster. Other setting accommodations may involve preferential seating or testing in a location with minimal distractions, which are especially important for students with ADHD.

Accommodations involving presentation may include having someone read the directions or test items to the student. Other accommodations may involve larger answer bubbles, additional space between lines, or reduced items on a page. Some of the major accommodations for student responses include having someone record the student's responses or use of a word processor, spell checker, calculator, or dictionary.

Testing accommodations need to be listed in a student's IEP. You and the student need to work together to identify the accommodations that would be helpful in improving test performance. These should be presented at the IEP meeting by the student after the student has role played with you how to make his presentation. However, it is important to keep in mind that the accommodations should maintain standard conditions (i.e., they allow the student to take the test in a different way without changing what the test is measuring; Virginia Department of Education, 1997). It is also important to avoid requesting accommodations that do not maintain standard conditions because these may prevent a student from receiving the benefits of the test (e.g., high school graduation for a high-stakes test).

WHAT ARE STRATEGIES TO REDUCE TEST ANXIETY?

There are two types of strategies used to reduce anxiety; one involves students preparing themselves before taking a test, and the other involves a specific self-talk strategy while taking a test. *To lessen the anxiety that builds up before taking a test,* students need to prepare themselves in the following ways:

• Get adequate rest the night before the test.

• Eat a good breakfast before the test.

• Lay out all materials needed for the test the night before.

• *Do not* cram at the last minute because the students become aware of the answers they do not know and this adds to their anxiety. Students should set an ending time for studying and not go beyond that time.

• Get a pep talk from a teacher, counselor, or friend who encourages the students about the benefits of test (e.g., high school graduation for a high-stakes test).

• Practice relaxation techniques such as those described in BRAVE before going in to take the test.

The second type of strategy to reduce anxiety involves the student's *self-talk while taking a test*. The BRAVE strategy is designed for this purpose. With this strategy, the students are to recall steps that will aid in minimizing anxiety that builds while taking a test. The students should also try to recall any graphics associated with each step so that they can practice the action required (e.g., re-calling the picture of the lungs as an aid to breathing deeply).

The steps in this strategy include well-accepted techniques for reducing anxiety, such as deep breathing, muscle relaxation, maintaining a positive atti-tude, visualization, and focusing on the end. Pauk (1997) found that deep breath-ing and muscle relaxation exercises reduced stress in college students. When practicing these steps in the resource setting, have the students close their eyes to help focus on breathing and muscle relaxation. Have them count the num-ber of breaths in a given period of time to contrast deep breathing with normal breathing. To help students relax their muscles, play quiet music or relaxation tapes. For training students to use visualization as an aid for relaxation, have them identify a favorite place (e.g., the beach), shut their eyes, and describe each aspect of a scene at this place, including people, position of objects, color, shape, and size of objects.

BRAVE:
TO OVERCOME NERVOUSNESS WHEN TAKING A TEST

Breathe deeply.
Relax.
Attitude is everything.
Visualize yourself in your favorite place.
End is in sight.

Breathe deeply.

- Take long, slow deep breaths throughout the test.

- Focus your attention on your breathing to make it steady.

Relax.

- When you feel your muscles tightening, try to slowly relax each muscle one at a time. Mentally tell yourself that you are relaxing each muscle one at a time. For example, relax your leg muscles by telling yourself, "I am now relaxing my leg muscles."

- Start relaxing your muscles from the top of your body and go down. Add extra focus to your neck muscles.

Attitude is everything!

- Maintain a positive attitude throughout the entire test.
- During the test, tell yourself that, "I can do it."
- Put a star next to answers that you are sure that you got right to show that you can do it!

Visualize yourself in your favorite place.

- When you find yourself becoming anxious, close your eyes for a few seconds and imagine yourself in your favorite place (e.g., at the beach, at the mall, watching television, playing sports).

End is in sight!

- Even if you feel that the test will last forever, remember that it will be over before you know it, and your anxiety will fade!

WHAT ARE STRATEGIES FOR TIME MANAGEMENT WHEN TAKING A TEST?

There are two approaches for developing time management when taking a test. The first involves explicit instruction on analysis of time factors before taking a test and the second involves a self-talk strategy–FLEAS. Development of time management for test taking must begin with students recognizing the following requirements:

- Students must wear a watch or have access to a clock while taking a test.
- Students must get to the test on time.
- Students must use all time available for the test.
- Students must check all answers if they finish the test early.

Explicit instruction is given in analyzing time limits in relationship to test content. Demonstrate how to analyze time in relationship to the number of items on a test. For example, if there are 60 minutes for a test and there are 20 multiple-choice items, demonstrate dividing 60 by 20 and arriving at the conclusion that the student can devote about 3 minutes to each question. Give different examples using different test formats (e.g., true/false, essay). Then, demonstrate with examples in which the items have different point values (e.g., 60 minutes for 10 multiple-choice questions and two essay questions). Give the student guided practice in solving division problems such as the ones that you demonstrated. It is not important that students know the exact amount of time to be devoted to each item; but rather, it is important to make students aware of time factors in relationship to the number and type of items on a test.

The second approach to developing time management skills for testing involves the FLEAS strategy, which is designed to help a student use self-talk to complete tests on time. This strategy gives the student an overall plan for managing time while taking a test. Most students with disabilities, especially those who are impulsive, just start with the first question and do not get an overall picture of the questions and time factors. If they find the first question hard to answer, then they may become frustrated and their anxiety may overwhelm them. If they scan the whole test, then they may see that there are questions that they can readily answer.

The first step in FLEAS requires the students to read the directions carefully. Then, they are to scan the entire test and consider the total number of test items in relationship to the time allowed. The next two steps have the students analyze the questions in terms of easy or hard and the amount of points associated with each question. The last step has the students skip questions they cannot answer and return to them if there is time at the end.

FLEAS:
TO HELP ME COMPLETE TESTS ON TIME

First read the directions carefully.
Look over the test.
Easiest questions should be answered first.
Answer questions that are worth more.
Skip a question if you are stumped.

First read the directions carefully.

- Read the directions and put them in your own words.

- If you do not understand a certain part of the directions, then ask the teacher for help before you begin the test. If this is not possible, then try to figure out the meanings of particular words by analyzing the context or the surrounding words.

Look over the test and decide how much time you should spend on each test item.

- First, figure out how much time you have to finish the entire test (e.g., 60 minutes).
- Next, figure out the total number of questions on the test (e.g., 30 questions).
- Then, divide the total time (60 minutes) by the total number of questions (30 questions). You have 2 minutes to spend on each test question.
- If you can't figure out how much exact time to spend on each question, just estimate. This will keep you aware of time and move you along so that you don't spend too much time on one question.

Easiest questions should be answered first.

- Answer the questions that are easiest for you and then answer the remaining questions.

Answer questions that are worth more points first.

- It is important to determine how many points questions are worth, and answer the questions that are worth more first.

Skip a question if you are stumped (just make sure to go back to it later).

- If you find yourself spending a long time answering a particular question, then mark the question and move on to the next question.
- Try to return to the question after you have answered the other questions. However, if you do not get back to that question, then chances are you will have answered many other questions instead of spending so much time on one particular question.

WHAT ARE STRATEGIES FOR CAREFULLY READING TEST DIRECTIONS AND QUESTIONS?

Students with mild disabilities may not read directions and questions carefully because of their learning style, which is superficial and not reflective. They may associate a question with the first response that comes to mind, they may not reflect on other possible responses, and they may have difficulty understanding some of the words in directions. To improve a student's ability to read test directions and questions, first teach words frequently found in directions. The RAINS strategy is designed to assist students to be more reflective in their approach to reading directions and questions.

Explicitly teach each of the words listed next and any others that have been used on tests that they have taken. Teach the students to decode each word as well as its meaning. Create practice questions with each of these words using the students' course content or use old tests students have taken with these words.

- Analyze: break into parts
- Categorize: place items under headings
- Classify: place items in related groups
- Compare: tell how things are the same
- Contrast: tell how things are different
- Criticize: present pros and cons
- Defend: prove an idea
- Define: give a meaning
- Describe: provide details
- Discuss: give the main idea and details
- Enumerate: list
- Evaluate: make a judgment based on evidence
- Explain: give reasons or causes
- Illustrate: give examples
- Justify: give evidence to support your ideas
- Prove: provide factual evidence to support your ideas
- Relate: show relationships
- Summarize: give main points
- Trace: describe steps in a process

Use the RAINS strategy to teach students to be more reflective and analytical when reading test questions and directions. The first step in this strategy requires the students to read the entire question and choices for multiple-choice tests. The second step requires them to identify any words that they cannot read or do not understand. They are to try to recall where they might have seen a particular unknown word before and figure out the decoding or meaning based on this. If this is not successful, then they are to use context clues and analyze surrounding words as aids to successfully read or understand the word. The next step has them identify keywords in the question or answer choices. The students are directed to pay special attention to negatives as these are often used to make questions harder. Students need to be explicitly taught words for negatives (e.g., *no, not, none, never*) as well as prefixes that represent negation (e.g., *un-, in-*). Finally, they are taught to use grammatical clues as aids for matching the correct answer choice with the question. All of these steps require students to develop the metalinguistic skill of carefully analyzing language.

RAINS:
TO HELP ME READ DIRECTIONS AND QUESTIONS CAREFULLY

Read the entire question.
Analyze the context.
Identify keywords.
Notice the negatives.
Search for grammatical clues.

Read the entire question and all choices before answering.

- Always reread the entire question and all choices.
- You may think the question is asking one thing, but after you read the complete question, you may realize it may actually be asking something else.

Analyze the context and figure out words that you do not know.

- Identify unknown words.
- Try to remember where you have seen these words before. Maybe you saw them in your textbook or your notes.
- Analyze the context by trying to use the words you do know in the sentences that surround the unknown words. By analyzing the surrounding words, you may be able to figure out the unknown word.

Identify the key words in the question and in the answer choices.

- These words are *often, most, all, some, equal, good,* and *sometimes.*
- Analyze the meanings of these words.

Notice the negatives.

- These words are *no, not, none, never,* and the prefix *un-* (e.g., *unimportant*) or *in-* (e.g., *incomplete*) in each question and answer.
- Negatives completely change the meaning of a question or an answer, so watch carefully for these words.

Search for grammatical clues.

• All questions follow the rules of grammar. Narrow your choices by eliminating possible answers that do not produce grammatically correct sentences.

WHAT ARE STRATEGIES FOR
TAKING MULTIPLE-CHOICE TESTS?

The most common type of test format on standardized tests, especially high-stakes tests, is the multiple-choice question. This type of test format is difficult for many students with disabilities because they are impulsive and just read the first or second choices. For other students, the difficulty lies in deciding between several choices that may be correct. When multiple-choice questions are constructed, two or three of the choices are usually similar, making it hard to distinguish the correct response. Students need to have good analytical skills to differentiate among the choices and decide which choice is closest to the correct one.

A number of strategies have been used to help students with learning disabilities to improve test-taking abilities with multiple-choice tests.

1. SCORER, one of the first strategies, was developed in 1972 by Carman and Adams (Sabornie & deBettencourt, 1997) and includes the following steps: scheduling time (S), looking for clue words (C), omitting difficult items (O), reading carefully (R), estimating the answer (E), and reviewing the work (R).

2. PIRATES uses similar steps: prepare for the test (P), inspect the instructions (I), read each question (R), answer or abandon each question (A), turn back (T), estimate answers for remaining questions (E), and survey the test (S) (Hughes, Ruhl, Deshler, & Schumaker, 1993).

3. DETER has the students read the directions (D), examine the entire test (E), decide how much time will be spent on each item (T), begin with the easiest (E), and review after finishing (R) (Strichart, Mangrun, & Iannuzzi, 1998).

CRAM[1], the Active Learner Approach strategy, is designed to improve students' ability to take multiple-choice tests. CRAM does not include as many steps as SCORER, PIRATES, or DETER because some steps are taught in other strategies (e.g., reading the question carefully is taught in RAINS) and because it emphasizes processes necessary to retrieve a response for a multiple-

---

[1]There is another strategy titled *CRAM* that is a generic learning strategy designed by Deshler, Ellis, and Lenz (1996). The Active Learner Approach CRAM was devised by Craig Stoll, a graduate student involved with our project with college students. He developed CRAM without prior knowledge of the Deshler, Ellis, and Lenz strategy. The reader should not confuse the two as they have different purposes.

choice test. CRAM was the most used strategy in our project with college students with disabilities, and the tutors found it easy to use and effective.

CRAM focuses on helping students select the best choice by having them use recall rather than recognition (i.e., have the students recall the answer and then compare this answer with the choices available). The students will be hesitant to cover the answer choices because this makes it harder to guess. Use practice tests in which the advantage of using this approach becomes evident (i.e., use items for which you know the students can retrieve the answers to). As students compare their answer with the answer choices, have them verbally describe why each choice can be correct or not. Have them check off each choice after it is discussed.

CRAM:
TO HELP ME WITH MULTIPLE-CHOICES TESTS

Cover the answers.
Read the question carefully.
Answer the question without looking at the choices.
Match your answer to one of the given choices.

Cover the answers.

- Use a blank card or your hand to cover the choices.

Read the question carefully.

- Highlight the important words.
- Put the question in your own words.
- Remember where you saw the answer in your textbook or notes.

Answer the question without looking at the choices.

Match your answer to one of the given choices.

- Select the choice that matches your answer.
- If no choice matches your answer, then try to eliminate some of the choices.
- Look for keywords to help you select the best answer.

WHAT ARE STRATEGIES FOR TAKING TRUE/FALSE TESTS?

Test questions with a true/false format are difficult for students with learning disabilities because the questions require the students to carefully analyze specific words. True/false questions are often constructed to confuse the test taker so that the answer is not obvious. Many students with disabilities, especially those who are not reflective, guess readily on true/false tests because they know that they have a 50% probability of being correct.

The SQUID strategy is designed to assist students with disabilities to carefully analyze different types of words frequently used in true/false questions and not be dependent on guessing. Tips that are frequently given for true/false tests were incorporated into the steps (e.g., looking for qualifying words, simplifying double negatives; Bos & Vaughn, 2002). SQUID develops the metalinguistic skill of analyzing language. The students are taught to look for words that are absolutes. When modeling this strategy, create many examples of questions that use absolutes with answers that are false. Likewise, teach students to analyze words on the basis of qualifications and show why the answers to these questions are usually true. Teach how negatives change meanings of sentences. Analyzing statements with two negatives is especially difficult. Having the students cross out each of the negatives and reading the remaining sentence shows the meaning. Finally, have the students analyze all parts of a statement to make sure that each part is true. Students who are impulsive may see that one part of the statement is true and mark the statement as true without reading on to a part that makes the statement false.

SQUID:
TO HELP ME WITH TRUE/FALSE TESTS

Statements that are absolute are usually false.
Qualified statements are usually true.
Underline the negatives.
If a statement has two negatives, then cross out both
   negatives.
Decide that a statement is true if everything is true.

Statements that are absolute are usually false.

- Words such as these represent absolutes and are usually *false*: *all, every, never,* and *no.*

- Examples: All animals are reptiles. Every person in Congress is a man.

Qualified statements are usually true.

- Words such as these represent qualifiers and are usually *true*: *some, most,* and *sometimes.*
- Examples: Some animals are reptiles. Most of the people in Congress are men.

Underline the negatives.

- Words such as these are negatives: *not, cannot, do not, no,* or the prefixes *in-* (e.g., *incomplete*) and *un-* (e.g., *unimportant*).
- Examples: Washington, D.C., is *not* the capital of the United States. Three hundred and sixty-five days is an *in*complete year.

If a statement has two negatives, then cross out both negatives.

- Cross out both of the negatives and read the sentence without them. This will clearly show the meaning.
- Example: People will ~~not~~ buy luxury goods if they do ~~not~~ have disposable income. People will buy luxury goods if they have disposable income.

Decide that a statement is *true* only if *everything* about the statement is true.

- Items on a test often include information that is true, except for a detail, so pay close attention to the complete statement.
- Example: Massachusetts, Virginia, and Pennsylvania were all part of the original 13 colonies (true, because all three were part of the 13 colonies). Massachusetts, Virginia, and Montana were all part of the original 13 colonies (false, because Montana was not one of the original 13 colonies).

WHAT ARE STRATEGIES FOR TAKING ESSAY TESTS?

A number of strategies have been used to help students with disabilities perform better on essay tests:

1. QUOTE involves the following steps: question and look at the direction words (Q), underline important ideas (U), organize and write (O), decide on time (T), and evaluate (E) (Strichart, Mangrum, & Iannuzzi, 1998).

2. ANSWER, which was developed by Hughes, Schumaker, and Deshler (Bos & Vaughn, 2002), has students analyze the situation (A), notice requirements (N), set up an outline (S), work in the details (W), engineer the answer (E), and review (R).

Essay tests are difficult for students with disabilities because they require the integration of four subskills: careful reading of the question, retrieval of the correct response, organization of the ideas involved in the response, and expressive writing of the response. We developed the RULE-WE strategy to overcome difficulties of reading the question and organizing the ideas. Retrieval of the correct response is taught with the SPORT strategy, which is designed to assist students to retrieve responses that they practiced while studying. SPORT is described in the next section on activating study strategies during testing. If a student has difficulty with essay tests because of expressive writing problems, then accommodations for oral testing might be requested. In addition, use of strategies to train the student to write essay responses should be provided (see the IBC strategy in Chapter 11).

The RULE-WE strategy is designed to guide the student in reading the question carefully, underlining keywords, outlining the response, and writing the answer from the outline. For the outline, the student must identify the main point as well as the details. Students need to practice writing these outlines with just a few keywords that represent the meaning and not complete sentences. They must learn to only write complete sentences when they write the answer.

RULE-WE:
TO HELP ME WITH ESSAY TESTS

Read the question.
Underline keywords.
List or outline major points.
Emphasize details for each point.
Write the answer.
Evaluate the answer.

Read the question.

- Read all parts of the question. Many essay questions include multiple parts. Be sure to answer all parts.

Underline keywords.

- Keywords for essay tests are: *analyze, categorize, classify, compare, contrast, criticize, defend, define, describe, discuss, enumerate, evaluate, explain, illustrate, justify, prove, relate, summarize,* and *trace.*
- Define the keyword to yourself before answering the question.

List or outline the major points.

- Write the major points you studied that relate to this question.

Emphasize the details for each of the points.

- Under each of the points, write *at least* two details.

Write the answer.

- First, read over your outline and organize the major points and details.
- Write an introduction to the major points.
- Check off each of the major points and details as you include them in your answer.
- Write complete sentences for each of your major points and details.
- Write an ending that summarizes or wraps up the ideas from your outline.

Evaluate your answer.

- Reread the question, and then read your answer to make sure that it matches the question.
- Add information to clarify points that were not adequately explained.
- Correct any grammatical or spelling errors.

WHAT ARE STRATEGIES FOR ACTIVATING STUDY SKILL STRATEGIES WHEN TAKING A TEST?

Use the SPORT strategy for students who have difficulty applying what they study to the testing situation. This self-talk strategy is designed to assist students in transferring what they studied and applying it to the testing situation. To facilitate this, students are instructed to visualize the material and try to recall where in a book or in their notes they saw it. Some students can be taught to recall the location of the material (e.g., whether they saw this information on the right or left page of a book or the top or bottom of a page). Then, they are taught to bring to mind any memory strategies they used, recall note cards that they used to study, or remember associations they made. Teaching them to "dump" information is exceedingly important. Have them write in the margin all the information that they recall relative to the question. Then, have them analyze the dumped material and select what they should include in their answer.

SPORT:
TO HELP ME REMEMBER WHAT I STUDIED WHEN I TAKE A TEST

> **S**ay to yourself—where?
> **P**icture in your head.
> **O**rganize in your mind.
> **R**emember to "dump" all the information.
> **T**ell yourself that you need to go back.

Say to yourself, "Where did I see this information when I was studying?"

- When you find yourself forgetting important information, think back to when you were studying.

- Try to think of where the information was located in a certain book, on a certain page of the book, in your lecture notes, or on your note cards.

Picture in your head what you read or wrote that might help.

- Close your eyes and picture yourself as you studied for the test.

- Try to visualize the information just as you saw it in your book or notes when you were studying. Try to remember what you said aloud when you studied.

Organize in your mind all of the study aids that you used.

- Study aids include memory strategies such as mnemonics and other techniques you used to help you memorize information.

- Think about any note cards that you made.

- Think about any keywords and pictures that you created.

Remember to "dump" all the information as you recall it.

- As you take the test, write everything you studied. Write this in the margin or on the back of the test.

Tell yourself that you need to go back and look at the "dumped" information.

- As you answer the questions, go back and look at everything you wrote in the margins or on the back of the test.

- As you look at each item in the margin, ask yourself if you included it in your answer and if not, do you want to include it.

BILL, A STUDENT WITH TEST-TAKING DIFFICULTIES

Bill is in the ninth grade and is having difficulty with weekly objective quizzes that he must take on one to three chapters of the textbook in his world history class. Bill has difficulties with test anxiety, being impulsive when taking multiple-choice tests, and using metacognitive strategies to activate study skills when taking a test. His world history class is the last period of the day, and his anxiety about the test builds up throughout the school day. Bill and his special education teacher, Ms. Fox, decide that he should request an accommodation involving taking the quiz before school so that his anxiety does not build. They role play a conversation in which Bill requests this accommodation from his world history teacher, Mr. Fairchild. Bill has a meeting with Mr. Fairchild and presents his reasons for wanting to take the test early in the day. Mr. Fairchild readily agrees to this. In addition to this accommodation, Ms. Fox teaches Bill to use BRAVE as a self-talk strategy to reduce his anxiety while taking the quiz.

Ms. Fox teaches Bill the CRAM strategy to improve his ability to take multiple-choice tests and overcome his impulsiveness in responding. During their resource period, Ms. Fox constructs practice multiple-choice tests and then models how to use CRAM. She finds that Bill does not read all the choices carefully and usually selects the first or second choice. They work on starting with the last choice and working up to the first choice as a way of making sure that Bill considers all the choices. Bill is taught to check off each choice as they read it to show that Bill is considering all choices.

To teach Bill to transfer the strategies that he used for studying to the test situation, Ms. Fox teaches him the SPORT strategy. She finds that he has the most difficulty with the step in which he has to organize the study aids that he used. Before taking a practice test, she has him verbally describe what mnemonics he used and then find the question that goes with the material that he studied. She teaches him to write the mnemonic cue on the test page as a guide for writing his answer.

Bill continues to work on mastering SPORT over the semester. By the end of the semester, he has mastered it at the independent level. He has learned to manage his test anxiety using BRAVE, and he reads all answer choices when he uses CRAM. His weekly quiz grades have improved significantly, and his average is at a passing level for the course at the end of the semester.

8

Study Skills

░ Why do students with learning disabilities and ADHD need to learn study skills?

░ What are the different subskills of study skills?

░ What is special about teaching study skills?

░ What are strategies to help get started studying?

░ What are strategies for staying focused while studying?

░ What are strategies for avoiding distraction when studying?

░ What are strategies for studying from notes?

░ What are strategies for studying from books?

░ What are strategies for organizing information from books and notes?

░ What are strategies for remembering information for tests?

WHY DO STUDENTS WITH LEARNING DISABILITIES AND ADHD NEED TO LEARN STUDY SKILLS?

Students with learning disabilities and ADHD find it difficult to meet the challenge of developing *independent* study skills because of the required attention, advanced cognitive processes, and memory skills that must be integrated. Learned helplessness, which may be fostered by parents and/or teachers, also makes independent study skills difficult. Many students with disabilities can study with other students or under the guidance of their parents or teachers. However, they must learn to study independently if they are to be successful at higher academic levels, especially postsecondary schooling. Many students with learning disabilities and ADHD find it difficult to get started studying and, once started, find it difficult to sustain attention. They have come to depend on their resource teachers to get them started and to help them stay on task during the resource period. Likewise, some students have their parents study with them at home. Teacher and parent assistance is important at the initial stages of learning but must be faded so that the students develop the ability to study independently. This is important for students who are planning to attend college. In our study of college students, we worked with a freshman who was at a residential college far from home and was having difficulty studying independently. He said that the thing he most disliked about college was that he couldn't bring his mother with him to help him study. He was not joking.

Students with learning disabilities and ADHD tend to be passive learners and do not lay out a study plan of how to organize their time and learning. When studying their notes or books, they simply read the material without imposing an overall structure on the material to increase their understanding and retention of the material. When studying for tests, they just read material and do not use cognitive strategies to aid their memorization of the material. A large number of students with learning disabilities have memory problems and yet they have not developed ways to compensate for them.

Many students in high school participate in study skills workshops. These are usually time-limited workshops (e.g., 1 or 2 weeks) and involve general rules for studying. In our study of college students with mild disabilities, we found that many of these students had received this instruction in high school. Most of them found these workshops of limited use because the workshops did not help them in applying the rules to the specific studying that they were doing for their classes. They did not have the required skills to generalize these rules and transfer their use to their specific needs. With the Active Learner Approach, all instruction on study skills is applied to the students' current demands to study for tests so they can avoid the gaps created by problems with transfer and generalization.

WHAT ARE THE DIFFERENT SUBSKILLS OF STUDY SKILLS?

There are three major areas of subskills of study skills: attention, advanced cognitive processes, and memory. The subskills involved in attention include coming to attention, sustaining attention, and overcoming distractions. These three subskills involving attention (and the corresponding Active Learner Student Questionnaire items found in Appendix A) are taught with the Active Learner Approach.

- Coming to attention: "I find it hard to start studying."

- Sustaining attention: "I can't stay focused when I study."

- Overcoming distractions: "I'm easily distracted by things that happen around me when I study."

A second area of subskills involves advanced cognitive processes. This area requires students to interact with the material to be learned. They need to analyze the demands of testing in relation to the material to be studied and develop and use strategies to enhance their mastery of the content. Devine (1981) pointed out the relationship between studying and advanced cognitive processes when he noted that studying becomes thinking when it involves noting inferences, seeing relations, identifying main points, predicting, relating, and so forth. The following three subskills involving advanced cognitive processes (with the corresponding Active Learner Student Questionnaire items found in Appendix A) are taught with the Active Learner Approach.

- Studying from notes: "I have difficulty studying from my notes."

- Studying from books: "I have difficulty studying from books."

- Organizing information: "I don't know how to organize information from books and notes."

The final subskill of study skills involves memorization. Rote memorization, or memorization without understanding, is avoided with the Active Learner Approach. Instead, meaningful memorization is emphasized. With the Active Learner Approach, students learn to try to understand the overall structure of the material and then memorize the parts of the structure. The following study skill involving memory (and the corresponding Active Learner Student Questionnaire items found in Appendix A) is taught with the Active Learner Approach.

- Memorizing information: "I have difficulty remembering information for tests."

The attention, advanced cognitive processes, and memory subskills are closely interrelated. If students have no plans for how to learn, then it is difficult to sustain attention—they are confused and at a loss for what to do. Likewise, if they cannot attend, then they have difficulty identifying and using strategies to enhance their learning and memorization. If they do not understand the material that they are studying, then it is difficult to memorize isolated, unrelated facts. Therefore, for some students with mild disabilities, it is necessary to provide instruction in the three areas of attention, advanced cognitive processing, and memory.

WHAT IS SPECIAL ABOUT TEACHING STUDY SKILLS?

With the Active Learner Approach to teaching study skills, the course demands placed on students for studying for tests are used as the content of the teaching. No general rules are provided unless followed up with application to specific course content. This makes teaching study skills harder because you must obtain the students' test schedules as well as descriptions of the tests or examples of test items. You must analyze the students' notes and/or readings in relation to the test demands. This requires extensive preplanning on your part, which will take time. Just as the student is expected to devote time to learning the strategies, you must be willing to devote time to preparing appropriate instruction.

Teaching study skills must be integrated with training of other related areas, such as organizing, notetaking, and test taking. The students must have adequate time laid out for studying, and they must have good notes for studying. They must be taught how to link what they studied to what they need to bring to mind when taking the test. This metacognitive skill is especially difficult to learn.

WHAT ARE STRATEGIES TO HELP GET STARTED STUDYING?

Many students sit down with the best intentions to study; however, they just can't get started. They may stare at their books or out the window for long periods of time. To overcome this, students need to identify environments that are best for them to study. Some students like to study in the library; others prefer to study at home. Some students prefer no noise; others like to have music or the television on. They find that the music or the television blocks out other sounds that might distract them. Some students like to have dim light when working; others like bright light. Have the students analyze where they prefer studying as well as the noise and light conditions they find most conducive to studying. Do not impose your study preferences on the students. Whatever works for them should be used.

If students find themselves distracted in a study situation, then they must be taught to remove themselves immediately. For example, they are studying in the library and some nearby students are talking. Instead of trying to get the other students to stop talking, your students can simply move to another place.

Teach the students to have everything that they need for studying ready before they start. If they have to get up and down to retrieve supplies, they will have difficulty actually getting started studying and their actual study time will be shortened.

Studying is hard for everyone but especially for students with mild disabilities. Have them set up a reinforcement plan in which they reinforce themselves to start studying as well as sustain their attention over a certain period of study time. The reinforcers need to be important to them. Guide them in selecting reinforcers such as eating a favorite food, playing a video game, listening to music, talking on the telephone, or using the computer. All of these reinforcers should have time limits on them (i.e., after studying for 30 minutes they can have 10 minutes of computer time).

The amount of time students see before them as the time for studying seems endless, so it is difficult for them to get started. To help with this, have the students make lists of what they have to study *before* getting started. Have them check off each task as they complete it. This will help them organize their study time and indicate that an end is in sight when they finish all of the tasks.

Some students are distracted by ideas that pop into their heads when they begin studying. To minimize these distractions, have them keep a worry pad while they are studying. Pauk (1997) suggested that college students improve their studying by keeping a concentration score sheet to develop self-observation and a worry pad to write down ideas that pop into their heads. We suggest that students jot down ideas that interfere with their studying and go back to them after they have finished studying. It is important to point out to the students that once they write an idea down, they have to let it go until after they have completed studying.

The CHECK strategy is designed to overcome difficulties that students have in getting started studying. When you teach this, have the students record the starting times for their studying to indicate that they are actually using the strategy effectively. For example, if they are at home studying, then they are to record the exact time that they sit down at their desks to begin. Then, they are to record the times that they actually started as represented by taking notes or some other physical action. They are to determine if there is a delay between the time they sat down and the time they actually got started. If there is a delay, this will indicate the importance of using a strategy to overcome it.

CHECK:
TO HELP ME START STUDYING

Change environments.
Have all equipment nearby.
Establish rewards for yourself.
Create a checklist of tasks to be done.
Keep a worry pad.

Change environments.

- Find the environment that is best for *you.* Consider whether you like to be away from people, whether you like noise, and whether you like bright or dim light.

- If you are distracted for some reason, then find a new place to study that will have fewer distractions.

- As soon as you are distracted, change environments. Do not waste time trying to shut out distractions or wait for the distractions to go away.

Have all equipment nearby when studying.

- Before studying, collect the materials that you will need (pens, pencils, paper, notebooks, books, paper clips, note cards, etc.).

- This will save time so you won't have to find equipment during your study time and then have difficulty starting to studying again after you find the equipment.

Establish rewards for yourself.

- You may have difficulty starting to study because it looks like you may never finish or because you keep thinking of other things you would rather do than study.

- To help, you need to set rewards for your yourself. For example, you may reward yourself after you finish reading a chapter, or you may divide your study time into shorter periods (e.g., 30 minutes) and reward yourself at the end of these periods.

- You can use rewards such as eating a favorite food, watching television, playing video games, using the computer, talking to a friend on the telephone, or using e-mail. If you are using a reward in the middle of your study time, then be sure to set a time limit for the reward (e.g., 10 minutes of talking on the telephone).

Create a checklist of all the tasks you need to do before you start studying.

- You may have difficulty starting to study because you think you have too many tasks to do or you have no idea of what you have to do so it seems like your studying will be endless.

- Make a list of what you have to study and prioritize these tasks starting with the most important tasks to be done.

- After completing each task, check it off to see how much you have accomplished. The list will also let you know what you need to finish.

Keep a worry pad.

- If distractions are keeping you from starting to study, then create a worry pad, which is a piece of paper on which you write all of the ideas that keep popping into your head.

- After you write an idea down, try to put it out of your mind until you are finished studying. Each time a worry interrupts your studying, write it on the paper.

WHAT ARE STRATEGIES FOR STAYING FOCUSED WHILE STUDYING?

Many students with mild disabilities are not aware that they are not focused while studying. They think that because they have sat at their desks with their books open for 2 hours, they have studied for 2 hours, even though they may have daydreamed for 1 hour of that time. To make them aware of this, have them record the time that they start studying and then record the times that they are not studying (e.g., going to the bathroom, getting some water, answering the telephone, daydreaming). Compare the actual amount of time that they devoted to studying with the amount of time that they thought they were studying. For example, if a student said that he studied for an hour, but it was found that he spent 20 minutes going to the bathroom, finding materials he needed, and daydreaming, emphasize that he only spent 40 minutes actually studying.

The S2TOP strategy is designed to make students aware of what they are doing when studying and help them to try to stay focused. This is an important strategy for students who are easily distracted.

S2TOP:
TO HELP ME STAY FOCUSED WHEN I STUDY

Set a timer.
See if you are off task.
Touch the circle.
Organize your thoughts.
Proceed again.

Set a timer and sit down to study.

- Use your watch or a kitchen timer and set it for a certain period of time that you plan to study.

See if you are off task.

- When you notice that your mind has drifted off task, tell yourself that you are not studying and that you have to go back to studying.

Touch the circle.

- Draw a circle on a piece of scratch paper.
- Every time you become aware that you are daydreaming, make a mark inside the circle.

Organize your thoughts.

- After you make a mark in the circle, take a few seconds to organize your thoughts.
- Shut your eyes and tell yourself to get back to studying.

Proceed again.

- Once you have organized your thoughts, begin to study again.
- After your study session is over, count the number of marks you made in the circle.
- Your goal is to decrease the number of marks you make in a circle the next time you study. Try to reach a point where you can study without making any marks in a circle. Then you will have overcome your problems with daydreaming!

WHAT ARE STRATEGIES FOR AVOIDING DISTRACTION WHEN STUDYING?

Students with mild disabilities are distracted by both external and internal stimuli. Making environmental changes is the most effective way for minimizing the effects of external distractors (e.g., visual and auditory stimuli). The PATS strategy is designed to help students learn to overcome being distracted by such stimuli. This strategy assists the student in identifying the best environment in which to study by using criteria such as having people or noise around or having bright or dim lighting. In addition, students are cautioned not to study in bed because it is usually associated with sleeping. The second step has them eliminate visual distractions by using techniques such as facing away from people and putting away things that the students might touch. The third step has them analyze whether they are distracted by auditory stimuli such as music or television. If they are distracted by auditory stimuli, then it is suggested that they should try using earplugs to block out such stimuli. The final step has the students use self-talk to identify and control internal distractions such as stomach rumbling and daydreaming.

PATS:
TO HELP AVOID DISTRACTION WHEN I STUDY

Pick the right environment.
Always reduce visual distractions.
Try to eliminate noise around you.
Self-talk to control internal distractions.

Pick the right environment to study.

- Choose a place to study where you feel most comfortable. You may like to study in a place with people around (e.g., the library) or with no people (e.g., your room at home). You may like music or television to drown out background noises, or you may want complete quiet. You also may like to study with bright light or dim light.

- Reserve a place for studying so that you associate that place *only* with studying. For example, if you study in your bed, you may confuse yourself because your bed is associated with sleeping and not studying.

Always reduce visual distractions.

- If you are visually distracted, then be sure to find a place to study where there is nothing to distract you (e.g., the desk in your room). If you are studying in the library, then make sure to sit away from the main desk and the door. If possible, sit facing the wall or the book stacks.

- Even if you like to study with people around, you need to be sure that you will not be tempted to watch people, rather than study. For example, if there is a baseball game happening outside the room where you're studying, then be sure to sit far from the window so that you're not tempted to watch the game.

- Do not study near things that you may be tempted to play with (e.g., a video game, a stapler).

Try to eliminate noise around you.

- If you are distracted by noises, then study in a quiet room. If you are still distracted by noises (e.g., the air conditioner), then use earplugs to block out all background sounds.

- If you like to study with music or television, then make sure that they are not distracting you. Find out if music helps you or not. If you listen to song lyrics while studying, then you are distracted by the music. If you ignore the lyrics, then you may be helped by the music. If you have the television on and you are listening to what people are saying, then the television is distracting you. If you don't pay attention to what people are saying, then the television may block out background noise.

- Use earplugs if necessary.

Self-talk to control internal distractions.

- Sometimes people are distracted by internal factors from their own bodies (e.g., grumbling stomach, itching, thinking about other things to do).

- When you become aware of internal distractions, talk to yourself and direct your attention back to studying. For example, if your stomach is grumbling, then say to yourself, "It's almost lunchtime and I'm hungry. I have to study for another 30 minutes before lunch, so I'll ignore my stomach noises."

WHAT ARE STRATEGIES FOR STUDYING FROM NOTES?

The purpose of teaching students to study from their notes is to understand the overall main ideas of the content and fit in facts that have to be memorized. However, teaching students how to study from their notes is dependent on them having good notes. Be sure to use strategies, such as the Cornell Method or I SWAM, which are described in Chapter 9, to teach students to take good notes. If students do not take good notes, then it will be impossible to teach them to study from them.

Many students think that the act of taking notes will result in learning the material. They must learn how to use their notes to improve their comprehension of the course content and memorize relevant information for tests. The R3 HI strategy is designed to assist students to achieve improved comprehension and memorization of material in their notes. They are taught to highlight important information in their notes so that they are actively engaged with the content as they reread it. They are also taught to predict what information in their notes might be on the test. This, too, encourages them to be actively engaged with the content of their notes.

R3 HI:
TO HELP ME STUDY FROM MY NOTES

Read after class.
Read before class.
Read before test.
Highlight important information.
Identify material that you think will be on the test.

Read your notes after class.

- This allows you to review the lecture and get clarification of any notes that are unclear.

- Reading your notes after class is helpful because the lecture is still fresh in your memory, and you can add any material that you did not write down.

Read your notes before class.

- This makes it easier for you to understand the new lecture because you can see the relationship to the previous lecture.

Read your notes before a test.

- This is a very important strategy for studying for a test.

- It is best to read the notes aloud. Hearing the information helps you to remember it.

- First, read all your notes. Then, read your highlighted notes. Read the highlighted notes as many times as necessary to recall the information.

- If you used the Cornell Method for taking notes, first read the right-hand side, then the left-hand side, and finally the summary at the bottom of the page.

Highlight important information.

- While reading your notes, highlight important information.

- Do not highlight everything. Try to limit your highlighting to specific words, phrases, or sentences. Never highlight an entire paragraph.

- The next time you read your notes, the highlighted text should speed up your review process.

Identify material that you think will be on the test.

- As you reread your notes, concentrate on material that you think will be on the test based on what the teacher told you or based on the types of tests the teacher has given in the past.

- It may be helpful to rewrite material that you think will be on the test and reread this several times. The act of writing will help you remember the information that you wrote.

WHAT ARE STRATEGIES FOR STUDYING FROM BOOKS?

Many students with mild disabilities believe that reading book material once or twice is sufficient for studying. They do not realize that they must interact with the material to comprehend and memorize it. Students are reluctant to review the chapters over and over until they master the organization of the material. They must be taught to use note cards so that they can extract the most important information and use these for studying. The CON AIR strategy is designed to improve students' understanding and memorization of reading material through the use of note cards. The tutors in our study of college students frequently used this strategy because note cards were found to be effective in mastering material. By using separate cards for the chapter headings and subheadings, the students can understand the overall organization of the materials. By writing questions and answers on the note cards, the students can better recall information that will be tested. Study cards have been a popular study technique for many years because they are portable, allow for self-testing, and help students prepare for tests using multiple-choice or recall formats (Pauk, 1997).

CON AIR:
TO HELP ME STUDY FROM BOOKS

Copy chapter headings and subheadings.
Organize note cards.
Number the cards under categories.
Arrange the note cards in columns.
Identify each card's correct place.
Review the note cards.

Copy chapter headings and subheadings onto note cards.

- Use different colored note cards to show that these are main ideas.

Organize important facts, definitions, and information onto white note cards.

- Use white note cards to indicate that these are specifics that go under different main ideas.
- On one side of the card, write a fact, definition, or information. On the other side, write a question that asks for this fact, definition, or information.

Number the white note cards to show the order they appeared in the book.

- Put a number on each card to show the order the material was given in the book.

Arrange the colored note cards in columns.

- Leave space under each colored card to place the white cards underneath.

Identify each card's correct place underneath the colored cards.

- Put the cards in numbered order under each colored card.
- Try to remember the location and order of the cards when you take a test.

Review information on each card.

- Shuffle the white cards and then place them under the corresponding colored cards.
- Test yourself on the information on the white cards. Read the questions, answer them, and then check for the correct answer on the backs.

WHAT ARE STRATEGIES FOR ORGANIZING INFORMATION FROM BOOKS AND NOTES?

In order to effectively study, students need to integrate information from two sources (i.e., material that they have read in books and material that they have included in their notes from lectures), which requires them to use advanced cognitive skills to identify common and different information from both sources. They need to recognize that the book often expands on the ideas of the lectures. Organizing information is necessary for students to gain comprehension of how all the information fits together. The WORRY strategy is designed to help students integrate content from reading and notes and arrive at an understanding of how all the ideas fit together. Memorization of facts is not involved here; however, memorization is made easier if the facts to be learned fit into an overall structure. Memorization of unrelated facts is much harder than memorizing facts that are part of an overall structure.

WORRY:
TO HELP ME ORGANIZE
INFORMATION FROM BOOKS AND NOTES

Work with note cards from reading and lecture notes.
Outline main ideas covered in reading and lectures.
Read note cards from reading for facts.
Read lecture notes for facts.
Yes, you're ready after one more reading of your outline.

Work with note cards from readings and lecture notes.

- Get your note cards from a specific reading and the related lecture notes on the same topic.

- You want to read through the note cards and lecture notes to find main ideas covered in both.

- Use skimming, or fast reading, to get these main ideas. Look at the left margin and bottom of the pages you took using the Cornell Method. Look at the colored note cards you made for the main ideas of the reading.

Outline key points covered in reading and lectures.

- Make an outline of the main ideas of the topic based on skimming the note cards from the reading and the lecture notes.

- As you go through the note cards and lecture notes, write down the main ideas included in both in your outline. If a main idea is included in one but not the other, then think about why this is. If you think that the idea is important, then include it in your outline.

Read your note cards for facts.

- After you have made your outline of the main ideas, read your note cards again to see where the facts fit in relation to the main ideas.

Read lecture notes for facts.

- Read your lecture notes on the right side of the pages using the Cornell Method to see where the facts fit in relation to the main ideas.

- If there are facts in the lecture notes that you want to memorize, then make note cards for them and add them to the note cards you used from the reading.

Yes, you're ready after one more reading of the outline.

- At the end of your studying, review your outline one last time to make sure that you have an understanding of the main ideas included in the reading material and lecture notes.

- For your last reading, read the outline aloud to help remember the overall meaning of the content you are studying.

WHAT ARE STRATEGIES FOR REMEMBERING INFORMATION FOR TESTS?

Many of the tests that students are required to take involve memorization of specific facts. This is especially true of the high-stakes tests that many students with disabilities are required to take for graduation. In order to effectively memorize facts, students must use strategies that fit the specific nature of the material to be memorized. For example, memorization of maps is facilitated using visualization techniques in which the students try to picture the maps in their minds. Whatever strategies they use, memorization is facilitated if students understand the content. For example, if a student understands the events that took place during the revolution (Boston Tea Party, signing of the Declaration of Independence, creation of the Constitution, etc.), then it will be easier to recall the dates associated with each of these. Therefore, always try to embed memorization of facts into a larger, meaningful picture.

The BREAK strategy includes five research-based strategies that students must master to become skilled at memorizing school content:

1. Use of short, spaced practice

2. Use of auditory and motor cues to reinforce learning

3. Use of mnemonics

4. Use of visualization

5. Use of keywords

Research has demonstrated that memorization is facilitated when there are short, spaced periods devoted to practice (Mastropieri & Scruggs, 2000). If a student tries to devote long periods to memorizing facts, then this may result in boredom and/or overloading. It is especially good to space practice over several days. Some students find it helpful to rehearse what they have to memorize before going to bed because they seem to rehearse while sleeping. It is important that the students use spaced practice and not try to cram. Cramming right before a test may be ineffective for students with disabilities because of the high level of mastery of memory techniques required and because of the anxiety that results from the students realizing that there is information that they have not memorized.

In order for students to memorize content, they must interact with the information. One way of doing this is to use verbalization and recite the information aloud. Students are taught to read their note cards or lecture notes aloud. If reciting the information is not sufficient, then they are instructed to write the information as well. This motor response reinforces the recall for some students by providing multisensory information.

One of the most effective methods for short-term recall of facts is the use of mnemonics (i.e., acronyms and acrostics that aid in the recall of information). With BREAK, students are taught to form words or sentences starting with certain letters to aid recall. Use of visualization or picturing information in one's mind is another recommended technique to aid recall. Finally, the keyword method for aiding retention of information is recommended. With this method, a keyword is associated with the word or fact to be memorized, and an interaction between these two words is pictured in the student's mind.

Students should be encouraged to use as many of these techniques as possible and try to fit a specific technique to the nature of the content. The BREAK strategy does not help students decide which memorization technique fits the content that they are to learn. You need to help them analyze this. For example, lists lend themselves to mnemonics. Visualization works for things that can be pictured (e.g., maps, science). The keyword method only works for certain words that can have associations. Reciting aloud and writing are techniques that can be used for many types of content. Demonstrate applying these to different content so that the students learn to match memorization techniques with the content.

BREAK is a complex strategy that includes a number of different skills. It will require that you devote extensive time to the modeling and guided practice stages. In addition, many of the techniques in BREAK are effective for short-term memorization (or working memory) of facts for use in school while a particular topic is being covered. They do not necessarily lead to long-term memorization of facts. For example, long-term memorization of the presidents of the United States is usually mastered by relating the terms of presidents to the history of events during that time period, rather than memorization using mnemonics or other such techniques.

The various memory techniques incorporated into BREAK are found in many other strategies. For example, Strichart, Mangrum, and Iannuzzi (1998) recommended the mind picture strategy for visualizing information, the abbreviation strategy for mnemonics, and the categorization strategy to make information meaningful.

BREAK:
TO HELP ME REMEMBER INFORMATION FOR TESTS

Break memorizing into short time periods.
Recite the information aloud as you write it.
Establish mnemonics.
Always try to visualize information in your mind.
Keywords help.

Break memorizing into short time periods.

- Never try to memorize a lot of information at one time. This leads to overloading, and your mind won't let you memorize any more information. Or, it leads to boredom and you can't get motivated to keep working on memorizing.

- Try to arrange short, frequent blocks of time for memorization. Spend a certain amount of time working on methods to memorize some information and then review these methods at certain times throughout your studying time.

- For example, you may devote 10 minutes to memorizing your Spanish vocabulary at the beginning of a 2-hour block of studying and then 10 minutes in the middle and another 10 minutes at the end. This will give you 30 minutes of studying your Spanish vocabulary. It is less effective to spend 30 minutes at one time working on the vocabulary because of overloading and boredom. It's easier to work on it in short time periods spaced out over time.

- Never cram! Don't try to memorize information you haven't worked on right before a test. If you do, this will make you anxious. However, before a test, you should review memorization techniques that you have been using while studying.

Recite information aloud as you write it.

- Read aloud the note cards you are studying from. Read the questions on one side and then the answers on the other side.

- After reading aloud, test yourself on the information by shutting your eyes and asking and answering the questions again.

- If you get the answer wrong, then write it several times as you say it over and over.

Establish mnemonics to help you remember information.

- Mnemonics are words and letters that help you remember information.

- To make up a mnemonic, make a list of the important facts you need to remember. Use the first letter of each fact to make up another word that will help you remember the ideas to be memorized. For example, the mnemonic HOMES was created to help students remember the names of the Great Lakes.

  - First, the Great Lakes were listed: Superior, Michigan, Huron, Erie, Ontario.

  - Next, the first letter of each word was written separately: S, M, H, E, O.

  - Then, the letters were moved around to create a keyword that would remind you of the names of the five Great Lakes. The word HOMES was created using H (Huron), O (Ontario), M (Michigan), E (Erie), and S (Superior).

- Another type of mnemonic involves using the first letters of the words or ideas to be memorized to create a "catchy" sentence. The sentence does not have to make sense as long as it sticks in your mind and you can remember it when taking a test. Using the first letters of the five Great Lakes— (Michigan), H (Huron), S (Superior), O (Ontario), E (Erie)—the following sentence can be made: "Monkeys have seven orange ears."

- It is important that you recall these mnemonic techniques when taking a test. Write down the keyword (HOMES) or catchy sentence (Monkeys have seven orange ears) in the margin of your test and then analyze the letters as an aid to recalling the facts.

Always try to visualize words or pictures in your mind to help you remember.

- As you study, try to visualize (picture in your mind) words and pictures that will help you remember. For example, if you are trying to remember the parts of an animal cell, then you may picture in your mind the diagram from your science book where the different parts were shown. If you used graphic organizers to help you learn, then picture the graphic organizer in your mind and recall each of the parts.

- After looking at the picture or graphic, shut your eyes and try to recall as much detail as possible. If you can't recall all the details, then study the picture or graphic again and shut your eyes and repeat the process. Do this until you can recall all parts to be memorized.

- When answering a test question involving material you visualized, shut your eyes for a second, and try to recall all aspects of the picture or graphic in your mind.

Keywords help.

- If you have to memorize words or facts that are new or hard for you, then it may help to associate these with keywords. For example, if you can't recall the meaning of the word *ziggurat* (i.e., a temple built in a series of terraces with each terrace smaller than the one below with a staircase and a shrine on top) for a world history test, then look at the word to find something that is related to the meaning. The small word *zig* appears in the word and the series of terraces zig-zag up.

- It is best to combine the keyword approach with visualizing. Once you identify a keyword, picture in your mind a relationship between the keyword and the original word (picture the zig-zag pattern of the ziggurat).

SAM, A STUDENT WITH STUDY SKILL DIFFICULTIES

Sam is a high school freshman who was diagnosed as having a learning disability when he was in second grade after he had difficulty learning to read. He has received resource special education services since that time and is now reading at grade level. Sam is a creative student who is a musician, artist, and writer. He has strengths in abstract thinking and is able to understand all of the content that he has to learn. He has been identified as gifted and talented; however, he has difficulty memorizing facts for his classes, especially biology and world history, which require him to use rote memory skills. He is in honors classes that require a great deal of memorization of facts as the basis for more advanced thinking.

Sam's resource teacher, Ms. Reed, and Sam decide that the BREAK strategy would be helpful to Sam, especially for the weekly quizzes in his biology class. Ms. Reed models this strategy and Sam responds very positively because he sees how he can apply his creativity to recall facts. He especially likes the use of visualization and mnemonics because he likes to create visual images to correspond to the material that he has to memorize. If Sam can't visualize material, then he likes to make up funny acronyms and acrostics. Ms. Reed and Sam have contests to see who can make up funnier acronyms and acrostics or more creative visual images. For example, when studying the food chain involving phytoplankton, zooplankton, mussels, and starfish, Sam associates phytoplankton with a visual image of a photo, zooplankton with a visual image of a zoo, mussels with a visual image of arm muscles, and starfish with a visual image of a star. He then makes up the silly acronym, "Pittsburgh's zoo may sink," as an aid to recalling the order of the four items on the food chain.

With this strategy, Sam is able to use his creative abilities as an aid to recalling rote information. Sam readily grasps the steps of the BREAK strategy and uses them independently to recall information for his weekly quizzes in biology as well as his tests in world history. His grades in biology and world history improve.

Sam also generalizes use of visualization and mnemonics to memorization of vocabulary for his French class. He likes to use these strategies so much that he decides to share a list of visual images and mnemonic aids that he has developed for the weekly French vocabulary assignments with his classmates. The other students find these aids helpful and begin to use them. The French teacher also likes the aids and asks Sam to keep a notebook of them so that she can share the aids with future students.

9

Notetaking

░ Why do students with learning disabilities and ADHD need to learn notetaking skills?

░ What are the different subskills of notetaking?

░ What is special about teaching notetaking strategies?

░ What are strategies to help take notes in lectures?

░ What are strategies to help take organized notes?

░ What are strategies to help take notes from a taped lecture?

░ What are strategies to help take notes when reading?

░ What are strategies for avoiding distraction when taking notes?

WHY DO STUDENTS WITH LEARNING DISABILITIES AND ADHD NEED TO LEARN NOTETAKING SKILLS?

Because lecturing is the primary mode of general education instruction at the secondary level, high school students must develop good notetaking skills.

Likewise, postsecondary students also need to take comprehensive notes from lectures to use for studying at a later time. If they do not take good notes, then they will not be able to study the material, regardless of how good their study skills may be.

Being able to take lecture notes involves integration of the ability to orally understand the language being heard, the ability to pick out the most important ideas to record, and the ability to write these ideas so that they can be understood at a later time. Notetaking, therefore, requires well-developed skills in receptive oral language, written language, and the abstract cognitive skill of selecting the most important ideas. In addition, a high level of sustained attention is required over a long period of time. Students with mild disabilities are often distracted by both internal and external stimuli in a lecture setting, which makes it difficult for them to sustain attention over time.

In addition to taking notes from lectures, students need to learn to take notes from tapes of lectures that they have made. Many students with mild disabilities often tape lectures. However, some do not listen to the tapes after they have made them because they do not know how to effectively take notes from the tapes. They tend to be passive learners and think that the act of taping will accomplish learning the material. Others may just listen to a tape once or twice without taking notes from the tape; however, this is not adequate for them to store information for future testing. They must be taught to listen to the tape and use the same oral and written language skills as required for listening to actual lectures. The advantage of the taped lecture is that the students can replay sections as many times as necessary in order to clarify meaning or compensate for lapsed attention.

Students must also take notes when reading materials. When students study, they must learn to take notes of important ideas as they read. In this case, reading skills, rather than oral language skills, are required, along with written language skills. The students must be able to read the material and use the abstract cognitive skills of selecting the most important information to record in their notes.

WHAT ARE THE DIFFERENT SUBSKILLS OF NOTETAKING?

The following five subskills of notetaking (with the corresponding Active Learner Student Questionnaire items found in Appendix A) are taught with the Active Learner Approach.

1. Notetaking with lectures: "I can't write down everything the teacher says because the teacher talks too fast."

2. Disorganized written notes: "The notes that I take are disorganized and hard to understand."

3. Notetaking with taped lectures: "I have trouble taking notes from a taped lecture."

4. Notetaking with reading material: "The notes I take when I read don't help me."

5. Distraction while taking notes: "I have difficulty taking notes because I get distracted."

WHAT IS SPECIAL ABOUT TEACHING NOTETAKING STRATEGIES?

It is imperative that you provide explicit instruction when teaching students to identify significant variables in understanding lectures. Tape-record the actual lectures of the students' teachers so you can use these to analyze how to develop skills in analyzing the following three types of cues: verbal, nonverbal, and body language. Obviously, you will need to get the approval and support of these teachers. Make clear that you are not judging the teachers' abilities to lecture but rather using their lectures as teaching content. Provide instruction by playing the teacher's lecture and stopping to explain various cues. You also need to provide instruction by reading the teacher's lecture and stopping to emphasize important cues, especially those involving body language.

To teach students to analyze verbal cues when taking notes from actual or taped lectures, teach them to listen for keywords, such as *important,* or key phrases (e.g., "This is the primary cause of the war") that the teacher uses to emphasize ideas. They should also be taught to monitor for lists that the teacher gives and write all parts of the list (e.g., "The *first* important event was . . . *Next* was . . ."). Also, teach the students to write down whatever the teacher writes on the chalkboard or includes in an overhead or PowerPoint presentation. Tell the students that the teacher only includes the most important points in these written presentations and, therefore, they need to write these down. If the teacher is delivering a lecture via the Internet, then make sure that the students write the exact web site name and URL so that they can go back to it to take more comprehensive notes.

Nonverbal cues include emphasis that the speaker places on certain words or phrases. For example, teach the students to attend to words or phrases that are spoken in a louder voice or are drawn out. Teach the students to attend to pauses, especially when the teachers stop to have the students write down important ideas. Point out that whenever teachers do this, they want the students to write down what was said. When you read a teacher's lecture notes, give exaggerated emphasis to words and phrases that the teacher emphasized so as to draw additional attention to these nonverbal cues.

The last type of cue that the students must learn to attend to involves the teacher's use of body language. You can only teach attention to these cues by reading the teacher's lecture yourself. Show how you might represent important ideas through hand movements, leaning your body forward, or facial expressions. Exaggerate these movements so that the students can more readily identify them and learn what they represent.

When teaching students to take notes from books, have them use all side and paragraph headings as major points in an outline. Then, have them read paragraph by paragraph to get the main ideas and write these down. Teach them to write down any bold-faced words, as these represent important concepts. It may be necessary to integrate teaching of notetaking from books with strategies to improve reading comprehension (e.g., see RAP-Q in Chapter 10).

In addition to explicit instruction on notetaking, it is important that students request accommodations to help them cope with lecturing demands. Any type of accommodation for notetaking needs to be included in the student's individualized education program (IEP). Students need to advocate for these accommodations with their general education teachers. You need to role play with them how to do this in a socially appropriate manner.

For many students with hard-to-read handwriting, it is important to get accommodations or have them learn to use a laptop to take notes. However, this requires accurate, fast typing abilities, especially in a lecture setting, which many students do not have.

A frequently used accommodation that students might request involves taping a teacher's lecture. In order to do this, the students should obtain the teacher's permission, even if this is an accommodation listed in the IEP. Teach the students that they must try to take notes even if they are taping a lecture. If they do not take notes, then they may not attend to the lecture, making it harder for them to understand it when they listen to the tape. When studying, the students need to read their notes as they listen to the taped lecture and insert points that they did not include or clarify those that they did not understand.

Another accommodation that students might request involves getting the teacher's PowerPoint presentation, overheads, or notes. Students can also obtain notes from other students. Students can ask friends for notes, or on a more formalized basis, borrow notes from a student who agrees to share all notes. A scribe (notetaker) can also be listed in the IEP as an accommodation for students with difficulties in notetaking.

WHAT ARE STRATEGIES TO HELP TAKE NOTES IN LECTURES?

Students often complain that their teachers talk too fast. This may be true, but this most often reflects the students' difficulties with notetaking for lectures. Explicitly teach the students to attend to verbal, nonverbal, and body language cues of the teacher. Also, tell students to sit close to the teacher so it is easier for them to attend and pick up all of the teacher's relevant cues.

It is important to teach students to be prepared for a lecture. This means that they are to read previous lecture notes or assigned readings before class. Many students do not like to do this, so it is important to help them realize that this will make it easier for them to understand the lecture.

The I SWAM strategy is used to teach students to take notes when they are having trouble understanding the teacher. The steps of this strategy include integrating previous notes and readings before the lecture, sitting close to the teacher, writing everything down that the teacher writes, analyzing cues sent by the teacher, and monitoring for attention. Some of the I SWAM skills are also taught in LINKS (listen, identify verbal cues, note, keywords, and stack information into outline form) and AWARE (arrange to take notes, write quickly, apply cues, review notes, and edit notes; Deshler, Ellis, & Lenz, 1996).

I SWAM:
TO HELP ME TAKE NOTES WHEN THE TEACHER TALKS FAST

Integrate previous notes and readings.
Sit close to the teacher.
Write down everything.
Analyze verbal, nonverbal, and body language cues.
Monitor for attention.

Integrate all previous notes and readings.

- Be prepared for the lecture. Don't go in "cold" and expect to understand the lecture.

- Read the previous lecture notes and any assigned readings for the lecture. If possible, do this right before the lecture so that you can relate the ideas you hear in the lecture to the ideas in your previous lecture notes and readings.

Sit close.

- Sit as close to the teacher as possible.

- Be sure that you can clearly see the chalkboard or screen if there are overheads, a PowerPoint presentation, or a computer screen used.

Write everything.

- Teachers write down the most important things to be remembered, so write everything from the chalkboard or screen.

- Write down the information the teacher gives when he or she pauses because it is expected that you will write this and learn it.

Analyze verbal, nonverbal, and body language cues.

- Teachers send messages about the most important parts of their lectures by sending verbal, nonverbal, and body language cues.

- Important verbal cues are keywords (e.g., *important*) or phrases (e.g., *primary cause of the war*). Listen for these words and write down the ideas being conveyed. Also, listen for lists (e.g., *the first characteristic*), and write down all items that are listed.

- Important nonverbal cues are conveyed by emphasis that the teacher places on words and phrases by talking louder, by drawing out words, or by pausing. Whenever a teacher pauses, it is usually to allow students to write down ideas, so be sure to write these down.

- Important body language cues are conveyed by the teacher's face, body movements, and posture. The teacher may lean forward or use hand motions to signal important information. Look at any change in emotion conveyed by the teacher's facial expression (e.g., when the teacher says "This was a tragic event," she may change her facial expression to show sadness).

Monitor your attention.

- If you stop writing for a period of time, then ask yourself why you haven't taken notes.

- If your attention has lagged, then change your position, or look more closely at the teacher.

- If you don't understand what the teacher is saying, then try to write as much as possible down. After the lecture, read what you have written and compare it with other students' notes or to the teacher's notes to add or clarify points you had difficulty with.

WHAT ARE STRATEGIES TO HELP TAKE ORGANIZED NOTES?

Many students take notes, but the final product is a mess and the students cannot read or understand what they wrote. This is true for students who have difficulty identifying the main ideas and important points in the lecture. They write down everything and can't identify what should be retained in the notes and what should be dropped.

There are a number of different formats for organizing notes. The Cornell Method, which is used with the Active Learner Approach, is a well-established best practice to assist students to develop notetaking skills that was developed by Pauk in 1984 (Pauk, 1997). However, any approach that helps students take organized notes is appropriate. With the Cornell Method, the page is divided into three sections. One section is for taking notes, the second section is for extracting the key points, and the last section requires students to review and clarify. Students need to draw lines to create these sections before taking notes. It is a good idea for the students to create a large number of sheets with this format so that they can readily use them for lectures whenever needed. In addition, the students should write the course name and date at the top of each page so that they can keep track of their notes sequentially.

CORNELL METHOD:
TO HELP ME TAKE ORGANIZED NOTES

Divide the paper into three sections.

- Draw a dark horizontal line about five or six lines from the bottom. Use a heavy magic marker to draw the line so that it is clear.
- Draw a dark vertical line about 2 inches from the left side of the paper from the top to the horizontal line.

Document.

- Write the course name, date, and topic at the top of each page.

Write notes.

- The large box to the right is for writing notes.
- Skip a line between ideas and topics.
- Don't use complete sentences. Use abbreviations, whenever possible. Develop a shorthand of your own, such as using & for the word *and*.

Review and clarify.

- Review the notes as soon as possible after class.
- Pull out the main ideas, key points, dates, and people, and write these in the left column.

Summarize.

- Write a summary of the main ideas in the bottom section.

Study your notes.

- Reread the notes in the right column.

- Spend most of your time studying the ideas in the left column and the summary at the bottom. These are the most important ideas and will probably include most of the information that will be tested.

WHAT ARE STRATEGIES TO HELP
TAKE NOTES FROM A TAPED LECTURE?

Students must be taught to take notes from taped lectures as soon as possible after hearing the lecture. They need to be strongly encouraged to take notes even though they are taping the lecture. Many students feel that they do not have to take notes because of the taping, but this usually results in them not attending to the lecture.

The PP 123 strategy is designed to help students take notes from taped lectures. This strategy is based on one that was developed by a college student with learning disabilities that one of us worked with. This young man produced extensive final lecture notes with color coding for his business major classes that he sold to his classmates without disabilities. This student had learning disabilities in listening and notetaking, but he obviously had abilities in entrepreneurial skills!

The PP 123 strategy has the students prepare for listening to the lecture by assembling the necessary materials and reviewing the information relative to it. Then, the students are to listen to the tape in small segments, either for a specified period of time (e.g., 2 minutes) or for the span of a particular topic. The students are then directed to listen to the tape three times. The first time is to get the ideas on the tape, the second is to take notes, and the third is to review the notes in relation to the tape. Taking notes from a taped lecture can be facilitated with use of a word processor if the student has the required typing skills.

PP 123:
TO HELP ME TAKE NOTES FROM A TAPED LECTURE

Prepare to take notes.
Play tape in small sections.
1. First listen.
2. Second listen.
3. Third listen.

Prepare to take notes.

- Get your writing or word processing material together.
- Before listening to the tape, read the notes that you took in the lecture or notes that you got from others. Try to make yourself familiar with the information that you will hear on the tape. This will make it much easier to understand.

Play the tape in small sections.

- Do not listen to the whole tape or large sections at one time.
- Listen for a particular amount of time (e.g., 2 minutes), or listen to the information on a specific topic.
- Take notes after each section. If you need to replay a section, then go back and replay it as many times as necessary.

1. First listen—listen for meaning.

- The purpose of the first listen is to get an overall picture of what is being said on this segment of the tape. Listen to get the main ideas.
- If the section doesn't make sense, then read the notes that you took on this topic, or look at the notes you have from the teacher or other students. Going back and listening to the previous section may also help.

2. Second listen—take notes.

- After you understand the section, take notes.
- Try to organize your notes in an outline form.

3. Third listen—review.

- Listen to the tape again as you read the notes you have taken.
- Make sure that you have included all the important materials.
- As you read the notes and listen to the lecture, color code the notes you have made. Use a highlighter with one color for main ideas and another for details.

WHAT ARE STRATEGIES TO HELP TAKE NOTES WHEN READING?

Taking notes when reading is important for studying and requires well-developed reading and expressive writing skills. The SCROL strategy is designed to help students take notes when reading textbooks. This strategy requires students to get the overall layout of the reading material by first surveying it. Then, the students are to try to make connections between the various chapters and sections. Next, they read and identify the most important information. Using this information, the students make an outline of the main ideas and supporting details. The students do not have to write complete sentences. Rather, they should use phrases containing essential information that will spark the ideas when they study the notes at a later time. Then, the students look back to make sure that all the important information has been included in the outline.

SCROL:
TO HELP ME TAKE NOTES FROM READING MATERIAL

Survey.
Connect.
Read.
Outline.
Look.

Survey the material to be read.

- Look at the section and paragraph headings to get an idea of what will be covered in the chapter. Look at side boxes and end-of-chapter activities to get additional information.

Connect the ideas.

- Look at how the section and paragraph headings relate to each other.
- Write down keywords to show how the sections are connected.

Read the material.

- Read the information under each heading.
- Pay attention to words and phrases that are in bold face or are italicized because these usually express important information about the heading.

Outline.

- Write down the main ideas and supporting details in outline form.

- Use your section and paragraph headings as main ideas, whenever possible. The topic sentence, or the first sentence of a paragraph, will often serve as a main idea.

- List *at least* two details under each main idea.

- You may want to list additional details under detail headings if you are studying for an objective test that will include many facts.

Look.

- Look back at each chapter and paragraph heading and information under each.

- Make sure that your outline contains all of this information.

- If you have omitted information, then add it.

- If there are relationships between the sections that you want to note, then draw arrows to show ideas that are related.

WHAT ARE STRATEGIES FOR AVOIDING DISTRACTION WHEN TAKING NOTES?

Taking notes in a lecture requires sustained attention for long periods of time. This is difficult for many students with mild disabilities, especially because they often find the content of the lectures boring and of little perceived use. The TASSEL strategy is designed to help students avoid distraction when taking notes. The first step of this strategy cues students to refrain from doodling, which is often distracting because students attend to aspects of the drawing instead of the lecture. The second step has students arrive to class prepared. If the students have read the previous notes and assigned readings, then it is more likely that they will understand the lecture and not be distracted. The less students understand a lecture, the more likely they will be distracted. The next step has the students sit in the front of the classroom, followed by the step in which they sit away from friends. When students sit near friends, they are tempted to talk and pass notes. The next step in TASSEL has the students monitor their attention to become aware when they are daydreaming. If they find that they are daydreaming, then they are to look at the teacher or the material being presented by the teacher and write down whatever the teacher is saying, even if at a later time they find that it was not important. The final step of TASSEL has the students look at the teacher and establish eye contact.

TASSEL:
TO HELP ME AVOID DISTRACTION WHEN TAKING NOTES

Try not to doodle.
Arrive at class prepared.
Sit near the front.
Sit away from friends.
End daydreaming.
Look at the teacher.

Try not to doodle while taking notes.

- Doodling breaks your concentration and takes your focus away from note-taking.

- Each time you feel yourself wanting to doodle, take that urge and write down what the teacher is saying.

Arrive at class prepared.

- Read all assigned readings and review all previous lecture notes so that you will understand what is covered in the lecture.

- If you are not prepared, then you will be more likely to daydream and become distracted.

Sit near the front of the classroom.

- Sit near the front so that you can clearly see the teacher, the chalkboard, the overhead, or PowerPoint or computer presentations.

Sit away from friends.

- If you sit near friends, then you will be tempted to talk or pass notes to them.

- If you have assigned seats and you have to sit near friends, then resist talking to them or passing notes during class.

End daydreaming.

- If you become aware that you are daydreaming, then immediately change your position. Sit forward and look at the teacher's eyes.

- Turn your attention to the teacher and write down whatever he is saying, even if later you find that it was not important.

Look at the teacher.

- Make eye contact with the teacher as much as possible. This will give the feeling that you are having a conversation with the teacher.

- Whenever you are not taking notes or looking at the chalkboard, overhead, PowerPoint presentation, or computer screen, keep your eyes on the teacher.

KIM, A STUDENT WITH NOTETAKING DIFFICULTIES

Kim is a junior who is in college preparatory classes. She plans to attend college and major in English. She has good oral language and reading skills but has difficulty with notetaking because of problems with attention and disorganization. She often daydreams and has difficulty turning her attention back to the lecture. Her notes are disorganized and messy. She doodles all over, and her handwriting is small and hard to read. She is having difficulty taking good notes in her U.S. history class. Because of this, she does not have adequate notes to use for studying and is getting low grades on all quizzes and tests in this class.

Kim's resource teacher, Mr. Lund, decides to teach Kim to use TASSEL to minimize her attention problems with lectures and to use the Cornell Method to help her organize her notes so that they are more usable for study purposes. In addition, they decide that she should use the accommodation of taping her U.S. history class. Because this accommodation is not in her IEP, an addendum to the IEP is made. Kim's mother readily agrees to this change in her IEP. Kim meets with Mr. Washington, her U.S. history teacher, and discusses how she can unobtrusively tape his class using a miniature tape recorder that will be on her desk.

When Mr. Lund presents TASSEL to Kim, he finds that in addition to doodling, she sits in the back of the class next to her best friend, with whom she likes to chat. This makes it hard for her to see the chalkboard, which is a problem because Mr. Washington frequently writes lists on the board. Kim and Mr. Lund discuss the changes she would like to make in her seating. When Kim meets with Mr. Washington about taping his lecture, she asks if she can move her seat to the front to the classroom, close to the chalkboard and away from her friend. He readily agrees to this.

Kim and Mr. Lund work on having Kim monitor when she starts to doodle and stop immediately. Using the Cornell Method format should also prevent her from doodling because she needs to write on all sections of the page. They also work on having her monitor when she starts to daydream. She practices this in the resource room and over the semester becomes more effective at minimizing doodling and daydreaming. She takes more comprehensive notes because she writes everything that Mr. Lund writes on the chalkboard.

Mr. Lund teaches Kim to use the Cornell Method to organize her notes. She takes notes in the right hand section and skips lines frequently to make her hand-writing more readable when studying. She finds that she is able to extract key points and write them in the left column and to summarize in the bottom section. As a result of using the Cornell Method, her notes are more organized and she finds them more useful for studying.

Kim also learns to use PP 123 to listen to her notes. She finds that her attention has improved with TASSEL, but she still has periods of lapsed attention. She finds use of taping very helpful, and every night she listens to the U.S. history lecture and uses PP 123 to enhance her Cornell notes.

Over the semester, Kim masters TASSEL, the Cornell Method, and PP 123. Her grades on all quizzes and tests in U.S. history improve. She also transfers use of these methods for her English literature class and finds that her notes get better in that class.

10
Reading

- Why do students with learning disabilities and ADHD need to learn reading skills?

- What are the different subskills of reading?

- What is special about teaching reading?

- What are strategies to help understand difficult words?

- What are strategies to help remember reading vocabulary?

- What are strategies to get the overall ideas of reading material for my classes?

- What are strategies for understanding main ideas of reading material?

- What are strategies for understanding details for reading material?

- What are strategies for understanding stories that are read?

- What are strategies for increasing reading speed?

- What are strategies for reading from computers?

- What are strategies for using aids to help reading?

WHY DO STUDENTS WITH LEARNING DISABILITIES AND ADHD NEED TO LEARN READING SKILLS?

Reading disabilities are among the most frequently identified types of problems for students with learning disabilities (Hallahan, Kauffman, & Lloyd, 1999). Of all the children identified with learning disabilities in the schools, 80% primarily have reading deficits (Foorman, Fletcher, & Francis, n.d.; Lyon, 1999). There is great variability in reading levels among secondary students with learning disabilities. Some students are nonreaders; others can identify advanced words at a secondary level but have little understanding of what they read. This chapter is targeted toward students who have mastered the early stages of reading and can decode words but have not attained the higher levels of reading comprehension that they can apply to learning school content. Most of these students have not learned to read strategically or to monitor their understanding (Vaughn, Gersten, & Chard, 2000).

Using a variation of Chall's six-stage model of reading (Chall, 1983) is the best way to understand these students' reading disabilities. The first, or prereading, stage of this model involves mastery of the prerequisites for learning to read (e.g., phonological awareness); whereas the second, or early reading, stage involves mastery of skills in literal comprehension and word identification through phonics and sight methods. At the third, or fluency, stage, the skills learned in the second stage become automatic. The fourth stage is reading-to-learn in which there is a significant developmental shift from *learning to read* to *reading to learn,* in which the previously mastered skills are applied to learning school content. This stage takes place in the fourth to eighth grades in students without reading disabilities. The fifth stage involves constructing knowledge and developing higher level cognitive and metacognitive skills using reading and occurs at the secondary level in students without reading disabilities. The last stage involves adapting and modifying one's reading abilities based on changing occupational, functional, and social demands throughout the life span.

The students for whom the reading strategies in the Active Learner Approach are designed are at the fourth and fifth stages of this model. They are learning to apply reading skills for mastery of school content, and they are learning to construct knowledge and develop higher level cognitive and metacognitive skills using reading. The reading strategies in the Active Learner Approach are designed to move the students through these two stages. The emphasis of the Active Learner Approach reading strategies is on comprehension of advanced reading vocabulary and comprehension of increasingly difficult materials. Secondary students who are at lower reading levels (prereading through the fluency stages) need another approach; namely, systematic reading instruction to master the basic skills of reading.

Once students with learning disabilities enter middle school, they usually are *not* given any reading instruction as many educators believe that these students do not need any additional instruction. However, students with disabilities need reading instruction until they attain the fifth stage of reading. Reading instruction for students who are beyond the fluency stage of reading does not have to involve a special methodology or special materials (e.g., phonics). Reading is more than just acquiring skills, it is applying these skills to school learning. The Active Learner Approach for reading instruction is designed to provide direct instruction for the development of advanced reading comprehension skills.

The assumption underlying the Active Learner Approach to reading instruction is that reading is a highly complex process that is dependent on environmental, experiential, cognitive, linguistic, instructional, genetic, and neurobiological factors (Lyon, Alexander, & Yaffee, 1997). There is a reciprocal relationship between reading and cognitive/linguistic factors over the life span. In the early stages of the reading process, cognitive and linguistic abilities are required for learning to read. After students learn to read, it increases their cognitive and linguistic abilities (Stanovich, 1986). Many of the strategies in the Active Learner Approach are designed to increase students' cognitive and linguistic abilities as well as their reading.

WHAT ARE THE DIFFERENT SUBSKILLS OF READING?

A task analysis of reading at the reading-to-learn stage and the knowledge construction stage must focus on the following comprehension subskills:

- Length of the unit to be understood

  - Word

  - Sentence

  - Paragraph

  - Passage

- Type of text to be understood

  - Narrative

  - Expository

- Type of cognitive process needed in order for students to understand the reading material

  - Literal (reading the lines or getting the main ideas, facts, and sequences)

  - Interpretive or inferential (reading between the lines, thinking using the reading material)

- Applied or evaluative (reading beyond the lines to form opinions and new ideas; Vacca & Vacca, 2002)

- Purpose of reading and speed
  - Recreational
  - Learning
  - Memorizing
  - Scanning
  - Skimming

With the strategies in this manual, reading instruction is provided for the different comprehension subskills of the previous task analysis. Comprehension of different units of length is provided at the word, paragraph, and passage levels. In terms of the subskill of type of text to be understood, comprehension of both narrative and expository text is developed. The various types of cognitive processes involving literal, inferential, and evaluative comprehension are systematically developed with the strategies in this manual. Finally, this manual includes strategies to help students adjust their speed of reading in relation to the purpose of the reading.

With the Active Learner Approach, comprehension of vocabulary is systematically taught to develop understanding at the word level. Comprehension at the sentence, paragraph, and passage level is also systematically taught through other strategies in other sections. The following two subskills of vocabulary (and the corresponding Active Learner Student Questionnaire items found in Appendix A) are taught with the Active Learner Approach.

- Understanding advanced vocabulary: "I have difficulty understanding difficult words that I read."

- Recalling advanced vocabulary: "I forget vocabulary words I learn."

The following two subskills of comprehension involving paragraphs and passages (and the corresponding Active Learner Student Questionnaire items found in Appendix A) are taught with the Active Learner Approach.

- Comprehension of main ideas at the paragraph level: "I have difficulty understanding the main idea when I read."

- Comprehension of details: "I have difficulty understanding the details when I read."

Both of the previous areas involve literal comprehension (i.e., understanding the main ideas and details). Interpretive and applied comprehension skills are systematically taught in the section on advanced thinking skills in Chapter 13.

Comprehension of the type of text—narrative and expository—is developed with the Active Learner Approach. One of the research-supported strategies for improving reading comprehension is teaching students to know text structure (i.e., whether they are reading narrative or expository text; Mastropieri, Scruggs, Bakken, & Whedon, 1996). Emphasis on narrative text is important for English classes as well as recreational purposes, whereas emphasis on expository text is important for all classes other than English as well as functional reading (e.g., the newspaper, directions).

Reading from the computer is a type of expository text but has many differences from textbooks, and, therefore, there is a separate strategy to develop reading skills for use with computers. The three following subskills of comprehension using different types of text (and the corresponding Active Learner Student Questionnaire items found in Appendix A) are taught with the Active Learner Approach.

- Expository text: "I have difficulty getting the overall ideas when I read material for my classes."

- Narrative text: "I have difficulty understanding stories that I read."

- Electronic presentations: "I have difficulty understanding what I read from the computer screen."

A strategy related to the purpose of reading and the relationship to reading speed is included in one item on the Learning Questionnaire in which the student must respond to, "I read slowly." The last area taught with the Active Learner Approach involves the use of aids to help with reading. This is a metacognitive skill that students need to develop to monitor their reading. The item on the Learning Questionnaire that corresponds to this is, "I don't usually use aids to help me read."

WHAT IS SPECIAL ABOUT TEACHING READING?

With the Active Learner Approach to teaching reading, the students' reading materials are their textbooks and the reading that they must do for their classes. There are no separate reading materials as in a systematic reading program that might be used at the lower levels of instruction. Use of reading materials other than those the students need to read for their classes would make it harder for the students to generalize and transfer reading skills developed with such materials to materials that they are using in their classes.

Many students at the secondary level will continue to make decoding or word identification errors when reading (e.g., they read the word *through* for the word *though*). In most cases, it is not appropriate to systematically teach reading skills related to these errors. Instead, try to have the students use context clues and other meaning strategies to compensate for these errors. For example, if a student read, "Through the U.S. lost the battle, it has become a historic event," have the student reread the sentence and ask herself if it made sense, and what word would have to be changed to make the sentence correct.

The use of graphic organizers is highly recommended when teaching comprehension skills with the Active Learner Approach. The reading content usually involves complex relationships that can be visually demonstrated with graphic organizers. These complex relationships usually involve advanced thinking skills (interpretive and applied comprehension skills). These skills are taught in Chapter 13, so integrate the teaching of the reading strategies with the teaching of strategies for advanced thinking.

It is especially important to use a scaffolding approach to reading instruction with the Active Learner Approach. Many students with reading disabilities have developed learned helplessness in which they read the material and expect the teacher to interpret it for them. Initially, you will need to support the students by demonstrating how to analyze texts, but you must get to the guided practice stage as soon as possible and make the transition from you interpreting the text to the student interpreting the text.

Finally, the students are encouraged to use think-alouds to guide their analysis of their reading. Think-alouds and giving students a plan of action have been identified as research-based best practices to improve reading comprehension (Bos & Vaughn, 2002; Kucan & Beck, 1997).

WHAT ARE STRATEGIES TO HELP UNDERSTAND DIFFICULT WORDS?

General education textbooks include large numbers of words that students do not understand, although they may be able to decode them (e.g., they may be able to pronounce the words *ratify* and *vector,* but they do not know their meanings). Many students with mild disabilities simply skip such words when they meet them. They do not use techniques to aid in determining the meaning because of their superficial approach to reading. They do not want to take the time for such analysis, or do not know how to do such an analysis.

The So We Go C strategy[1] is designed to help students understand difficult words by skimming text for words that they do not understand. Then, they are taught to create note cards with these words so that they can study them and master their meanings. They are to find the meanings of these words through context clues, a glossary, a dictionary, or as a last resort, asking the teacher. This strategy trains students to do prereading so that when they do read, they understand the words that they encounter in the text.

---

[1]This strategy was developed by Clinton Sower, a graduate assistant on our project on college students.

SO WE GO C:
TO HELP ME UNDERSTAND DIFFICULT WORDS THAT I READ

Skim the text.
Write unknown words.
Go back and define.
Create two piles of cards.

Skim the text for words you do not understand.

- Skim or quickly look over what you have read.

- Skim one section or paragraph at a time.

- Highlight or write down any unknown words. You may be able to read these words, but you do not understand their meanings.

Write the unknown words on one side of the note cards.

Go back and write the definitions for the terms on the other sides of the cards.

- Read the text around the unknown word to see if you can figure out what it means. This is called using *context clues.* If you can figure out the meaning, then write the definition on the back of the card.

- If you can't figure out the meaning from the context clues, then see if the word is in the glossary at the back of the book. If you find it, then write the definition on the back of the card.

- If you can't find the definition in a glossary, then look the word up in the dictionary, and write the definition on the back of the card.

- If you still can't find the definition, then ask your teacher.

Create two piles of cards.

- Review the cards. If you understand the definitions for the words, then put them in a pile and study them so that you can remember the meanings of the words.

- If you do not understand the definitions you have written, then ask your teacher to explain them. Use self-talk to explain the meaning to yourself.

WHAT ARE STRATEGIES TO HELP
REMEMBER READING VOCABULARY?

Some students can learn to decode and understand the meaning of a difficult word that they read, but they cannot retain the definition. To aid in long-term recall of such words, it is best to fit the word into understanding of the overall ideas of the content area. For short-term retention of such words, the IF IT FITS strategy should be used. This strategy is based on the research-supported IF IT FITS strategy developed by King-Sears, Mercer, and Sindelar (1992). This strategy integrates the use of the keyword method (Mastropieri & Scruggs, 2000) that is embedded in the BREAK strategy, which is designed to aid in memorization (see Chapter 8). With IF IT FITS, the students identify an unfamiliar word, find the definition, isolate the word, tell the definition by speaking it aloud, find a keyword, imagine an interaction between the unfamiliar word and the keyword, think about the strategy, and then study it. This is a complex strategy with eight steps that takes considerable time for teacher modeling and guided practice.

IF IT FITS:
TO HELP ME REMEMBER NEW VOCABULARY

Identify each unfamiliar word.
Find the definition of the word.
Isolate the word.
Tell the definition.
Find a keyword.
Imagine an interaction.
Think about your strategy.
Study the strategy.

Identify each unfamiliar word (e.g., the word *perspicacious*).

Find the definition of the word.

- Read the text around the unknown word to see if you can figure out what it means. This is called using *context clues* (If you are *perspicacious,* then your keen sense for detail may find the meaning from context clues).

- If you can't figure out the meaning from the context clues, then see if the word is in the glossary at the back of the book.

- If you can't find it in the glossary, then look it up in the dictionary (*perspicacious:* able to understand or perceive keenly).

- If you still can't understand the definition, then ask your teacher to explain it.

Isolate the word.

- Write the word on the front of a note card.

Tell yourself the definition of the word.

- Say the definition aloud.
- Write the definition on the back of the note card.

Find a keyword.

- Associate a keyword with the word you are trying to learn.
- The keyword should sound or look like the word you already know (e.g., *perspicacious* looks like the word *perspective*).

Imagine an interaction.

- Think of an interaction between the word you are trying to remember and the keyword (A *perspicacious* person has a keen *perspective*).

- Try to picture the interaction in your mind (Picture the statue of The Thinker as a *perspicacious* person who has a keen *perspective*).

Think about your strategy.

- Think of the keyword.
- Then say the definition of the word aloud.

Study the strategy.

- Study your note cards with unfamiliar words.

- Close your eyes and test yourself. Read the word and try to recall the definition on the back. Then, check yourself to see if you are correct. If not, try to recall the keyword and imagine the interaction between the keyword and the word you are trying to remember.

WHAT ARE STRATEGIES TO GET THE
OVERALL IDEAS OF READING MATERIAL FOR MY CLASSES?

Students with disabilities approach a reading task by just starting to read. They do not preview what they have to read, which makes it difficult for the students to relate the reading content to what they already know and does not give them an explicit purpose for reading the material. To teach students to see the act of reading a particular passage as an event with three separate parts—a beginning, a middle, and an end—use the BCDE strategy. This approach is similar to the well-accepted best practice directed reading–thinking activity (DR–TA) that has been successfully used in the field of reading for many years (Vacca & Vacca, 2002). However, the difference between BCDE and DR–TA is that the student is responsible for directing the teaching process with BCDE, whereas the teacher is responsible with DR–TA. With the BCDE strategy, the student is taught to self-question, whereas the teacher always asks the questions with DR–TA.

BCDE is especially useful for reading expository text. With this strategy, the student can see the overall layout and plan for presentation of the material and the continuity between sections of text. Subject matter textbooks have different layouts, and students must learn the plans for each of the textbooks used in their courses.

The first step in BCDE has the student survey the material to be read and make predictions. Based on the previously read material, the students create prediction questions as well as questions dealing with the headings, pictures, graphics, and study questions. Prediction has been identified as one of the best practices for teaching reading comprehension to older students because it activates prior knowledge and encourages students to use this to facilitate their understanding of the ideas in the text (Duke & Pearson, 2001; Mastropieri et al., 1996). At the next stage, the students read in order to answer the questions they constructed. At the final stage, after the reading is completed, the students answer the questions posed in the first stage and also summarize the material they read.

BCDE:
TO HELP ME GET THE OVERALL IDEAS WHEN I READ

Before reading—survey.
Create questions to ask yourself.
During reading—answer the questions.
End of reading—summarize.

Before reading, survey the material to be read.

- Always look over the pages you have to read before you actually start reading.

- If you are reading a textbook, read the title, side headings, paragraph headings, pictures, graphics, bold-face words, and study questions. Think of how this chapter is related to previous chapters.

- If you are reading a story, look back at the previous section you read and predict what you think will happen in this section. Skim the paragraphs to get some ideas of what might be in the section you will be reading. Make predictions about the characters and the actions that you think will take place.

Create questions to ask yourself while you read the material.

- For textbooks, create questions about the material based on the title, side headings, paragraph headings, pictures, graphics, bold-face words, and study questions. Write these on the front of note cards.

- For stories, write questions based on the predictions that you made. Make predictions about the characters and actions.

During reading of the material, answer the questions you wrote on the note cards.

- As you read the material, keep in mind the questions that you wrote.

- When you find the answers to the questions, write them on the backs of the cards.

End of reading—summarize.

- After you have finished reading, look over all the questions you wrote. If you did not find an answer to a question, then go back and try to find it.

- Ask yourself the questions and try to answer them.

- Say a summary of the main ideas of what you just read aloud to yourself.

- Ask yourself how the material you just read is related to material that you read before this.

- Predict how the material you just read will be related to the material that you will read next.

WHAT ARE STRATEGIES FOR
UNDERSTANDING MAIN IDEAS OF READING MATERIAL?

Getting the main idea of material that has been read is one of the most important comprehension skills. To help students get the main idea, the RAP-Q strategy is used with the Active Learner Approach. In our study with college students, RAP-Q was one of the most used strategies by the tutors, who cited its ease of use and effectiveness as reasons for their frequent use of it. With this strategy, the students are required to read one paragraph or short section at a time and create questions concerning the main idea of the passage. This approach should not be used for long passages because the student may lose the continuity of the paragraphs or sections and not get the overall idea. This requires students to analyze each passage, which slows down their reading. Many students with disabilities do not like this strategy because they want to move quickly through the reading material. They must be made to realize that they cannot master main ideas by reading quickly.

The first step in RAP-Q has the students read the paragraph or section. In the second step, the students ask themselves what the main idea of the passage was. The third step is the most difficult because they must paraphrase the main idea. By putting the main idea into their own words, it indicates that they understand the material they read and are not just parroting the words from the text. The last step has them creating questions about the main idea and writing the questions and answers on note cards for later study use.

RAP-Q is based on a well-researched paraphrasing strategy called RAP, developed by Schumaker, Denton, and Deshler (1984). The difference in the two strategies involves the use of note cards to record questions so that they can be used for study purposes at a later time. These cards can also be used to understand the continuity between the paragraphs or the sections and, therefore, lead to an understanding of the overall main idea of the reading material.

RAP-Q:
TO HELP ME UNDERSTAND THE MAIN IDEAS OF WHAT I READ

> **R**ead a paragraph or a section.
> **A**sk what the main ideas are.
> **P**ut the ideas in your own words.
> **Q**uestions about the reading.

Read a paragraph or a section of the material you are working on.

- Do not read long sections because you may not be able to understand the material if you don't break it up into smaller parts.

Ask yourself what the main ideas are.

- Try to find the sentence or sentences that give the most important ideas in the section that you read.

Put the main ideas in your own words.

- *Paraphrasing* is when you put material that you read into your own words.
- When you paraphrase the main ideas, make sure you try to think of other words to say the same thing as in the book.

Questions about the reading.

- Based on your paraphrasing of the main ideas, write a question and an answer on the back of a note card so that you can use this for studying.
- Compare the note cards that you wrote on the main ideas of previous paragraphs or sections so that you can see how the ideas of one section are related to the next.

WHAT ARE STRATEGIES FOR UNDERSTANDING DETAILS FOR READING MATERIAL?

Reading for the purpose of learning and memorizing requires attention to details. The Ask 5 W's & 1 H & Answer strategy is designed to assist the students to organize the details to see how they fit into the overall structure of the reading and to retain them for study purposes. This strategy is based on the six question words: *who, what, where, when, why,* and *how.* Students are to ask themselves these questions in relation to chapter headings and side headings so that they can see how the specific details are related to main ideas. This strategy is best used in conjunction with RAP-Q and/or BCDE so that they first get the overall ideas or main ideas and then fit the details into these overarching ideas. Use graphic organizers to visually depict the relationship between the main ideas and the details as well as among the various details. In addition, use of color coding for the main idea and the different types of details aids students in seeing the interrelationship between them.

ASK 5 W'S & 1 H & ANSWER:
TO HELP ME UNDERSTAND DETAILS OF WHAT I READ

Ask detailed questions to go with the main ideas.

- **W**ho?
- **W**hat?
- **W**here?
- **W**hen?
- **W**hy?
- **H**ow?

Answer the questions using an outline or graphic organizers.

Ask detailed questions to go with the main ideas.

- For each of the main ideas that you have identified in a reading, ask your-self questions starting with the 5 W's and 1 H question words.

Who?

- Identify and list the characters in the reading.
- Draw connecting lines between the characters, and describe to yourself the relationship between the characters.

What?

- Identify and list the events or actions in the reading.
- Draw connecting lines between the events or actions to show the relation-ship between them.
- Draw connecting lines between the characters and the events as you describe to yourself the relationship between them.

Where?

- Identify and list all the places in the reading.
- Draw connecting lines between the places, events, and characters as you describe to yourself the relationship among them.

When?

- Identify and list all the time factors in the reading.
- Draw connecting lines between the time factors, places, events, and characters as you describe to yourself the relationship among them.

Why?

- Identify and list causes for events or actions.
- Draw connecting lines from the causes to the effects on the characters, events, places, or times as you describe the relationship among them.

How?

- Identify and list the way events took place.
- Draw connecting lines between the way the events took place and other factors as you describe the relationship to yourself.

Answer the questions using an outline or graphic organizers.

- Review all the details you listed.
- Make an outline of the overall or main ideas, and then select details from your lists that are important and write these under the main ideas. You don't have to include every detail that you identified. You may want to use different colored pens (or fonts if you are using a word processor), and write the main idea in one color (green), the *who* details in another color (red), the *what* details in another (blue), and so forth. This helps you see the relationship between all the information. When you finish your outline, you should have a complete picture of the overall ideas and how the details relate to these.
- It might also be helpful to draw lines integrating all the details.

WHAT ARE STRATEGIES FOR
UNDERSTANDING STORIES THAT ARE READ?

Some students with disabilities do not understand that texts are organized differently and, therefore, they must use different strategies to understand them. Explain to the students that the stories they read usually have a particular format and they can best be understood by analyzing the format that the students will be taught. The SPORE strategy gives the basic format for understanding stories. SPORE is almost identical to the STORE strategy, except that P is used for problem and T is used for trouble. STORE was developed by Bos to improve student performance with narrative text (Bos & Vaughn, 2002). It has been long recognized that student self-questioning using this format leads to improved reading comprehension (Mastropieri et al., 1996; Richeck, Caldwell, Jennings, & Lerner, 1996).

With SPORE, you lead students in analyzing the setting of the story, problem, order of action, resolution, and ending. You can guide them in making a story web with the title in the center and each of the five aspects in surrounding circles. Story webs can be developed for chapters and then combined for the entire book. This helps students see the continuity between the chapters and better understand the overall ideas in the book.

SPORE is used as a reading strategy to help students understand the organization of narrative text and also as a writing strategy to help students write stories. For some students, it is useful to combine reading and writing instruction using this same strategy.

SPORE:
TO HELP ME UNDERSTAND STORIES THAT I READ

Setting.
Problem.
Order of action.
Resolution.
End.

Setting.

- Make a story web with the center circle containing the name of the story or chapter of the story that was read. Then, make five circles radiating from this center circle. Each of these five circles should have one of the parts of the SPORE strategy. Just write a word or phrase in each circle. Do not use complete sentences.

- Put the information on the setting in one circle. Write the word *setting* at the top.

- Identify the setting in terms of *who* (people), *what* (animals), *where* (places), and *when* (times) in the story.

- To write a full description of *who, what, where,* and *when,* create additional circles or boxes to fill in as much detail as possible.

Problem.

- Identify the major problems in the story or chapter.

- Analyze the *who, what, where,* and *when* in relation to the problem.

- Write words or phrases in the circle to represent the problems.

Order of action.

- In this circle, write all the events that occurred.

- Number the events in the order they occurred.

Resolution.

- In this circle, write *how* the problems were solved.

End.

- In this circle, identify how the story was wrapped up and what happened to the different characters.

- Review the story web and reread what you have written in each of the circles so that you can get the overall picture of what was included in the story.

WHAT ARE STRATEGIES FOR INCREASING READING SPEED?

Students with disabilities may read slowly or may not know how to vary their reading speed based on the type of material that they are reading. Teach them that it is not productive to read everything quickly and that when you are studying or memorizing, it is important to read slowly to understand the material and to use strategies to recall the content. They should be taught that they can read quickly when they are reading for pleasure or when they are looking for specific information.

The WARF strategy[2] is used to teach students to increase their reading speed. With this strategy, they are taught to widen their eye span and not read word by word. They are taught to group words so that they do not read the articles (e.g., *the, a*) or auxiliary verbs (e.g., *is, are*) because these do not give meaning. They are to look for the words that give meaning. They are taught to try to group words meaningfully (e.g., group the words *the last emperor* and concentrate on the words *last* and *emperor*).

The second step in this strategy instructs the students to avoid skip backs. If they don't understand something, then they are told to keep reading and try to use context clues to gain understanding. If this is not successful, then they are to go back. The next step has them read silently. Some students with disabilities who are at the fourth and fifth stages of the reading model continue to read aloud in a whisper. They must be taught to avoid this by pressing their lips together. The last step has them learn to flex their reading rate depending on the type of material that they are reading.

WARF:
TO HELP IMPROVE MY READING SPEED

Widen your eye span.
Avoid skip backs.
Read silently.
Flex your reading rate.

Widen your eye span.

- Do not read one word at a time.

- Read groups of words. Try to group words starting with *the* and *a* with nouns. Just look at the nouns. Don't look at the words *the* and *a* because they do not add any meaning. Group words starting with *is, are, was,* and *were* with verbs. Just look at the verbs because they are the words that give the meaning.

---

[2]This strategy was developed by Clinton Sower, a graduate assistant on our project on college students.

Avoid skip backs.

- If you do not understand an idea, then do not reread the words immediately. First, keep reading and try to get the meaning by using context clues.

- If you can't get the meaning from the context clues, then go back and reread to try to understand the material.

Read silently.

- Try not to read aloud unless you are trying to memorize material or you are trying to focus your attention on the material and not be distracted.

- Reading aloud slows you down. To stop yourself from reading aloud, press your lips together to prevent yourself from mouthing the words.

Flex your reading rate.

- When you read important information that you need to understand or memorize, then read slowly.

- When you read information that you understand and know well, then read faster.

- If you are looking for information, then read quickly as you search for that word on the page.

WHAT ARE STRATEGIES FOR READING FROM COMPUTERS?

Material on computer sites is a form of expository text because it usually gives information. However, it is organized differently from textbooks, and students need to learn how to understand the different parts of a computer page and how to read the page effectively. Many web pages are cluttered and have many moving distractions, making it especially difficult for students with ADHD to focus on the important elements of the web site. The RUD PC strategy[3] is designed to assist students to more effectively understand material that is presented on web pages. First, the students need to focus on the title, which is usually centered on the page. Then, they need to use the cursor to skim the different parts of the page. They need to be instructed that skimming is different from reading because they are just reading to answer specific questions. If they find that the material is important, then they need to systematically analyze information in each of the sections. They should generally start at the top and read across content that spans the width of the page. For material that is

---

[3]This strategy was developed by Clinton Sower, a graduate assistant on our project on college students.

presented in boxes or circles, they need to be taught to systematically analyze each of these. They may do this in a left-to-right fashion or may first analyze the bigger boxes and then the smaller ones. If there are pop-ups with ads or material unrelated to the web site, then students need to learn to click these off as soon as they appear.

Because there is so much information on a page, students need to decide if they need to read the entire page. If they are doing research, then they may find from reading just the first few lines that the material is not relevant and may stop reading. If they find that it is relevant, then they are to print the pages or bookmark the page for more in-depth analysis. For some students, printing the page is advisable because they may be distracted by the web site graphics or may find the small font difficult to read. The final step has them collecting bibliographic information on the site. They need to be taught that this is imperative if they are to get back to the site and if they are to correctly cite it for any research that they may do.

RUD PC:
TO HELP ME READ FROM THE COMPUTER SCREEN

Read the title and headings.
Use the cursor to skim the page.
Decide if you need the page.
Print the page.
Copy the bibliographic information.

Read the title and headings.

- Read the title and headings.
- See how the page is organized. Some pages have boxes or circles containing information and some have information presented in book form. If there are boxes, then pay special attention to the bigger boxes, which usually have more information.

Use the cursor to skim the page.

- Do not read everything on the page carefully.
- Read quickly to find what is included in the web site.

Decide if the page is worth reading completely.

- If you need the information for an assignment, then read it carefully. If there are a lot of boxes and circles on the page, then figure out a system so that you read all of them. It may help to start with the biggest box and then go to each of the smaller ones, or it may help to start at the left and move to the right.

- If you find that the information is not important to you because it is not related to what you have to do, then keep surfing.

Print the page.

- If you decide that you need to read the information in more detail, then you can print the page, or you can bookmark the site and read it again later.

- Sometimes it is easier to read print copies of pages because the print is bigger and because there may be less distractions.

Collect bibliographic information.

- Copy the web site address and URL so that you can cite it for any research that you are doing.

- Find the author and title (if available).

- Find the date of publication (if available).

WHAT ARE STRATEGIES FOR USING AIDS TO HELP READING?

Many students with disabilities do not use aids to help them systematically increase their comprehension of what they are reading. They do not have an overall plan for how to attack the material that they have to read because they lack metacognitive skills. The PASTE strategy is designed to make students aware of aids that will increase their reading comprehension. This strategy is designed to develop self-monitoring in the students, which is perhaps one of the most essential reading comprehension strategies (Mastropieri et al., 1996). These aids apply to both narrative and expository text. The first step instructs the students to preview the text. Then, the students are instructed to take notes on main ideas. Next, the students need to get the meanings of unknown words. Highlighting material is strongly recommended if students own their own books. If they do not, but find highlighting helpful, then photocopies of their reading material should be provided. Finally, they are taught to examine ideas for relationship. This last step is a metacognitive skill that they are to apply as they read so they find connections between ideas.

PASTE:
TO HELP ME READ BETTER BY USING AIDS

Preview the text.
Always take notes on main ideas.
Save time by analyzing unknown words.
Try to highlight important information.
Examine ideas for relationships.

Preview the text before reading.

- Always look over the pages you have to read before you start reading.

- Focus on headings and subheadings.

- Also, focus on words that are in bold face or have definitions in parentheses.

Always take notes on main ideas.

- Write down the main ideas and important facts on notes cards so that you can study these in the future.

Save time by analyzing unknown words.

- If you do not know the meaning of a word, then try to figure it out using context clues. If this doesn't work, then look it up in the glossary or a dictionary.

- If you think this is an important word, then write it on the front of a note card and the definition on the back.

Try to highlight important information.

- If you own the book you are using, then highlight the important ideas. If you find highlighting helpful for understanding a book and the book is not your property, then photocopy the pages and highlight them.

- If you do not own the book and have taken notes on what you have read, then highlight the important ideas in your notes.

- *Never highlight everything.* The idea behind highlighting is to identify the most important information. If you highlight everything, then you will not be able to pick out the most important information.

Examine ideas for relationships.

- As you read, try to think about the "big picture." Try to figure out how the information you are reading is related to other information on this topic.

- Try to think about what you have read before on this topic.

- Use graphic organizers to help you show these relationships. For example, if this chapter contains causes for events described in previous chapters, then use cause-and-effect graphic organizers with arrows going from the causes to the effects.

MARK, A STUDENT WITH A READING DISABILITY

Mark is a high school sophomore who was diagnosed with a learning disability in fourth grade. He had no difficulty learning to read in the early grades but did have problems with reading comprehension in his subject matter classes. He has a non-reflective learning style and is in a rush to finish all academic tasks, especially reading. He usually gets the main ideas of what he reads but does not retain details because he reads material only once and at a fast pace. He has an excellent auditory memory and has been able to retain facts that his teachers impart in lectures. However, his world history teacher, Mr. Leigh, does not lecture on facts. His class involves discussion of important issues and role plays of historical events, whereas his weekly quizzes assess facts from the textbook. Mark does well in the class discussions and fully understands the issues being taught. However, he does poorly on the quizzes because he reads the textbook chapters quickly and does not use any strategies to retain facts and details. Based on his failing grades on the quizzes, he is in danger of getting a D or F in the class, although he is getting an A average for his classroom participation.

Mark does not receive a regular period of special education help, but he can consult with the special education resource teacher, Ms. Santos, whenever he has a problem. He meets with Ms. Santos to decide what he should do about his performance in his world history class. He reluctantly agrees to use the Ask 5 W's & 1 H & Answer strategy to help him understand and retain the details of the world history textbook chapters he reads. He does not like the idea of spending a lot of time reading, so Ms. Santos and Mark work up a contract in which he agrees to try the strategy for 3 weeks to see if it helps him get better grades on his quizzes. Ms. Santos spends five class periods with Mark modeling and giving guided practice on how to use this strategy. Mark uses the strategy at home for 3 weeks, and his quiz grades improve to a passing level. Mark says that he will continue to use the Ask 5 W's & 1 H & Answer strategy on his own.

Ms. Santos checks back with Mark 2 weeks later and finds that he has not used the strategy and his quiz grades have dropped again. He says that he hates to spend all that time studying. Ms. Santos and Mark decide to involve his parents to see if they can help him spend more time on his studying at home. Mark's parents meet with Ms. Santos and Mark and they agree to reward Mark if he spends 30 minutes using this strategy every night that he has to read the world history chapters. They agree to reward him with money to put toward buying a new skateboard. Mark uses the strategy as long as he is rewarded. Fortunately, the skateboard he wants is expensive and he will need a lot of money to get it, which means that he will be using the strategy for most of the semester. Hopefully, after he gets all the money he needs, he will have enough intrinsic motivation to continue using the strategy.

11
Writing

- Why do students with learning disabilities and ADHD need to learn writing skills?

- What are the different subskills of writing?

- What is special about teaching writing?

- What are strategies for spelling?

- What are strategies for capitalization?

- What are strategies for using commas?

- What are strategies for using colons and semicolons?

- What are strategies for writing grammatically correct advanced sentences?

- What are strategies for proofreading for mechanics?

- What are strategies for writing paragraphs?

- What are strategies for finding words to fit one's ideas when writing?

- What are strategies for organizing ideas when writing stories?

■ What are strategies for organizing ideas for research papers and essays?

■ What are strategies for writing introductions and conclusions?

■ What are strategies for finding information when writing papers?

■ What are strategies for keeping to the topic when writing?

■ What are strategies for proofreading for clear presentation of content?

WHY DO STUDENTS WITH LEARNING
DISABILITIES AND ADHD NEED TO LEARN WRITING SKILLS?

The demands for written communication become greater as students progress through the grades. By the time they reach the secondary level, it is expected that they will be able to write well enough to meet the composition demands of their English classes as well as the composition and test demands of their other classes. In addition, many high-stakes tests require writing essays as a measure of writing ability rather than tests of isolated mechanics skills, such as spelling, punctuation, and capitalization. Written communication skills are also of great importance for many jobs because they require the use of electronic communication (i.e., e-mail).

Writing requires students to seamlessly integrate different complex skills. They must think of the ideas they want to express, find sentences and words to express these ideas, organize these sentences into a cohesive arrangement, write grammatically correct sentences, spell words, capitalize, use appropriate punctuation, and proofread what they have written for clarity and mechanics. A weakness in any one of these required skills may result in the inability to use that skill when it must be integrated with the other skills. When a skill is needed in an isolated situation, the students may be able to use it, but when that skill must be integrated with others, the students may not be able to do so. For example, students may be able to spell 10 words correctly on a spelling test; however, they may not be able to spell these same words correctly when they must use them in spontaneous writing. When the necessity of integrating these different skills into the spontaneous act of writing is considered, it becomes evident why so many students with learning disabilities have writing problems.

Students with learning disabilities have been identified as having problems with the mechanics (e.g., grammatically correct sentences, spelling, punctuation, capitalization) and composition aspects of writing (Bos & Vaughn, 2002). Composition is more important than mechanics because it carries the meaning that the writer wants to convey. However, errors in mechanics detract from the readability of the writer's message. Most secondary students with disabilities have been taught the rules underlying the mechanics of writing; however, they have not retained them adequately enough to use them when writing. When these skills are assessed in isolation, many students can gain access to them; however, students cannot gain access to the skills when they are assessed in combination with other skills in a complex writing task.

Many secondary students with learning disabilities do not have difficulty constructing grammatically correct sentences when they speak but cannot do so when they express these sentences in writing. There is a breakdown in the connection between the idea the student wants to express and the motor act of writing the response. At the secondary level, many students with learning disabilities can write grammatically correct simple sentences but cannot do so with compound and complex sentences, which are required for higher level writing tasks.

Problems with spelling are among the most frequently reported of students with learning disabilities, and some suggest that spelling is more difficult than reading (Bosman & Van Orden, 1997). Although the use of spell check has allowed some students to compensate for their poor spelling, many students with learning disabilities still perceive spelling as a major obstacle to achieving in school.

Spelling abilities are dependent on mastery of phonics and structural analysis rules as well as good memory skills. Mastery of phonics is necessary to encode phonetically regular words, and mastery of structural analysis is necessary to encode multisyllabic words. Phonics and structural analysis are developed on a decoding basis for reading but must be used on an encoding basis for spelling. For words that cannot be sounded out phonetically, students must have good visual memory skills so that they can recall the order of the letters for words to be spelled. Students with reading disabilities will, in all likelihood, have spelling problems because they will not be able to encode phonics and use structural analysis skills if they have not mastered these at the decoding level. However, there are students with spelling problems who do not have corresponding reading problems. They have been able to master the decoding aspects of phonics and structural analysis and apply their visual memory skills to recalling nonphonetic words. However, they have deficits in the encoding of such skills, and this is reflected in spelling problems.

Some students with spelling problems have difficulty using spell checks on word processing programs because they have problems at the recognition and recall levels. Students who can effectively use spell checks have problems at the recall level but not the recognition level (i.e., they cannot retrieve the correct spelling of a word, but when they see the correct spelling, they can recognize it).

Students who have problems learning and applying rules will have difficulty with punctuation and capitalization. Some students can master these skills in isolation and can do worksheet-type activities requiring correct punctuation and capitalization, but when they must combine these skills with other writing skills, they have difficulty applying the rules. Some students are aided by grammar checks on word processing programs; however, others are not because they do not know the grammatical rules that they are violating.

There are three major requirements for students to effectively write compositions: background knowledge, language abilities, and metacognitive skills. The students must have adequate background knowledge in order to have the necessary content to write about. Many students with disabilities have not been exposed to adequate instruction in various content areas, so they do not have prior knowledge about the topic on which they are to write. When giving writing assignments, make sure that the students have adequate background knowledge and can retrieve it for the purpose of writing. Help them use brainstorming to produce as many ideas as possible whenever they are required to write. In addition, integrate the teaching of writing with the teaching of content (i.e., make sure the students are given a sufficient base of information to use for their writing).

Strong oral language abilities are necessary for mastery of composition. Some students have weak oral language skills and, consequently, do not have the prerequisites necessary for written composition. Other students have strong oral language abilities but cannot apply these to their writing. Students need extensive, abstract vocabularies and mastery of complex syntactical structures for expressive writing. However, some students have limited expressive vocabularies and have difficulty finding words to express their ideas or use simple words that do not clearly represent the complexity of their ideas. Use of the thesaurus on a word processor may help some students broaden the vocabulary that they use. Other students are not helped by this because they do not understand the nuances in the different word choices listed in the thesaurus. Some students with limited syntactical abilities use repetitive simple sentences, which do not adequately represent the complexity of their ideas.

Another requirement for mastery of composition abilities is effective metacognitive skills. The students need to have an overall picture of what they want to express in their writing. They need to identify a beginning and an end and organize the body of writing using a logical, sequential order. Many students with metacognitive deficits have difficulty brainstorming and organizing a number of ideas. Students with ADHD often have difficulty with composition because they do not keep to the topic. As they write, they are distracted by ideas that are tangentially related to the topic.

WHAT ARE THE DIFFERENT SUBSKILLS OF WRITING?

Teaching writing using the Active Learner Approach is divided into two major areas: mechanics and composition. Under mechanics, the following subskills are included:

- Spelling
- Capitalization
- Punctuation
- Grammar/syntax
- Proofreading for mechanics errors

The following subskills involving the mechanics of writing (and corresponding Active Learner Student Questionnaire items found in Appendix A) are taught with the Active Learner Approach.

- Spelling: "I have difficulty spelling."

- Capitalization: "I have difficulty using correct capitalization."

- Punctuation with commas: "I have difficulty using commas correctly."

- Punctuation with colons and semicolons: "I have difficulty using colons and semicolons correctly."

- Grammar/syntax: "I have difficulty writing good sentences."

- Proofreading for mechanics: "I have difficulty proofreading for spelling, punctuation, capitalization, and sentences."

A task analysis of the composition subskills of writing considers the following aspects of length of the unit of writing, just as length of unit was a subskill considered for reading comprehension:

- Word

- Sentence

- Paragraph

- Passage

With the Active Learner Approach, strategies for each of these composition subskills are provided. Strategies for improving students' written vocabularies are based on semantic training (i.e., expressive mastery of words through expressive oral language is used as the basis for expressive mastery of words through expressive written language).

The Active Learner Approach includes instruction on helping students retrieve words to fit the ideas they want to express. The following vocabulary subskill of written language (and the corresponding Active Learner Student Questionnaire item found in Appendix A) is taught.

- Word retrieval: "I have difficulty finding the words to say what I mean."

Strategies for improving students' ability to write complex sentence structures are based on their expressive oral language skills in the area of syntax. There is instruction about sentences in the mechanics area, but this instruction is focused on correct grammar (e.g., noun–verb agreement). Instruction about sentences in the composition area focuses on use of sentences to fit the students' ideas. Instruction on this permeates most of the composition strategies.

Strategies for writing paragraphs involve teaching students to structure and organize one or several main ideas in a paragraph using a beginning, middle, and end; whereas strategies for writing passages involve teaching students to apply this same beginning, middle, and ending structure using multiple paragraphs and multiple ideas. The strategies for writing passages are listed in the next section under strategies for teaching narrative and expository text. The following composition subskill involving the paragraph length of the unit (and the corresponding Active Learner Student Questionnaire item found in Appendix A) is taught with the Active Learner Approach.

- Writing paragraphs: "I have difficulty writing paragraphs."

The type of text to be written by the students is also analyzed with the Active Learner Approach. Students are taught to write organized, sequential papers with clear introductions and conclusions with narrative and expository text. In addition, the students learn how to acquire information as the basis for their expository writing. The following subskills (and the corresponding Active Learner Student Questionnaire items found in Appendix A) are taught with the Active Learner Approach.

- Narrative writing: "I have difficulty organizing my ideas when I write stories."

- Expository writing: "I have difficulty organizing my ideas when I write research papers and essays."

- Researching for expository writing: "I have difficulty finding information when I write research papers and essays."

- Organized, sequential writing: "I have difficulty writing introductions and conclusions."

Another subskill of composition involves monitoring for meaning. This involves the metacognitive skill of monitoring to keep to the topic when writing as well as attend to organizational factors when proofreading. The following subskills involving monitoring for meaning when writing (and the corresponding Active Learner Student Questionnaire items found in Appendix A) are taught with the Active Learner Approach.

- Keeping to the topic: "I have difficulty keeping to the topic."

- Proofreading for content: "I have difficulty proofreading to see if my writing makes sense."

WHAT IS SPECIAL ABOUT TEACHING WRITING?

With the Active Learner Approach to teaching writing, the students' writing assignments should be used as the content of their instruction. This should include the writing that is necessary for English papers as well as essays and research papers in other content courses. In addition, they should be given practice in writing essay responses for tests they take in their courses.

For some students, teaching writing is most effectively presented when integrated with teaching reading. When students learn to read new vocabulary (using the So We Go C strategy), they should also be taught to include these words in their writing (using the SAT strategy). When students are taught to write paragraphs (using the IBC strategy), they should be taught to analyze paragraphs that they are reading using the model of topic sentence, details, and concluding sentence (using the RAP-Q strategy). Not all paragraphs are written in this manner so you have to be careful to find paragraphs that fit this model. Students are taught to use different strategies when reading narrative and expository text. They should also be taught to use different strategies when writing narrative and expository text. The SPORE strategy used to teach reading of narrative text is also used to teach writing of narrative text.

The decision to teach the mechanics skills of writing should be based on the demands on the student for correct mechanics skills. If students can effectively use the spell check and the grammar check on the word processor, then these accommodations should be included in the students' individualized education programs (IEPs) and used whenever appropriate. When students cannot use these accommodations, they should be required to keep written copies of the mechanics strategies handy whenever writing.

The composition subskills of writing are more important than the mechanics subskills because they convey the meaning, and there are few accommodations available to compensate for deficits in composition. Although, in some cases, a student can make an oral response instead of a written response (e.g., short responses on tests), this is not effective for writing lengthy papers or essay responses that require organization of complex ideas. Therefore, emphasis on composition should be greater than emphasis on mechanics when teaching writing to students with disabilities.

The best practices in expressive writing instruction reported by Vaughn, Gersten, and Chard (2000) have been integrated into the composition strategies of the Active Learner Approach. These best practices include explicit teaching of the critical steps in the writing process supported by a "think sheet" or mnemonic and explicit teaching of the conventions of the writing genre (i.e., text structures are provided to guide the writing). In addition, the plan, write, and revise approach to writing instruction has been shown to be effective with students with learning disabilities (Harris & Graham, 1996; Sexton, Harris, & Graham, 1998). All composition strategies in the Active Learner Approach incorporate these best practices.

Whenever possible, students should be allowed to use word processors rather than to handwrite. Many students who find it hard to write for long periods of time do not find it difficult to use word processors for long periods of time. Making corrections and rewriting are easier with a word processor than writing by hand. In addition, students often find using different fonts and print colors helps them maintain attention to a writing task.

WHAT ARE STRATEGIES FOR SPELLING?

Spelling problems continue to plague many students with learning disabilities through high school and college. Of the various mechanics of writing, spelling problems seem to stand out more than other types of problems. This may be true because many of the words that students with learning disabilities spell incorrectly are considered simple (e.g., use of the word *to* for the word *too*). When students spell these words incorrectly, they often receive teacher responses such as, "I can't believe that you can't spell such easy words." Homophones, or words that sound the same but are spelled differently, are particularly difficult for such students.

Students with learning disabilities are often reluctant to write because of the negative feedback that they have received about their writing due to their spelling errors, even when their composition was good. It is important to work with the students' general education teachers to make sure that their grades are not lowered because of poor spelling or other mechanics errors when their compositions are good. If necessary, add separate grading for mechanics and for composition as an accommodation in students' IEPs. When working with students who are frustrated when they can't spell words, encourage them to write the words as best they can so that they can get their ideas down. Tell them that as long as they can read these words, they can go back later and try to spell them correctly. Explain to them that their ideas are most important, not their spelling.

The We See Dark Light strategy is designed to teach students to improve their spelling when writing. It is *not* a strategy for systematically teaching spelling using phonological or visual approaches that are usually taught at the lower grade levels. Rather, it is a strategy to aid students in recalling how to spell words they need to use when composing. With this strategy, the students are taught to write the words that they cannot recall how to spell. They are taught to write a word different ways to see which spelling "looks right." This is helpful for students who have difficulty with recall but not with recognition of correct spelling. The second step has them use the spell check of a word processor if they have access to one. The third step has the students look the word up in the dictionary and analyze the uniqueness of the word (e.g., identifying the root or definition). The last step has the students make a list of words that they frequently forget how to spell and keep this list handy whenever they write. They should highlight the letters that are hard for them to remember (e.g., highlighting the *a* in *separate* for students who frequently spell the word *seperate*).

WE SEE DARK LIGHT:
TO IMPROVE MY SPELLING

Write the word.
Spell check.
Dictionary.
List words that are hard.

Write the word.

- When you can't think of how to spell a word, or someone has pointed out a word that you spelled incorrectly, or the spell check shows that a word is spelled incorrectly, try writing it several ways to see what "looks right."

- When you write it again, try to think of the sounds of the letters or how the word looked when you read it. Try to use the same cues you used to figure out how to read the word to help you figure out how to spell the word.

Spell check.

- If you are using a computer, then run the spell check.

- Look at each of the choices and try to figure out which is spelled the way you want it to be spelled. If necessary, write down the choices to see which "looks right."

Dictionary.

- If you don't have a computer or if the spell check doesn't help, then look the word up in the dictionary.

- It may be hard to look a word up if you don't know how to spell it. Write the word in different ways and look up each spelling until you find the word.

- If you can't remember which spelling goes with two words that sound alike (e.g., *pail* versus *pale*), then look both of them up in the dictionary and check which definition fits the word that you want to use.

- Once you find the word, look at the spelling, the syllables, the root word, and the definition as ways to help you remember.

List words that are hard for you.

- Make a list of words that you need to write a lot but can't remember how to spell.

- Highlight the letters that are hard for you to remember. For example, if you have difficulty remembering the spelling of *separate* because you usually write it as *seperate,* then underline or color code the first *a* to help you remember it.

- Keep this list in a handy place so that you can refer to the spelling of these words whenever you need it.

WHAT ARE STRATEGIES FOR CAPITALIZATION?

Students with learning disabilities in writing often have difficulty understanding what classes of words to capitalize. They usually master elementary capitalization rules, such as capitalizing the word *I* or the first letter of a sentence. However, more advanced categories, such as titles, are more difficult because they are not used as frequently, and the categories that they represent are more abstract (e.g., special events).

The PACKED strategy is designed to help students recall the categories of words that need to be capitalized. First, students are taught to capitalize proper nouns and distinguish them from other nouns. Then, they are taught to look for names and titles of family members and also titles for people. Next, they are taught to capitalize important words in a title. This is difficult because the students have to decide what words are important. Then, they are taught to capitalize words that represent special events (e.g., Christmas). Finally, they are taught to capitalize names of the days of the week and the months. For all of these categories, you should contrast examples and nonexamples (i.e., examples that represent the correct capitalization and examples that represent the incorrect capitalization). As an example, contrast capitalizing all of the words in *Gone With The Wind* versus only capitalizing the important words in *Gone with the Wind*.

PACKED:
TO HELP ME REMEMBER
WHAT WORDS NEED TO BE CAPITALIZED

Proper nouns.
All names and titles of family relations.
Capitalize important words in titles.
Keep titles of people capitalized.
Extra special events.
Days and months.

Proper nouns.

- All proper nouns should be capitalized.

- Proper nouns are names for people, places, or things.

  - People: George Washington (don't capitalize the word *president,* but capitalize the name of a president), Ricky Martin (don't capitalize the word *singer,* but capitalize the name of a singer), Tom Cruise (don't capitalize the word *actor,* but capitalize the name of an actor).

- Places: Disneyland (don't capitalize the words *amusement park*, but capitalize the name of an amusement park), White House (don't capitalize the words *president's house*, but capitalize the name of the house), Virginia (don't capitalize the word *state*, but capitalize the name of a state), Chicago (don't capitalize the word *city*, but capitalize the name of a city).

- Things: Pepsi-Cola (don't capitalize the words *soda pop*, but capitalize the name of a brand of soda pop), Nike (don't capitalize the word *shoe*, but capitalize the brand name of a shoe); Chicago Bulls (don't capitalize the words *basketball team*, but capitalize the name of a basketball team).

All names and titles of family members.

- Names of family relations: Mom (don't capitalize his *mother*, but capitalize *Mom* when it is used as a name), Dad (don't capitalize her *father*, but capitalize *Dad* when it is used as a name).

- Titles of family relations: Uncle Joe (don't capitalize my *uncle*, but capitalize uncle when it is used with a name), Aunt Emma (don't capitalize the word *aunt*, but capitalize aunt when it is used with a name).

Capitalize important words in titles of books, stories, or songs.

- The important words are the words that carry the meaning. The words that are not important are usually short words that don't carry meaning (e.g., the words *the, a, and, with*).

- Only capitalize important words or words that start the title:

    - *When I Was Young in the Mountains*

    - *Gone with the Wind*

    - *Songs to Grow on for Mother and Child*

Keep titles for people capitalized.

- Capitalize titles before and after a person's name.
- These titles might stand for their gender (e.g., Mr., Mrs.), their jobs (e.g., Dr.), their academic titles (e.g., M.Ed. for Master of Education), or others (e.g., Jr.).

    - Examples: Ms. Smith, Dr. Jones, Harry Connick, Jr., John Evans, Ph.D.

Extra special events.

- Capitalize special events such as holidays.

    - Examples: Christmas, Easter, Labor Day

- Capitalize special events such as historical events.

  - Examples: World War II, the French Revolution

Days and months.

- Capitalize days of the week.

  - Examples: Tuesday, Friday

- Capitalize months of the year.

  - Examples: May, August

WHAT ARE STRATEGIES FOR USING COMMAS?

Some students with writing disabilities omit commas from their writing because they do not see their importance. To help students understand the purpose of a comma, have them read aloud a sentence using a pause for a comma and then read the sentence without a pause. Show them how analysis of commas can help the reader. The AS I WAIT strategy is designed to assist students in using commas appropriately. First, they are taught to use commas for addresses and dates. Then, they are taught to use commas to set off nonessential information. Making a judgment as to whether information is essential is difficult. You need to give the students a lot of practice in determining whether information is vital to the meaning of the sentence. The third use of commas involves setting off introductory words or clauses. When teaching this, emphasize the two parts of sentences with introductory words and clauses. Words in lists are taught next. For lists, students may choose whether to use a comma before the last item in a list (e.g., *apples, pears, and plums* or *apples, pears and plums*). Point out both options, but have the students consistently follow one. In most cases, teach the students to use the comma before the last item in the list because this is more commonly used. Next, students are taught to separate two or more adjectives describing the same noun using commas. Commas are taught for use with independent clauses and coordinating conjunctions. Explain the meaning of both of these phrases. They are abstract and hard to teach, so use many examples. Finally, teach students to use commas to separate titles that follow a name.

AS I WAIT:
TO HELP ME REMEMBER WHEN TO USE COMMAS

Addresses and dates.
Set off nonessential information.
I ntroductory words or clauses.
Words in lists.
Adjectives (two or more).
I ndependent clauses.
Titles that follow a name.

Addresses and dates.

- Addresses need commas between the city and the state.
  - Example: Richmond, Virginia
- Addresses need commas between the city and the country.
  - Example: London, England
- Dates need commas between the day and the year.
  - Example: February 14, 2025

Set off nonessential information.

- Commas are needed to set off nonessential information in a sentence.
- Nonessential information is not important for the meaning of the sentence. You can omit this information, and the sentence will still have the same meaning.
  - Example: The ice sculpture, however, melted before the party began.

Introductory words or clauses.

- Use a comma to separate an introductory clause from the rest of the sentence. The clause is not a complete sentence and cannot stand alone. The remainder of the sentence is complete and can stand alone.
  - Example: After waiting in line for hours, we finally got to see the movie.

- Use a comma to separate an introductory word at the beginning of the sentence from the rest of the sentence.
  - Example: Consequently, the war was lost.

Words in lists.

- Use a comma to separate lists in which there are three or more words.
  - Example: Please bring your notebook, textbook, and pencil to class.

Adjectives (two or more) for the same noun.

- Use a comma to separate adjectives that describe the same noun.
  - Example: She likes pretty, frilly dresses.

Independent clauses with coordinating conjunctions.

- An independent clause contains a noun and verb and can stand alone as a complete sentence.
- Coordinating conjunctions are words that separate the two independent clauses (e.g., *and, but, or, for, nor, so*).
  - Example: The fire alarm went off, but there was no fire.

Titles that follow a name.

- Titles are abbreviations for degrees that people have (e.g., Joseph Wilson, M.D.) or for people who have the same names (e.g., Tyrone Johnson, Jr., versus Tyrone Johnson, III).

WHAT ARE STRATEGIES FOR USING COLONS AND SEMICOLONS?

The correct use of colons and semicolons is required for students who have school demands for advanced writing skills. These students are usually required to write research papers in various courses. Because these two forms of punctuation are not as frequently used as periods and commas, many students are not familiar with their correct usage. Use of the colon and semicolon is related to the writing of advanced, complex sentences.

The LSLT strategy is designed to help students remember when the use of colons and semicolons is appropriate. The use of colons is taught for presentation of lists and for salutations, whereas the use of semicolons is taught for separating long items in a list in which the use of commas might be confusing. The semicolon is also taught as a means of separating two independent clauses.

LSLT:
TO HELP ME REMEMBER
WHEN TO USE COLONS AND SEMICOLONS

Lists and colons.
Salutation and colons.
Lists and semicolons.
Two independent clauses and semicolons.

Lists and colons.

- Use a colon to set off a list if the clause introducing the list can stand as a sentence by itself.

    - Example: We will study all five Great Lakes: Huron, Ontario, Michigan, Erie, and Superior.

- Do not set off a list if the clause introducing the list cannot stand as a sentence by itself.

    - Example: The five Great Lakes are Huron, Ontario, Michigan, Erie, and Superior.

Salutation and colons.

- Use a colon following the salutation or greeting in a business letter.

    - Example: Dear Mr. Wilson:

Lists and semicolons.

- Use semicolons for items that would be confusing if they were set apart by commas.

    - Example: We invited Mrs. Jones, Karen's mother; Mrs. Smith, Karen's aunt; and Mrs. Parker, Karen's teacher.

Two independent clauses and semicolons.

- Use a semicolon with two independent clauses that are not connected by a conjunction.

    - Example: Think carefully before responding; your future may depend on your answer.

WHAT ARE STRATEGIES FOR WRITING
GRAMMATICALLY CORRECT ADVANCED SENTENCES?

Most secondary students with learning disabilities can write grammatically correct simple sentences, but they have difficulty with advanced sentence structures. It is not uncommon for these students to produce papers with short, repetitive sentences of four and five words. The goal of the strategy in this area is to have the students think of more complex sentences while they are composing. In addition, they are to consider common rules for sentence construction (e.g., subject–verb agreement) because many students fail to consider these rules when constructing sentences.

The CC-CIA strategy is designed to assist students to construct complex, grammatically correct sentences. Obviously, constructing sentences intertwines composition skills with mechanics skills, but the emphasis here is only on the mechanics. Another well-known strategy for developing sentence writing is PENS, which has the students pick a formula for a particular type of sentence, explore words to fit the formula, note the words, and determine subject–verb identification (Deshler, Ellis, & Lenz, 1996).

The first step in CC-CIA has the student think about constructing complete sentences, whereas the second step involves construction of compound sentences, and the third step involves complex sentences. The fourth step has the students include only related ideas and avoid constructing run-on sentences with unrelated topics. The last step has the students looking for agreement among the various parts of the sentence. This strategy is designed to help students construct complex sentences but also make sure that the parts of the sentence are grammatically consistent.

CC-CIA:
TO HELP ME CONSTRUCT
GRAMMATICALLY CORRECT ADVANCED SENTENCES

Construct complete sentences.
Construct compound sentences.
Construct complex sentences.
Include only related ideas.
Agreement of sentence parts.

Construct complete sentences.

- Make sure that each sentence that you write is a complete sentence. It must have a complete thought and have a subject and a verb.

- Example: "Using only men for all roles in Shakespeare's plays" is not a complete thought. It has to be changed to a complete thought such as, "It was necessary to use only men for all roles in Shakespeare's plays."

- Read your sentences aloud to make sure that you are writing a complete thought. Ask yourself if the sentences sound right.

Construct compound sentences.

- Make your sentences more interesting by using compound sentences. Compound sentences include two independent clauses, both of which are sentences that can stand alone.

  - Example: The armies fought for 2 weeks, but there was no clear winner.

- Avoid using short simple sentences.

  - Example: The armies fought for 2 weeks. There was no clear winner.

- Use conjunctions such as *but, and,* and *so* to connect the two independent clauses.

Construct complex sentences.

- Make your sentences more interesting by constructing complex sentences. Complex sentences include an independent clause, which is a complete sentence that can stand alone, and a dependent clause, which cannot stand alone.

  - Example: New diseases were introduced in the Indian population after Columbus came to the New World. *New diseases were introduced in the Indian population* is a complete sentence and can stand alone, but *after Columbus came to the New World* is not a complete sentence that can stand alone.

- Avoid use of simple sentences.

  - Example: Columbus came to the New World. He introduced new diseases in the Indian populations.

- Use conjunctions such as *when, after,* and *before* to connect the clauses.

Include only related ideas.

- Avoid run-on sentences that have unrelated ideas in them.

  - Example: The ships were the Niña, Pinta, and Santa Maria, but Columbus didn't know that the world was round.

- Make sure all the ideas in your sentences are related to a main topic. If not, use two sentences.

Agreement of sentence parts.

- Make sure that the subject and the verb agree.

  - Example: In the sentence "Use of tools were important to the cave-man," the subject is *use of tools* and the verb should be *was,* not *were.* "Use of tools was important to the caveman."

- Make sure that pronouns agree.

  - Example: In the sentence, "Everyone was happy because he (should be *they*) were going to get money."

- Make sure that articles (i.e., *a, and, an*) agree.

  - Example: In the sentence, "A equal society begins with equally excel-lent schools" should be "An equal society begins with equally excel-lent schools."

WHAT ARE STRATEGIES FOR PROOFREADING FOR MECHANICS?

Students with learning disabilities and ADHD have difficulty seeing their errors. This may be due to their cursory style of analyzing information or their inability to consider several variables at one time (e.g., punctuation, capitalization, spelling). To compensate for students' difficulties with considering several variables at a time, they are taught to look for one type of error at a time. This requires them to make multiple sweeps of their writing, and with each sweep they look for a different type of error. Some students do not like this because it requires more time, but they must be led to understand that this will result in identifying more errors in their writing. Also, reading their writing aloud is helpful for identifying errors. As they read aloud, they are to point to each word. In this way, they can identify words that have been omitted, duplicated, or are in the wrong order.

The SCOPE strategy is designed to assist students to more effectively proofread their writing for mechanics errors. SCOPE is similar to other frequently used proofreading strategies, such as COPS, which has the students edit for capitalization, overall appearance, punctuation, and spelling. SCOPE requires the students to reread the paper five times, looking for a different type of error each time. The first reading is to check for spelling, the second for capitalization, the third for order of words, the fourth for punctuation, and the last is to check to see if all sentences express complete thoughts.

SCOPE:
TO HELP PROOFREAD PAPERS FOR SPELLING, PUNCTUATION, CAPITALIZATION, AND SENTENCES

Spelling.
Capitalization.
Order of words.
Punctuation.
Express a complete thought.

With this strategy, you reread your paper five times. Each time you look for a different type of error. The first time you read your paper, you check for spelling errors. You find each of these and correct them. The second time you check for capitalization, the third time for order of words, the fourth time for punctuation, and the fifth time for grammatically correct sentences. It may take a long time to reread your paper five times, but it may be the only way to concentrate on certain types of errors and find them. It may be too hard to try to find five different types of errors at one time.

Spelling.

- Reread your paper for misspelled words.
- If you have a spell check, then use it.
- If you do not have a spell check, then try writing the misspelled words in different ways to see if one looks "right."
- If necessary, use a dictionary to find correct spellings.

Capitalization.

- Reread your paper to make sure all words that have to be capitalized are capitalized.
- Words that need to be capitalized are:
  - Proper nouns
  - First letters of names and titles of family members
  - Important words in titles
  - Titles of people

- Special events
- Days and months

Order of words.

- Reread your paper to make sure that words in each sentence are in the correct order and no words have been omitted.
- It may be helpful to read your paper aloud. Point to each word as you say it to make sure that no words have been omitted, added, or mixed up.

Punctuation.

- Reread your paper to make sure that you have used correct punctuation.
- Remember to check each of these types of punctuation mark:
  - Periods
  - Question marks
  - Commas
  - Colons
  - Semicolons

Express a complete thought.

- Reread each sentence aloud to make sure that you have used grammatically correct sentences.
- Reread for each of the following:
  - Complete sentences: each sentence has a complete thought.
  - No run-on sentences: all parts of the sentence are related.
  - Agreement: all parts of the sentence are in agreement (e.g., subject, verb, pronoun).
- It may be helpful to reread the sentences aloud to make sure that they sound "right."

WHAT ARE STRATEGIES FOR WRITING PARAGRAPHS?

Many students with learning disabilities write papers that contain one long paragraph, or they have paragraphs with single sentences. They do not understand that a paragraph contains one central idea and that all sentences within the paragraph are to be related to that idea. When teaching students to write paragraphs, they should organize all the ideas in the paper and then separate these into more specific ideas, which are represented by paragraphs. It is a good idea to use an outline with all the ideas in the paper represented by headings and subheadings. Show how the subheadings are converted to paragraphs.

In addition, integrate the teaching of reading paragraphs with writing paragraphs. Show the continuity between paragraphs and how each paragraph is written with a topic sentence, a body of descriptive sentences, and a concluding sentence. Obviously, not all paragraphs in reading material are written in this manner, so be careful to select only those paragraphs that fit this model.

The IBC strategy is designed to assist students in writing well-organized paragraphs. The first step has the students write a topic or introductory sentence that presents the main idea or ideas of the paragraph. The second step has them list sentences that describe the topic sentence in detail, which constitutes the body of the paragraph. The final step is to write a concluding sentence that wraps up the information presented in the paragraph.

Many teachers use the hamburger strategy to graphically represent the relationship between the three parts of the paragraph. The topic sentence is compared with the top part of the bun, and the concluding sentence is compared with the bottom of the bun. The details are compared with the hamburger, cheese, tomato, and so forth. For each part of the sandwich, the students must have corresponding sentences. The students are guided in building paragraphs using visual representations of these hamburger parts. We have found that students particularly like using the hamburger strategy when writing paragraphs.

IBC:
TO HELP ME WRITE PARAGRAPHS

Introduction with topic sentence.
Body with descriptive sentences.
Concluding sentence.

Introduction with topic sentence.

- Start with a topic sentence that presents the main idea to be discussed in the paragraph.

- Link the ideas in the paragraph to the ideas in the previous paragraph, if appropriate.

Body with descriptive sentences.

- Write sentences that explain the topic sentence by giving details and examples.

- Give three or more sentences to fully explain the main idea of the paragraph.

Concluding sentence.

- Summarize the main idea and main descriptive points.

WHAT ARE STRATEGIES FOR FINDING WORDS TO FIT ONE'S IDEAS WHEN WRITING?

Some students have difficulties retrieving exact words to fit their ideas when they write. In some cases, they can retrieve the words when they say the sentence aloud because they do not have a word retrieval problem with oral language. In other cases, this does not help, and they need to make associations as aids for finding words to fit the ideas that they want to express in writing. If these techniques are not helpful, then students are to use a thesaurus—either a hard copy or on a word processor. The SAT strategy is designed to help students learn to gain access to words to fit the ideas that they want to express through writing.

SAT:
TO HELP ME FIND THE RIGHT WORDS
TO SAY WHAT I MEAN WHEN WRITING

> **S**ay the sentence aloud.
> **A**ssociate the idea with words and pictures.
> **T**hesaurus.

Say the sentence aloud.

- If you can't think of a word to fit your idea, then read the sentence that you have written and say the word *blank* for the missing word. Then, try to think of words that might fit the sentence.

- If you write a word that doesn't sound right, then read the sentence aloud and listen to whether it sounds right. If it doesn't, then try to think of other words that might fit better.

Associate the idea with words and pictures.

- If you can't think of a specific word, then brainstorm and list as many words as possible that might fit the sentence. Read the sentence with each of the words you listed and decide on the word that best fits.

- If you can't brainstorm words, then try to associate a picture in your head with the idea that you are trying to express. See if the picture helps a word come into your mind.

Thesaurus.

- If associations do not help you think of words, then use the thesaurus on your word processor or in book form. Read the different choices, putting each in the sentence as you read it aloud. Decide which best fits the meaning that you want to express.

WHAT ARE STRATEGIES FOR ORGANIZING IDEAS WHEN WRITING STORIES?

Students with learning disabilities often write short stories with ideas that are unconnected or undeveloped. To help students organize their ideas to write narrative text, the SPORE strategy is used. This strategy is also used to teach students to understand stories that they read. If students are being taught to read narrative text and write summaries of the text (e.g., book reports), then coordinate the use of SPORE for both reading and writing purposes.

With SPORE, use a story web with the title in a center circle and five circles radiating from the center circle. Each of the five circles corresponds to the five parts of the SPORE strategy. In each circle, students are to write a word or phrase as a cue to what they want to include in their stories. In the first circle, the students are to identify the *who, what, where,* and *when* of the setting. To elicit as much detail as possible for the setting, create a new graphic for each aspect. For example, to describe the characters in more detail, have the students list the characters, how they look, their special characteristics, and so forth. For the *where,* have students describe the places in detail (e.g., the neighborhood in the city in terms of the houses and people).

At the second step, the students are to identify the major problems they are going to present involving the *who, what, where,* and *when* described under the setting. Elicit as much detail as possible. If necessary, have the students create a new graphic for the problem so that it can be described more fully. The third step has the students write the order of action, whereas the fourth step presents the resolution to the problem. The last step presents the ending and wraps up with a resolution of the problem and a description of the various aspects of the setting. At this stage, students are to review all the graphics they have completed to evaluate whether they have provided enough detail, whether there is unnecessary information, and whether the ideas flow continuously. After they have completed these five steps, they are to write their papers. They are to construct sentences for each of the words and phrases in the circles and graphics.

SPORE:
TO HELP ME ORGANIZE IDEAS TO WRITE STORIES

Setting.
Problem.
Order of action.
Resolution.
End.

Use the SPORE strategy to help write stories, book summaries, or any other assignments that require you to create detailed descriptions of people and events. With this strategy, you will construct a story web. In the center of the web is a circle in which you write the title of the story, chapter, or book that you are reviewing. Then, you will draw five circles radiating from this center circle. Each of these five circles should contain one of the parts of the SPORE strategy. Fill in each circle with phrases or words. Do not use complete sentences. You will write complete sentences at a later time when you write your paper from this story web. The idea of the story web is to get all the information down in an organized manner so that you can expand on the information when you actually write your paper.

Setting.

- Write the title of the paper in the center circle.

- Draw a line from the center circle. Make a smaller circle and write the word *setting* in it.

- From this circle, draw lines to smaller circles where you list the *who* (people), *what* (animals, events), *where* (places), and *when* (times) in the story.

- Fill in as much detail as you will need to use when writing your paper.

Problem.

- Make another circle and write the word *problem* in it.

- Think of the major problems that will occur in the story.

- Analyze the *who, what, where,* and *when* in relation to the problem.

Order of action.

- Make another circle and write the words *order of action* in it. List all the events that you want to include in the story.
- Number these in the order in which they will happen.

Resolution.

- Make another circle and write the word *resolution* in it.
- Describe how the problem will be solved.

End.

- Make the last circle and write the word *end* in it.
- Identify how the story will be wrapped up. Describe what happens to the various characters.
- Review the story web and reread what you have written in each circle so that you can see if you have an organized story, if you have enough detail, and if there are no unrelated ideas.
- Now you are ready to write your paper. Write complete sentences for each of the words and phrases in each of the circles of your story web. As you write sentences, check off the items in the circle to make sure that you have included everything in your story.

WHAT ARE STRATEGIES FOR ORGANIZING IDEAS FOR RESEARCH PAPERS AND ESSAYS?

Secondary students with learning disabilities have many demands in their general education classes to write research papers, essays, and responses to essay test questions. They must know how to organize information to create expository text, which requires metacognitive abilities in planning, executing, and evaluating. The POWER strategy, which is a well-accepted strategy that was developed by Englert and her colleagues in 1991, is used to develop this ability.

With the POWER strategy, there are three stages: prewriting, writing, and postwriting. At the prewriting stage, the students plan and organize what they are to write; at the writing stage, they write based on their planning; and at the postwriting stage, they edit and revise. This three-stage process requires a reflective learning approach that many students with learning disabilities and ADHD do not like because they just want to get to the writing stage. They must learn that expository writing entails an involved process that must be followed if they are to produce effective products.

At the first stage of POWER, the students plan by getting a clear picture of what they need to do for the assignment. Then, they brainstorm ideas. In order to do this, they may have to gather information from various sources, such as the Internet and the library. If they have problems with gathering information, then they need to be taught the TB NAIL strategy, which is described later in this chapter. They record this information on note cards using phrases but do not use complete sentences at this stage. At the second stage, they organize the information from the previous stages. They can use an outline for this, or they can arrange the note cards that they used to record information for the planning stage. At the next stage, they write from the outline or the note cards. They convert the phrases into complete sentences. At the fourth stage, they edit what they have written for mechanics and content. If they have difficulty with editing for mechanics, then they should use the SCOPE strategy described previously in this chapter. If they have difficulty with editing for content, then they should use the FAST strategy described later in this chapter. At the final stage, they revise based on the editing that they did. It should be apparent that teaching this type of writing involves the integration of different subskills and strategies for each of the subskills.

POWER:
TO HELP ME ORGANIZE IDEAS
WHEN WRITING RESEARCH PAPERS AND ESSAYS

Plan.
Organize.
Write.
Edit.
Revise.

The POWER strategy has three stages. The first stage is a prewriting stage and includes the planning and organizing steps. The second stage is actually writing and includes the writing step. The third stage is the postwriting stage and includes the editing and revising steps.

Plan.

- First start with a clear topic. Be sure you know exactly what you want to write about.

- At this stage, you need to gather all the information that you will need for your paper.

- Brainstorm and list all of the ideas you know about this topic.
- Make a list of topics for which you need to get more information.
- Gather the information from different sources, such as the Internet and the library.
- Take notes on all of the information that you want to include in your paper. Write down as much information as possible so that you will not have to go back later and get more information. Do not write complete sentences; just write phrases representing the ideas.
- Be sure to write complete references for all the information that you gather so that they can be included in a bibliography.

Organize.

- Review notes of your ideas and your note cards.
- Organize these in an outline using the main ideas of your paper as the major headings.
- You can write each of these main ideas on large or different colored note cards.
- Arrange each of the note cards from the planning stage under each of the main idea cards.
- Arrange the note cards in order and number them.
- Go back and make an outline of major headings, subheadings, and details.

Write.

- Use your outline and note cards as guides for writing your paper.
- Write complete sentences for the phrases on the note cards.
- Do not pay attention to mistakes at this stage. Just make sure that you include all the ideas and that you state these clearly and in order.

Edit.

- Check all spelling, capitalization, punctuation, order of words, and grammar using the SCOPE strategy.
- Check whether your ideas are well-stated using the FAST strategy.
- It may be helpful to read your paper aloud as a way of checking for errors.

Revise.

- Based on your editing using SCOPE and FAST, revise your paper.
- Reread it one last time before turning it in.

WHAT ARE STRATEGIES FOR
WRITING INTRODUCTIONS AND CONCLUSIONS?

Some students with learning disabilities have difficulty with organizing information in an integrated manner. They can write narrative and expository papers, but their ideas are disjointed. They do not lay out a beginning or end, nor do they link paragraphs in a meaningful way. A major reason for this is lack of metacognitive skills in seeing the overall picture of the final product that they want to produce. The OSWALD strategy was created to assist students in writing in an organized manner and can be used for either narrative or expository writing.

In the first step of OSWALD, the students make an outline of the main ideas and details of what they want to write. In the second step, they say the parts of the outline and explain the relationship between the main ideas and the parts as well as each of the main ideas. In the third step, they write an introduction to the paper in which they present all the main ideas that will be covered in the paper. In the fourth step, they add connecting words and sentences to link the main ideas. They use these as topic sentences for each of their paragraphs. In the fifth step, they look at their paper to see if everything has been linked in terms of the introduction and the supporting paragraphs. At the final stage, they draft a conclusion. This should summarize the ideas that were presented and should tie in with the introduction.

OSWALD:
TO HELP ME WRITE INTRODUCTIONS AND CONCLUSIONS

Outline.
Say the outline aloud.
Write introduction.
Add connecting information.
Look over the connections.
Draft conclusion.

Outline.

- Make an outline of the major points and details that you want to include in your paper.

Say the outline aloud.

- Read the outline over so that you see the relationship between the ideas.
- As you read the outline, think of the main ideas that are most important for your paper.

Write introduction.

- Write a paragraph introducing your paper.
- Include the main ideas that you picked out when you read the outline aloud.

Add connecting ideas.

- As you write your paper, write sentences to connect the ideas from one paragraph to another.
- Think of words that help show the relationship between ideas (e.g., *therefore, after, before*).

Look over the connections.

- Reread your paper starting with the introduction. Make sure each of the paragraphs is connected to the introduction and to each other.

Draft conclusion.

- Based on your introduction and the ideas you presented in the body of your paper, write an ending that will wrap up all the ideas.

WHAT ARE STRATEGIES FOR FINDING INFORMATION WHEN WRITING PAPERS?

In order to write good papers, students must have a fund of knowledge and facts on which to base their writing. Some students with learning disabilities have difficulty finding information to use for writing. They do not know how to organize the background information that they have and use this as a basis for acquiring additional information.

The TB NAIL strategy is designed to help students find information when they write research papers and essays. The first step in this strategy has the students clearly identify the topic about which they are writing. Some students are unclear of the specific topic and only have a general understanding of what they want to write about. The next step has them brainstorm the information that they already have on the topic. The next step has them narrow their search by analyzing the information they brainstormed. They identify the areas in which they have no information and those areas in which they have incomplete information. Next, they ask themselves where they might get such information. They can consider their textbooks, notes, the Internet, the library, interviews, and other sources. Then, they investigate these different sources and get all the information possible. The last step has them look at all the information they have gathered and fit the facts into the paper they plan to write.

TB NAIL:
TO HELP ME FIND INFORMATION
TO WRITE RESEARCH PAPERS AND ESSAYS

Topic.
Brainstorm.
Narrow the search.
Ask yourself where to get information.
Investigate sources of information.
Look over all information.

Topic.

- Clearly identify the topic that you are to write about.

- If you are choosing a topic, then make sure that it is broad so that there is a lot of information available on it.

- If you are given a topic, then make sure that you understand it fully. If necessary, ask your teacher to explain it.

Brainstorm.

- Brainstorm what you already know about this topic.

- When you brainstorm, think about possible sources of information:
  - Class discussions
  - Readings

- Media (e.g., movies, television, radio)
- Research

Narrow your search.

- Analyze the information you brainstormed to narrow your search.
- Identify specific subtopics that you need to research from other sources.

Ask yourself where to get the information.

- Think of the types of sources you need to investigate to get the information.
  - Internet search engines
  - Library books
  - References (e.g., encyclopedias, public documents)
  - Interviews
  - Media (e.g., movies, radio, television)

Investigate sources of information.

- Gather information from these sources.
- Take notes and record references for use in a bibliography.

Look over the information.

- Review all the information you have gathered to make sure that you have enough information on all subtopics. Do this so that you can fully discuss the overall topic in your paper.
- If you need additional information, then return to your sources and gather more.
- If you have information that does not seem to be important, then keep it until you write your paper before discarding it.

WHAT ARE STRATEGIES FOR KEEPING TO THE TOPIC WHEN WRITING?

Many students with learning disabilities and ADHD have difficulty keeping to the topic. They are easily distracted by other topics that result in a disjointed paper with the main topic not being fully discussed and unimportant topics being included. The TREE strategy is designed to help students stay focused on the topic on which they are writing. There is another strategy with the title TREE that is used to help students plan and take notes about what to say in their essays (Harris & Graham, 1992), which should not be confused with the TREE strategy of the Active Learner Approach.

The first step in TREE has the students clearly identify the topic of the paper as well as each paragraph. For the topic of the paper, they use the title to clearly focus on the main idea of the paper. For paragraphs, they clearly identify a topic sentence. The second step has them react to each paragraph in terms of whether it relates to the main idea of the paper. The third step has them analyze each paragraph to make sure that each sentence in the paragraph is related to the topic sentence. The last step has them write a conclusion that integrates the main topics and the subtopics of the paragraphs.

TREE:
TO HELP ME STAY ON TOPIC WHEN WRITING

Topic identification.
React to each paragraph.
Examine each sentence.
End.

Topic identification.

- Clearly identify the topic of the paper you are writing. Make sure that your title clearly reflects this topic.

- If you are selecting a topic for a paper, then make sure that it is a topic that is wide enough to get information on and not too wide that there will be too much information.

- If you are given a topic on which to write, then make sure that you understand it. If not, ask the teacher to fully explain it.

React to each paragraph.

- Examine each paragraph of the paper in relation to the topic. Either do this as you write the paper, or do it after you have written the paper.

- Ask yourself why this paragraph is included in the paper and how the paper would be without this paragraph.

- If a paragraph does not seem to be related to the topic of the paper, then either drop it or change the content so it more closely matches the topic.

Examine each sentence in each paragraph.

- As you write each paragraph or after you have written a paragraph, read it and ask yourself if each sentence is related to the topic sentence of the paragraph.

- If a sentence does not seem to be related to the topic of the paragraph, then either drop it or try to change it so that it is related to the topic.

End.

- Write a concluding paragraph or read the one that you have already written, and ask yourself if it summarizes the main ideas of the paper or comes to a conclusion based on the information presented in the paper.

- Make sure that you do not introduce any information that has not been covered before.

- If the ending includes information that is not relevant, then drop it or change it to make it relevant.

WHAT ARE STRATEGIES FOR PROOFREADING FOR CLEAR PRESENTATION OF CONTENT?

Students with learning disabilities and ADHD find it difficult to proofread for content because they understand what they want to say but cannot put themselves into the role of the reader and evaluate whether their writing indeed says what they want to say. Proofreading for mechanics is easier because there are explicit rules that can be used to determine whether a word is spelled incorrectly or the wrong punctuation is used. Proofreading for content involves judgments that are based on whether something could be understood by someone else. This requires the students to take the cognitive perspective of potential readers of the paper being written. This is a rather nebulous criterion and difficult to explain to students.

The FAST strategy is designed to help students proofread for content. Other strategies, such as DEFENDS, which are often used for proofreading, encompass editing for both content and mechanics (Deshler, Ellis, & Lenz, 1996). With FAST, the students are taught to use the standards of whether they clearly presented their ideas and whether someone without their knowledge could understand the ideas that they presented in their papers. They are instructed to take the role of the reader and assume that the reader knows little of the content in the paper. Taking the role of the reader requires advanced metacognitive skills and may be difficult for many students with learning disabilities. They are to ask themselves whether the reader could understand the ideas in the paper using three criteria: keeping to the topic; organizing a beginning, middle, and end; and clearly using words and sentences to explain the meaning of the ideas in the paper. In the first step, the students are asked to proofread their paper to determine whether they stayed on topic. The second step has them analyze the organization of their paper to see if there is a beginning, middle, and end and if ideas are interrelated. The third step has them look at the words and sentences to see if they clearly represent the ideas intended by the writer. The last step has them reread for a last time and ask themselves, "Is this paper as clear as it could be?"

FAST:
TO HELP ME PROOFREAD TO SEE IF MY WRITING MAKES SENSE

Find the main ideas and topics.
Ask yourself if the paper is well-organized.
Scan each word and sentence.
Take the time to rewrite.

With this strategy, you are to read your paper four times, each time looking for a different way of evaluating whether the ideas are clearly presented. You are to read your paper from the perspective of a person who does not know anything about the topic you are writing about. You are to ask yourself if this person could understand the topic based on how you wrote your paper.

Find the main ideas and topics.

- First, read your title and ask if it clearly presents the topic of the paper.

- Then, read your paper and ask yourself if each paragraph is related to the topic and contributes to the overall meaning of the paper.

Ask yourself if the paper is well-organized.

- Read the paper to make sure that it has a clear beginning, middle, and end.

- Make sure that the ending is not underdeveloped. Sometimes, writers are eager to finish their papers as they get near the end, and they don't develop their ideas adequately at the conclusion.

Scan each word and sentence.

- Read your paper and ask yourself if each of the words and sentences clearly present the ideas you want.

Take the time to rewrite.

- If you find any words, sentences, or sections that would not be clear to the reader, then rewrite them.

- Reread your rewritten paper to make sure that it would be understandable to any reader.

BRAD, A STUDENT WITH WRITING DIFFICULTIES

Brad is a high school junior who is having difficulty writing research papers for his English and psychology classes. Brad has no problem with the mechanics of writing but does have difficulty with two areas of composition: organizing his ideas for writing research papers and essays and writing introductions and conclusions. When he writes research papers, he usually collects information and presents it in an unintegrated manner.

Brad plans to attend college and eventually become a lawyer. He realizes that he needs to improve his expository writing for school and career purposes and is motivated to learn strategies for this purpose.

Brad has selected capital punishment as the topic for a paper that he has to write for his English class. He and Ms. Bennett, his resource teacher, decide that the POWER strategy will help Brad organize his ideas to help write his paper. They also decide to use the OSWALD strategy to help Brad connect his ideas when he writes his paper.

Ms. Bennett models POWER and then guides Brad to use the strategy. At the writing stage of POWER, she introduces OSWALD to help him write in a more connected manner. Ms. Bennett gives Brad a lot of support in writing his paper. He receives an *A-* on it.

Later in the semester, Brad is required to write a research paper on child abuse for his psychology class. Ms. Bennett does not model POWER or OSWALD but has Brad attempt to use these independently. Brad is not ready to use these independently and needs assistance from Ms. Bennett, especially with writing introductions, connecting sentences, and conclusions. Brad receives a *B+* on this paper.

Brad's next assignment involves writing a persuasive paper for his English class. He selects legalizing cloning for all purposes as his topic. Brad is able to independently use POWER but continues to have difficulty writing introductions and conclusions. Ms. Bennett needs to give him a lot of support and guidance in writing these. Brad receives an *A* on this paper.

For the next semester, Brad will continue to work on using OSWALD to make his ideas more connected.

12

Mathematics

- Why do students with learning disabilities and ADHD need to learn mathematics skills?

- How do the learning characteristics of learning disabilities and ADHD impact learning mathematics?

- What are the different subskills of mathematics?

- What are some important ideas about teaching mathematics strategies using the Active Learner Approach?

- What are strategies for whole number and fraction computations?

- What are strategies for determining place value?

- What are strategies for determining greater than and less than?

- What are strategies for solving word/story problems involving addition, subtraction, multiplication, and division of whole numbers and fractions?

What are strategies for properties of rational numbers (commutative, associative, distributive)?

What are strategies for order of operations?

What are strategies for adding positive and negative integers?

What are strategies for determining square root?

What are strategies for one-variable algebra equations?

What are strategies for solving algebra word problems?

WHY DO STUDENTS WITH LEARNING DISABILITIES AND ADHD NEED TO LEARN MATHEMATICS SKILLS?

Although more emphasis has traditionally been placed on the reading difficulties students with learning disabilities and ADHD encounter, many students with learning disabilities and ADHD struggle with mathematics as well. There are three reasons students with learning disabilities and ADHD need to learn mathematics. First, mathematics is integral to many important *life skills*. Everyday life skills such as determining how much change one should receive when paying cash for a product or service, balancing a checkbook, determining how much a product actually costs when it is on sale for "25% off," and reading and appropriately paying credit card bills are examples of essential mathematics life skills. Without mathematics skills such as these, students will find it difficult to live independently.

Second, high-stakes testing at the secondary level, which includes advanced mathematics skills (i.e., algebra), has become the benchmark for obtaining a standard high school diploma. Therefore, students with learning disabilities and ADHD must have mastery of these skills if they hope to pass these tests and receive a standard diploma. Students with learning disabilities have difficulty passing such tests (Disability Rights Advocates, 2001) as well as the core courses on which these tests are based (i.e., algebra). Students who are able to pass testing competencies in other content areas may still be denied a standard diploma because they cannot pass one or more math competencies. Algebra is one such mathematics competency, and passing it is a common diploma requirement for most school districts in the United States of America. It is conceivable that students could pass all other diploma competencies and still be denied a standard diploma because they are unable to pass this single mathematics competency.

Third, mathematics is integral to success in other subject areas (i.e., physical sciences, economics, computer literacy). Students with significant mathematics deficiencies will find it difficult to learn these important subjects. Without an adequate knowledge of mathematics beyond a basic skill level, students will struggle to pass courses and standardized tests involving these subjects. Again, deficiency in mathematics can potentially result in students not receiving a high school diploma.

HOW DO THE LEARNING CHARACTERISTICS OF LEARNING DISABILITIES AND ADHD IMPACT LEARNING MATHEMATICS?

Although any of the learning characteristics discussed in Chapter 2 can negatively affect students' ability to learn mathematics, several characteristics that can be especially problematic are passive learning, memory problems, metacognitive deficits, and attention problems. *Passive learning* in mathematics is characterized by students who do not actively apply information they already know to new problem-solving situations. The multiplication process of repeated addition—an important foundational mathematics concept—is a good example. Students are presented with the basic multiplication fact 3 x 4. The students may be able to say the product with little difficulty. They also may understand that 3 x 4 means three groups of four. However, when presented with the multiplication fact 4 x 4 they may not be able to recall the product. Instead of using their prior knowledge of repeated addition (i.e., that 4 x 4 equals one more group of four), they become frustrated and give up because they cannot recall the correct fact. A secondary level example of how passive learning impacts learning mathematics can be found when working with variables or unknowns. At the elementary level, students learn to solve equations containing unknowns (e.g., $2 + 3 = a$; $2 + a = 5$). Although they may be able to manage these problems, students with learning disabilities and ADHD have difficulty actively using their prior knowledge of variables or unknowns (i.e., that the letter simply represents a value that completes the math statement) to solve more sophisticated algebra situations (e.g., $7a + 5a - 2 = 46$). Unfortunately, students will often either stare at the problem, as if somehow the solution will "jump" into their heads, or automatically raise their hand for help. Neither strategy is an effective one. Teaching students a math strategy that provides them with an efficient way to gain access to their prior knowledge of variables or unknowns allows them to actively apply this prior knowledge to new problem-solving situations.

Memory problems affect mathematics in a number of ways. Memory retrieval problems have a detrimental impact on learning mathematics because mathematics knowledge and skills build on each other as students move through school. Middle and high school students increasingly need to use previously learned mathematics concepts and skills to perform higher level mathematics. Without the ability to retrieve prior knowledge efficiently or accurately, these students are at a distinct disadvantage. For example, students early on learn that the "x" symbol means multiplication. Later, students learn that the "•" symbol also means multiplication. Eventually, students learn that a number next to a letter (e.g., 6a) means "six times *a*." Students continue to be confronted with additional number–symbol associations as they progress through the mathematics curriculum, such as 3/4, which could mean "three fourths" or "three divided by four." As students are confronted with such number–symbol relationships, which can have one or more meanings, memory retrieval problems can become a significant issue. Say, for example, a student is confronted with the problem $6a = 12$. As they retrieve from memory what $6a$ means, their memory retrieval process may actually "mistakenly" retrieve the meaning for another number–symbol relationship (e.g., $6/a$). The solution to the problem will be different and thus inaccurate ($a = .5$ versus $a = 2$).

Another possibility is that they simply do not have a retrievable association for what a number and a letter together represent. Perhaps they learned it at one time, but when they need it in the present, they cannot retrieve its meaning. Memory retrieval problems also impact mathematics success when students have difficulty retrieving from memory particular steps to a problem-solving procedure. For example, when solving the equation $4a + 3a + 8 = 36$, a student may fail to remember to combine like variables. This lapse in memory will result in either frustration because he will not be able to solve for a, or he will resort to a faulty procedure in order to isolate the variable (e.g., subtract $3a$ from both sides of the equation). In either of these situations, memory problems can make mathematics frustrating and difficult to master.

Metacognitive deficits have to do with a student's inability to apply appropriate strategies for math problem solving and evaluate the success of those strategies. When confronted with a mathematics equation or a problem-solving situation, students with learning disabilities and ADHD often do not systematically apply successful strategies for solving the equation or problem. Consider the following word problem that involves solving for an unknown or variable.

Carlos and Debbie each visited the local music store. Carlos likes hip-hop music and bought two CDs of his favorite singers. Debbie bought three R & B CDs that featured some of her favorite singers. All CDs cost the same amount. Together, they spent a total of $45.00 for their CDs. How much did each CD cost?

One potential strategy for solving this word problem involves the following steps:

1. Find what you are solving for (i.e., how much each CD cost).

2. Determine what information in the word problem will help you solve it (e.g., number of students who bought CDs, how many CDs each student bought, the total amount spent).

3. Set up an equation that incorporates the important information.

4. Solve the equation to determine the solution for the word problem.

5. Check the solution using the story problem.

Although the previous strategy, or something like it, might typically be used, students with learning disabilities and ADHD will not employ such a strategy. It is likely that they will guess a solution and move to the next word problem, use a strategy or procedure that is not appropriate for this type of word problem, or fail to even attempt an answer. The first two responses will likely result in inaccurate solutions because the student did not evaluate the success of the strategy that he used (e.g., by checking the reasonableness of his answer). The third response automatically results in an incorrect solution. Students with learning disabilities and ADHD do not use appropriate strategies and do not evaluate the success of the strategies they do use because of several factors, including their prior experiences with failure (learned helplessness), memory retrieval problems, and attention problems. Metacognitive deficits are especially problematic for middle- and secondary-level students because the nature of the mathematics content requires these students to be proficient at applying problem-solving strategies.

Attention problems can also have a significant effect on learning mathematics. For example, students may "miss" an important step in a multistep problem-solving procedure (e.g., long division, one-variable algebra equations, word problem solving) as it is being presented. As students try to use what they have previously learned, they will not be successful because they are using a faulty procedure. In addition, students may be distracted by various features of a mathematics equation (e.g., multiple operations signs and symbols, particular number patterns, the color of the print) or problem-solving situation (e.g., the context in which the "problem" is situated may include many distracting qualities—the color and texture of concrete materials, the "story" in which a word problem is set). Moreover, for mathematics equations or problems in which a solution requires a systematic procedure, students may not focus on the important cues that guide their use of an appropriate procedure. Consider the following fraction multiplication problem:

$$2/6 \times 4/7 = 8/42, \text{ or } 4/21$$

Students may not differentiate between the numerator and denominator (due to their inability to filter out all of the information they are receiving from their various sensory modes) as they multiply. They may inadvertently multiply numerator by denominator, thereby reaching an incorrect solution.

$$2/6 \times 4/7 = 14/24, \text{ or } 7/12$$

WHAT ARE THE DIFFERENT SUBSKILLS OF MATHEMATICS?

Although there is a wide array of important mathematics concepts and skills for sixth through twelfth grades, the primary emphases in this chapter are pre-algebra and beginning algebra. Unfortunately, research on instruction for students with learning disabilities and ADHD in other secondary-level mathematics content areas is limited. However, a foundation for teaching pre-algebra and algebra to students with learning disabilities and ADHD is provided in the literature and can be effectively applied using the Active Learner Approach.

The strategies and resources described in this chapter represent strategies that assist students to learn and effectively use pre-algebra and beginning algebra mathematics concepts/skills as well as several relevant foundational concepts/skills taught at the elementary level. The elementary-level skills included are relevant because these represent basic skills that secondary students must possess in order to be successful in secondary-level mathematics. Unfortunately, many secondary students with learning disabilities and ADHD lack proficiency in these skills. Instructional assistance for students with learning disabilities and ADHD in these mathematics areas is crucial because passing the algebra I competency is an imposing barrier for many of these students. Students with learning disabilities and ADHD are capable of learning mathematics and obtaining a standard diploma.

In this age of high-stakes testing and "accountability," schools are attempting a number of different strategies to assist students with passing algebra I (Rettig & Canady, 1998). Some schools and districts have "double blocked" their algebra I courses (2-hour classes compared with 1-hour classes). Others have made algebra I a 2-year course in which students take algebra I part 1 during the first year and then algebra I part 2 the second year. Although these delivery systems increase the amount of time students spend in class, they do not necessarily result in instructional changes that meet the learning needs of students with math learning problems. By equipping your students with the specific mathematics strategies they need based on the Active Learner Student Questionnaire in Appendix A and by teaching them these strategies using the Active Learner Approach, your students will have the mathematics foundation necessary for them to successfully manage an algebra I course.

The standards of the National Council of Teachers of Mathematics (NCTM) identify the knowledge and skills students must possess to be proficient in mathematics from pre-K through the twelfth grade (NCTM, 2000). A task analysis of two NCTM standards, *Number and Operations* and *Algebra,* reveals a set of essential skills students must have to successfully meet an algebra I competency. These skills can be divided into two areas: 1) knowledge and skills that are foundational to pre-algebra/algebra and 2) pre-algebra and beginning algebra knowledge and skills. These skills comprise both *procedural* (the process for solving a problem) and *conceptual* (what the mathematics concept and/or procedure represents) understanding. Teaching students *both* procedural and conceptual understanding is essential for mathematics success at the secondary level. The following are elementary mathematics skills that are foundational to success in pre-algebra and algebra:

- Basic whole number operations
  - Addition
  - Subtraction

- Multiplication
- Division
- Place value
  - Ones
  - Tens
  - Hundreds
- Comparing integers
  - Greater than
  - Less than
  - Equal to
- Operations involving fractions
  - Addition
  - Subtraction
  - Multiplication
  - Division
- Solving word/story problems that represent mathematical statements involving whole numbers and fractions
  - Addition
  - Subtraction
  - Multiplication
  - Division

The following skills represent pre-algebra and beginning algebra skills that are essential for success in algebra I:

- Understanding properties of rational numbers
  - Commutative
  - Associative
  - Distributive
- Order of operations
  - Involving four operations without parentheses and exponents
  - Involving four operations with parentheses and exponents
- Adding positive and negative integers
  - Adding a positive integer and a negative integer
  - Adding two negative integers

- Determining square roots
- Solving one-variable algebraic equations
  - $4n = 12$
  - Combining like terms (e.g., $4a + 2a = 24$)
  - Adding and subtracting integers, including fractions (e.g., $7c + 3c + 4 - 1 = 53$)
- Solving word/story problems representing algebraic situations
  - $4n = 12$
  - Combining like terms
  - Adding and subtracting integers, including fractions

Knowledge and Skills Foundational to Pre-Algebra/Algebra

With the Active Learner Approach, students are systematically taught strategies that emphasize both procedural and conceptual understanding for elementary level skills that represent the NCTM area of *Number and Operations*. Students with learning disabilities and ADHD often have significant gaps in their knowledge and skills for this important area. These knowledge and skill gaps negatively impact their ability to understand and perform pre-algebra and beginning algebra mathematics. This is one reason these students often have difficulty succeeding in an algebra I course. The following four foundational subskills of *Number and Operations* (and the corresponding Active Learner Student Questionnaire items found in Appendix A) are taught using the Active Learner Approach:

- Solving problems involving whole number operations and fractions: " I have difficulty calculating answers to problems with whole numbers or fractions (addition, subtraction, multiplication, division)."

- Determining place value: "I have difficulty deciding the place value of digits in a number (e.g., that the 7 in 33,700 means seven hundreds)."

- Determining greater than, less than, and equal to: "I have difficulty determining greater than, less than, and equal to when comparing numbers."

- Solving word/story problems (whole numbers and fractions): "I have difficulty solving word or story problems with whole numbers or fractions."

Pre-Algebra and Beginning Algebra Knowledge and Skills

When students possess strategies for successfully managing the foundational skills listed previously, then they are ready to manage basic pre-algebra and beginning algebra skills. The Active Learner Approach can be effectively used to teach strategies for the following six pre-algebra/beginning algebra subskills that represent both the NCTM areas of *Number and Operations* and *Algebra:*

- Recognizing the commutative, associative, and distributive properties: "I have difficulty using the commutative property, $25 + 49 = 49 + 25$, to help me calculate or solve problems." "I have difficulty using the associative property, $(2 \times 45) \times 12 = 2 \times (45 \times 12)$, to help me calculate or solve problems." "I have difficulty using the distributive property, $8(7 + 6) = 8 \times 7 + 8 \times 6$, to help me calculate or solve problems."

- Order of operations: "I have difficulty solving problems using order of operations (e.g., problems that have more than one operations sign: $3 + 5 \times 6 - 2 \div 5$)."

- Adding positive and negative integers: "I have difficulty adding positive and negative numbers."

- Square roots: "I have difficulty determining square roots of numbers."

- Solving one-variable equations: "I have difficulty solving one-variable algebra equations."

- Solving word/story problems that represent one-variable algebra situations: "I have difficulty solving algebra word or story problems."

WHAT ARE SOME IMPORTANT IDEAS FOR TEACHING THE MATHEMATICS STRATEGIES USING THE ACTIVE LEARNER APPROACH?

Teach Both Procedural and Conceptual Understanding

Most important, an emphasis must be placed on both procedural and conceptual understanding. One type of understanding without the other will make success at the secondary level unlikely. The strategies described in this chapter, when taught using the Active Learner Approach, provide students with the steps for solving particular problems (procedure) and the cognitive (thinking) practice to understand the concept represented by the strategy steps (conceptual understanding).

Teach Using a Concrete-to-Representational-to-Abstract (C-R-A) Sequence of Instruction

Teaching mathematics from a concrete (using hands-on materials) to representational (drawing simple pictures that represent the concrete materials and your movement of them) to abstract (using numbers and mathematics symbols only) level of instruction greatly enhances students' conceptual understanding of mathematics. It also provides students with important kinesthetic (movement) and tactile (touch) experiences that help make the problem-solving steps more memorable due to the motor-memory feedback that can occur. At the *concrete level,* the use of simple objects such as plates, counting chips, cups, and so forth can provide students multisensory learning experiences that make the mathematics concepts accessible. Because of the learning needs of students with learning disabilities and ADHD, they are more likely to understand the mathematics concept when they can see it, hear it, touch it, and move it. Concrete level instruction allows this important learning experience to occur.

At the *representational level* (drawing), students are taught to draw solutions to mathematics problems based on their concrete experiences and understanding. Simple pictures such as tallies, dots, and circles can be drawn and manipulated so that students can solve problems without concrete materials. By drawing solutions, students are provided with three important learning tools. One, they are able to extend their concrete understanding to a level of understanding that is more abstract but not so abstract as to be nonmeaningful. Second, drawing solutions is an excellent general problem-solving strategy that can be generalized to other problem-solving situations. Third, they always have a strategy to use if at the abstract level they get "stuck." They can continue to problem solve independently without asking the teacher for help.

Once students have a solid concrete and representational understanding, then they are ready to extend this understanding to the *abstract level* in which they use only numbers and symbols. At this level of understanding, they internalize what they understand from their concrete and drawing experiences into their thinking processes and begin to solve problems, as we like to say, "in their heads." Most of the strategies described in this chapter can be used for at least two and sometimes all three levels of understanding. The descriptions for each strategy will provide guidance regarding which levels of understanding the strategy is appropriate for.

Explicitly Relate Computation Skills to Meaningful Contexts

Teaching mathematics through a C-R-A sequence of instruction will greatly enhance your students' conceptual understanding of mathematics. However, just how meaningful mathematics is to your students also depends on the degree to which mathematics skills are learned within contexts that are meaningful to them. Whether you are teaching mathematics strategies at a concrete, representational, or abstract level of understanding, always teach them within meaningful contexts. One way to do this is through simple word/story problems that include contexts matching your students' interests and experiences. Including the actual names of your students in word/story problems is also helpful. Remember, though, that due to possible reading problems, students with learning disabilities and ADHD need explicit instruction in actually solving word/story problems (see both FASTDRAW strategies later in this chapter). At times, it may be your goal to teach word/story problem-solving strategies, whereas at other times you may simply want to use word/story problems to show the relevance of a particular computational procedure. Both uses of word/story problems are helpful for students with learning disabilities and ADHD. The next time you find yourself teaching your students a particular mathematics skill or concept, ask yourself whether you provided them with an appropriate context for making the mathematics skill/concept meaningful. Doing so will pay great dividends for your students.

Provide Both Receptive and Expressive Practice Opportunities

Another helpful mathematics learning experience for students with learning disabilities and ADHD occurs during student practice. Providing students with multiple chances to practice the mathematics knowledge/skills they acquired during teacher instruction is a powerful teaching strategy (Vaughn, Gersten, & Chard, 2000). *How* this practice occurs can also be important. Sometimes students first need practice recognizing examples of mathematics concepts and procedures before they are ready to express the concepts and procedures themselves. Therefore, it can be helpful to some students if you separate practice into two stages. At the *receptive stage* of practice, students are presented with a problem or prompt and are asked to determine which of the choices provided is the solution. Or, they can be asked to determine which choice is representative of the learned mathematics concept. Students then can use language to describe why a particular choice is or is not the solution. This can be a valuable learning experience for both you and the student. The student has the chance to use her language and higher order thinking skills to describe why her choice is best, and you get excellent insight regarding what the student actually has learned.

At the *expressive stage* of practice, students solve problems themselves or they can develop examples of a learned mathematics concept (e.g., write word problems or draw pictures that represent a particular algebra equation). The expressive stage of practice is the most typical one, but sometimes students with learning disabilities and ADHD require receptive level practice before expressive level practice. This makes sense if we remember that learning does occur in stages and that students with learning problems often need different types of instruction to help make important transitions between learning stages. Because students are both solidifying conceptual understanding as well as building proficiency with practice, it is important that you provide them with the necessary experiences and instruction that make true learning occur.

Provide Students with Periodic Maintenance Opportunities for Knowledge and Skills They Have Previously Mastered

A last important consideration for teaching mathematics strategies using the Active Learner Approach is that previously learned strategies should be periodically revisited through the use of maintenance activities. Maintenance activities simply provide students opportunities to "revisit" mathematics strategies for which they have previously become proficient. Because many students with learning disabilities and ADHD have memory difficulties, periodic review and use of previously learned mathematics strategies is vital. Math maintenance activities do not have to be long and involved. If planned, they can take as little as 5 minutes of class time. A good example is "Problem of the Day." At a particular time during class, you present students with a prompt that requires them to use all or part of a previously learned strategy. Students can work independently or in small groups to respond. After a few minutes, solicit responses from your students and provide appropriate feedback. For example, you could write a word problem on the board and then write FAST from the FASTDRAW strategy (discussed later in this chapter) beside it. Include each step and circle the A step. Students can be asked to describe how to perform the step and then perform it using the word problem. Daily maintenance activities can greatly enhance students' memory of previously learned strategies as well as help them strengthen their understanding of the mathematical concepts they represent.

Final Thoughts About Teaching Mathematics Strategies Using the Active Learner Approach

Above all, remember to always emphasize the procedure outlined by the strategy *and* the concept that the mathematics strategy represents. With both procedural and conceptual understanding, it is more likely that students with learning disabilities and ADHD will be able to independently problem solve when either their procedural or conceptual understanding is "blocked" due to the learning characteristics they possess (e.g., memory problems). Teaching mathematics strategies using the Active Learner Approach and incorporating the additional instructional ideas described previously will help you effectively teach the mathematics strategies to your students with learning disabilities and ADHD.

MATHEMATICS STRATEGIES

The following strategies represent essential foundational mathematics skills, pre-algebra skills, and beginning algebra skills. Although certainly not exhaustive, the skills represented will provide your students with a solid foundation for success in an algebra I course. The strategies are organized into two sections: 1) strategies that have to do with elementary-level concepts/skills foundational to pre-algebra/algebra success (concepts/skills that many secondary-level students with learning disabilities and ADHD continue to struggle with) and 2) strategies that have to do with specific pre-algebra and beginning algebra concepts/skills. Table 12.1 summarizes these mathematics concepts/skills and their corresponding strategies.

STRATEGIES FOR FOUNDATIONAL MATHEMATICS CONCEPTS/SKILLS

What Are Strategies for Whole Number and Fraction Computations?

Many middle and high school students with learning disabilities and ADHD demonstrate difficulty with basic whole number and fraction computation. Their difficulties are the result of any one or a combination of learning problems. Memory retrieval problems make it difficult for some students to efficiently retrieve facts. This situation affects computation fluency because the ability to recall facts quickly and accurately greatly impacts the timeliness and

Table 12.1. Mathematics skills and corresponding strategies

Mathematics skill	Corresponding strategy
Foundational skills	
Whole number computation	DRAW FOR BASIC MATH
Place value	FIND
Greater than/less than	SPIES
Fraction computation	DRAW FOR BASIC MATH
Word problems (whole number and fractions)	FASTDRAW FOR BASIC MATH
Pre-algebra/beginning algebra skills	
Properties of rational numbers	COMAS, ASSOC, DIST
Order of operations	ORDER
Adding positive and negative integers	ADD
Square root	ROOT-IT
One-variable algebra equations	DRAW FOR ALGEBRA
Algebra word problems	FASTDRAW FOR ALGEBRA

accuracy of doing whole number computations. In addition, memory problems can make recalling particular procedural steps difficult. For example, missing the multiplication step in the long division process (divide, multiply, subtract, bring down) will result in inaccurate solutions. Difficulties with whole number and fraction computation can also be the result of a lack of conceptual understanding of the addition, subtraction, multiplication, and division processes. Without this understanding, it is difficult for students to estimate solutions and, therefore, have a basis for evaluating answers to computation problems. The following strategies provide students with memorable procedures for completing whole number and fraction computations as well as practice for the thinking processes that underlie each operation.

The DRAW FOR BASIC MATH strategy (Mercer & Mercer, 2001) provides students with a strategy for solving addition, subtraction, multiplication, and division problems at the representational level (by drawing) or at the abstract level ("in" students' "heads"). Examples for drawing solutions (Step A) for each computation process are provided in Figure 12.1. Students who do not need to draw the solution can bypass the drawing process and move directly to writing the answer. The DRAW FOR BASIC MATH strategy can also be taught at the concrete level of instruction. An excellent teaching technique at the concrete level of instruction is to replicate the steps of DRAW FOR BASIC MATH as you demonstrate and model the addition, subtraction, multiplication, and division processes. You can do this indirectly or directly. Simply use suitable concrete materials (e.g., plates for circles and counting chips for tallies) as you replicate Step A of the DRAW FOR BASIC MATH strategy.

Example: Addition

WHOLE NUMBERS   **FRACTIONS**

8 |||||||| 1/4
+3 ||| +2/4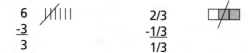
11   3/4

Example: Subtraction

6 |||||| 2/3
-3   -1/3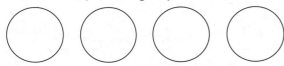
3   1/3

Example: Multiplication

4 x 5 = ___ – "four groups of five equals…"

1. Student represents groups with circles.

2. Student represents objects within groups with tallies.

3. Student totals tallies and writes answer.

4 x 5 = 20 – "four groups of five equals twenty"

Example: Division

24 ÷ 4 = ___

1. Student draws tallies to represent dividend ("24").

2. Student circles tallies by the value of the divisor ("4").

3. Student counts number of circles that represent the quotient ("6").

24 ÷ 4 = 6

Figure 12.1.   Examples for drawing solutions for each computation process.

DRAW FOR BASIC MATH[1]:
TO HELP ME CALCULATE ANSWERS TO PROBLEMS
WITH WHOLE NUMBERS AND FRACTIONS (+, −, x, ÷)

Discover the sign.
Read the problem.
Answer, or draw and check.
Write the answer.

Discover the sign.

- Scan the problem and find the operation sign (+, −, x, ÷).
- Circle and say the name of the operation sign.
- Say what the sign means.

Read the problem.

- Read the whole problem.
- Say the problem aloud as you read it.

Answer, or draw tallies and/or circles and check your answer.

- Answer the problem if you know how to solve it.
- If you don't know how to solve the problem, then draw pictures to solve it.
- Check your answer.

Write the answer.

- Write down the answer to the problem.

A helpful visual cueing strategy for long division that can be used in conjunction with DRAW FOR BASIC MATH is the face (with goatee or beard) strat-

[1]From TEACHING STUDENTS WITH LEARNING PROBLEMS: 5/E by Mercer/Mercer, © 2001. Reprinted by permission of Pearson Education, Inc., Upper Saddle River, NJ.

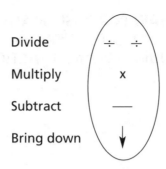

Divide

Multiply

Subtract

Bring down

Figure 12.2.   The face strategy. (*Source:* Mercer & Mercer, 2001.)

egy (Mercer & Mercer, 2001; see Figure 12.2). This picture provides students with a visual cue for solving long division problems. Each feature of the face is represented by an appropriate symbol. As a student moves from top to bottom, the appropriate procedure for solving long division problems is represented. The "eyes" represent *divide,* the "nose" represents *multiply,* the "mouth" represents" *subtract,* and the "goatee" or "beard" represents *bring down* (Students may find either *goatee* or *beard* more meaningful depending on their own experiences. Whichever term is most meaningful is the term that should be used). Students can be provided with cue sheets with the visual cue already drawn (with accompanying words that identify each step), or students can be taught to draw the face on their own papers. As students solve long division problems, they simply look at or visualize the face and perform each procedure as appropriate.

What are Strategies for Determining Place Value?

Place value is an essential mathematics concept and often is misunderstood or not understood by students with learning disabilities and ADHD. Nonunderstanding of place value is a primary cause for later problems with a variety of mathematics concepts and skills (e.g., computation involving regrouping, decimals). A student's ability to complete procedural processes that involve place value (i.e., regrouping) does not guarantee that they really understand place value. For example, a student may be able to accurately regroup when subtracting two multidigit numbers:

$$
\begin{array}{r}
4\ 12\ 1 \\
5\ 3\ 1 \\
-\ 3\ 9\ 2 \\
\hline
1\ 3\ 9
\end{array}
$$

However, if asked to estimate the difference of the numbers without working the problem procedurally, then they may be unable to do so. For example, they may base their estimation on the hundreds place only.

To estimate efficiently, students need to have a solid concept of place value. Estimation is an essential problem-solving skill because it provides students with a reliable way to determine whether their solution to a given problem is reasonable. As you have probably already experienced, students with learning disabilities and ADHD often do not check their solutions once they have performed the relevant mathematical procedure. One reason for this is that they are unable to estimate the reasonableness of their answer; therefore, they do not recognize when their solution is obviously incorrect. A solid understanding of place value will greatly help your students become better estimators and it will assist them to better grasp later mathematical concepts such as decimals and working with positive and negative integers.

The FIND strategy helps students determine the place value of digits in numbers representing 10 or greater (Mercer & Mercer, 2001). Although FIND is especially helpful at the abstract level of understanding, it also can be taught as students learn place value at the concrete and representational levels of understanding. Teaching the FIND strategy from a C-R-A sequence of instruction will help students develop a firm understanding of place value. The FIND strategy can be taught using concrete materials by using a place value mat and base-10 materials to represent the value of each digit in a multidigit number (see the concrete level example in Figure 12.3 for an illustration). Encouraging students to verbalize the values of each digit can be a very effective way to enhance understanding.

Once students demonstrate mastery at the concrete level, they can be taught to draw the place value of digits (representational level). Students can be taught to draw a place value mat and then represent the value of each digit by drawing simple symbols using tallies or dots (see the representational level example in Figure 12.3 for an illustration). Again, students should verbalize the values of each digit represented by their drawings. Last, students can determine place value at the abstract level of understanding by simply inserting a "t" between digits and naming the value of each column (see the abstract level example in Figure 12.3 for an illustration). Abbreviations can be used as students name place values (e.g., "O" for ones, "T" for tens). Students should continue to verbalize values of each digit at this stage. By inserting a "t" between digits, the student creates the columns of a simple place value mat. Students then name the place value of each object by writing it above each column. You will find that the wording of the FIND strategy represents its use at the abstract level of understanding. There are slight variations among steps of the FIND strategy for each level of understanding—concrete, representational, and abstract. This is necessary due to the different mediums used at each level of understanding (i.e., tangible materials, drawings, numbers, symbols). These variations are highlighted in italics in Figure 12.3.

Concrete example

Find the columns (between the numerals). *Write the digits above the appropriate columns of the place value mat.*

Insert the "t's." *(Students run their fingers along each "t" created by the lines that demarcate the place value columns.)*

Name the columns. *(Write the letter/word that represents the place value above each digit.)*

Determine the place value of individual digits. *(Represent each digit using the appropriate base-10 materials, count the value, and say the value for each digit.)*

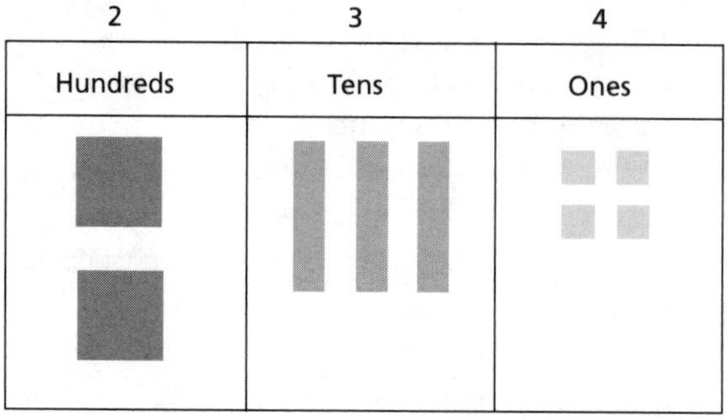

Representational level

Find the columns (between the numerals). *Students point to each "space" between each digit.*

Insert the "t's." *Students draw columns of the place value mat beneath each digit (if students are drawing their own place value mats); or, students run fingers along each "t" created by the lines that demarcate the place value columns (if students are provided with place value mats already drawn).*

Name the columns. *(Write the letter that represents the place value above each digit.)*

Determine the place value of individual digits. *(Represent each digit drawing representions for the value of each digit.)*

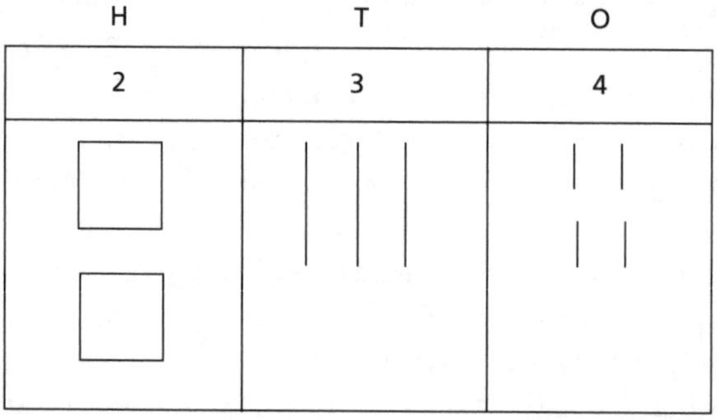

Abstract example

Find the columns (between the numerals).

Insert the "t's."

Name the columns (by place value).

Determine the place value of individual digits.

$$234 \longrightarrow \begin{array}{c|c|c} H & T & O \\ \hline 2 & 3 & 4 \end{array}$$

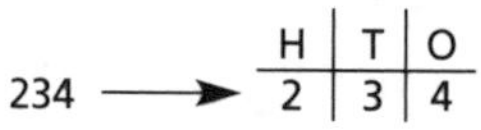

"2 hundreds, 3 tens, and 4 ones"

Figure 12.3. Teaching the FIND strategy at the C-R-A levels of understanding.

FIND[2]:
TO HELP ME DETERMINE
PLACE VALUE OF DIGITS IN MULTIDIGIT NUMBERS

Find the columns.
Insert the "t's."
Name the columns (by place value).
Determine the place value of individual digits.

Find the columns (between the numerals).

- Look for the spaces between each digit.

- Look for a decimal (underline or circle with decimal).

- For example, 3 4, 7 8 3 ⸳ 2 9

Insert the "t's."

- Write a "t" in the spaces between each digit.

- For example,

| 3 | 4, | 7 | 8 | 3⸳ | 2 | 9 |

Name the columns (by place value).

- Start with the last digit and write the place value above the digit.

- Remember to LOOK for a decimal point!

- Digits to the right of the decimal point (⸳→) are fractional parts of a whole number (tenths, hundredths, thousandths).

- Move to the next digit and write the place value above the digit.

- Continue until there are no digits remaining.

---

[2]From TEACHING STUDENTS WITH LEARNING PROBLEMS: 5/E by Mercer/Mercer, © 2001. Reprinted by permission of Pearson Education, Inc., Upper Saddle River, NJ.

- For example,

Ten Thousands	Thousands	Hundreds	Tens	Ones	Tenths	Hundredths
3	4,	7	8	3.	2	9

←—————————————————————————————— *START

Determine the place value of individual numbers.

- Select the digit and say its value.
- For example, "The digit 9 is in the hundredths place; therefore, its value is nine-hundredths."

What Are Strategies for Determining Greater Than and Less Than?

Students with learning disabilities and ADHD often have difficulty comparing the relative values of integers because they do not relate the value of abstract symbols to the concrete experiences that give the abstract symbols meaning. For example, when presented with a negative integer and a positive integer such as –24 and 3, students may choose –24 as the integer of greatest value. They do this because the abstract symbol – has little or no meaning for them. They see the number 24 and automatically believe it is greater than the number 3.

Students with learning disabilities and ADHD may also have difficulty with this skill because they do not attend to the relevant cues. Staying with the previous example, the student may not actually process that there is a – symbol in front of the number 24. They simply believe they are comparing 24 and 3. Students can benefit from instruction that provides them a C-R-A sequence of learning as well as a strategy that cues them to important cues for determining greater than and less than.

The SPIES strategy (Allsopp, 2001) provides a process for recognizing important cues using multiple senses and can be taught at the concrete, repre-

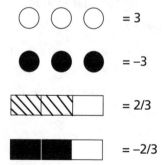

Figure 12.4. Comparing positive and negative integers.

Table 12.2. Teaching tips for using the alligator/shark picture cue

Cut out pictures of an alligator, shark, or other memorable character whose jaws or mouth open wide.

Paste two pictures together.

Initially use alligators or sharks to teach identifying greater than/less than (tell students that the alligator or shark has to open its mouth wider for the integer that has the greatest value).

Students use pictures to identify the larger integer.

Teach association of "<" and ">" to pictures.

Fade pictures to use of symbols only.

Encourage students to think of pictures when using "<" and ">."

Provide the pictures as cues for students who need them periodically.

sentational, and abstract levels of understanding. The first two steps provide auditory and kinesthetic (movement) ways to recognize cues that will help students determine each integer's value. The I step reminds students to determine whether integers are positive or negative based on what students have done during the first two steps. The E step prompts students to use their thinking skills to evaluate the actual value of each integer, whereas the S step cues students to select the integer of greatest value based on the decision they have made.

When initially teaching this strategy at the concrete level of understanding, you can model the E step by using concrete materials as you (and your students) evaluate the value of the integers being compared (e.g., counting objects, base-10 materials, fraction circles). Color coding concrete materials so that light colors depict positive integers and dark colors depict negative integers can be a helpful cue when comparing positive and negative integers (see Figure 12.4). At the representational level, students can draw simple pictures that represent the values of integers (e.g., circles for whole integers, boxes with shaded areas to represent fractions). Drawings can be shaded dark to depict negative integers. Drawings that depict positive integers can be left unshaded. Two additional cueing mechanisms can be used with the SPIES strategy and can be helpful at the abstract level. The alligator/shark picture cue (see Table 12.2) can be used during the last step, "Select the integer of greatest value." The picture will help some students attach meaning to the abstract symbols used for greater than and less than (i.e., $<$, $>$). The whole number greater than/less than number line visual cue and the fraction greater than/less than number line visual cue, shown in Figure 12.5, can also be used during the last step. Students can refer to the cues as they evaluate the relative values of the integers they are comparing. Students can find where each integer resides on the number line and then use the greater than or *jaws* symbol to determine which integer is greater (the integer that resides at a point where the jaws are wider is the integer of greatest value). Number lines can be modified to match the particular integers students are working with. A number line that depicts both whole numbers and fractions could also be used when students are working with both types of integers (see Figure 12.5).

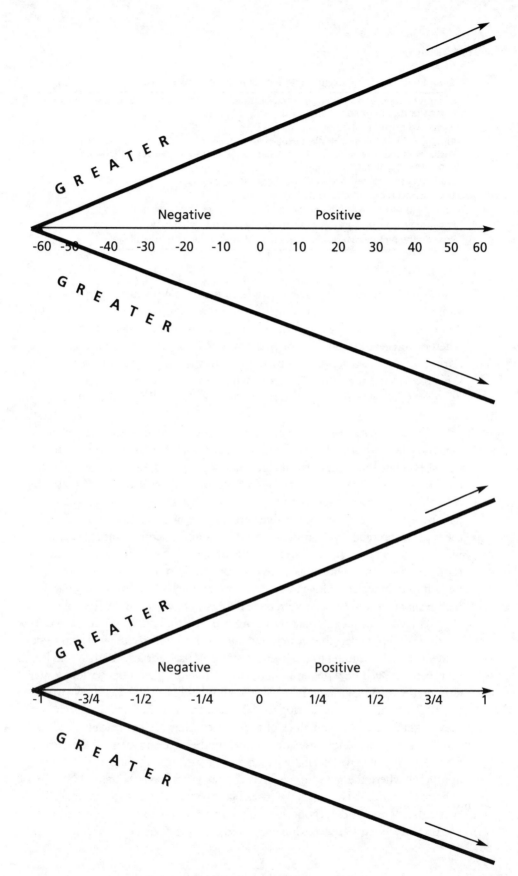

Figure 12.5. Whole number and fraction greater/less than number line visual cues.

SPIES:
TO HELP ME DETERMINE WHICH NUMBER IS GREATER THAN, LESS THAN, OR EQUAL TO WHEN COMPARING NUMBERS

Say each integer aloud.
Point to each integer and circle negative signs.
Identify whether integer is positive or negative.
Evaluate the magnitude of each integer.
Select integer of greatest value.

Say each integer aloud or to yourself.

Point to each integer and look for *negative* signs.

- Check for and circle negative integers by looking for the – symbol.

For example:

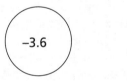

–3.6   2.5

- Integers that are positive will likely not have a sign.

Identify whether each integer is positive or negative.

Estimate the value of each integer using the rules of value.

Rules of value

- Rule 1 (positive number and negative number): Positive integer is always greater in value.

- Rule 2 (all positive numbers): Integer that is farther from zero on a number line is of greater value.

- Rule 3 (all negative numbers): Integer closest to zero on a number line is of greater value.

Select integer of greatest value.

- Use alligator/shark picture cue (Bernard, 1990). Think of < and > signs as the mouth of an alligator or shark—it has to open its mouth wider for the "bigger" integer.

What Are Strategies for Solving Word/Story Problems Involving Addition, Subtraction, Multiplication, and Division of Whole Numbers and Fractions?

Solving word/story problems can be a difficult task for students with learning disabilities and ADHD who may have reading problems or lack mathematical understanding. Reading skills deficits in areas such as decoding, fluency, vocabulary, and reading comprehension make word/story problem solving difficult because students have great difficulty comprehending the text. Understanding text is an essential component for solving word/story problems. In particular, students must be able to understand the context within which the problem to be solved is set. Without understanding the context of the word/story problem, it is hard for students to derive any meaning.

Mathematical understanding is also important. Students must be able to make mathematical sense from the words they read. To do this, students must cognitively process important "mathematical" cues revealed in the text (e.g., keywords—How many *altogether?* How many are *left?*; questions that reveal what is to be solved; number statements). These textual cues help students make "mathematical sense" of the text. Once students know what mathematical process is needed for solving the problem, they must be able to carry out the correct procedure to solve it. If a word/story problem calls for multiplication of fractions, then students must know how to multiply using fractions. If a word/story problem calls for long division, then students must know how to divide.

The FASTDRAW FOR BASIC MATH strategy provides students with a process for gaining meaning from the text as well as providing guidance for completing the mathematical procedure needed for solving the problem (Mercer & Mercer, 2001). FAST provides students with a strategy for finding the important information in a word/story problem and setting up an equation. DRAW FOR BASIC MATH can be used to solve the equation.

The F step, "Find what you are solving for," reminds students to look for cues in the text that signal, "This is the problem to be solved." For example, you can teach your students to look for the question mark. Once they've found the statement or statements that signify the problem to be solved, then they can underline it. Students can be taught important keywords that signal particular operations (e.g., *altogether* = addition or multiplication; *left* = subtraction). These keywords can be highlighted (e.g., underlined twice) as they appear in the underlined sentence.

The A step, "Ask yourself what is the important information," reminds students to read the text carefully, looking for important cue words (e.g., number phrases—*12 CDs; three fourths of a pizza*). A helpful technique to teach students is to read each sentence and ask themselves, "Is there a number phrase?" Then, they can circle any important information.

The S step, "Set up the equation," reminds students to set up an equation that allows them to solve the problem (underlined sentence). Students can be taught to look back at the underlined sentence to remind themselves what they are solving. Then, they take the important information they circled during step A and place the appropriate numbers and symbols below the word/story problem. Based on the problem they need to solve (determined by the underlined sentence), students use their mathematical understanding to place numbers in appropriate positions (e.g., for addition or multiplication, numbers can be placed in any order: $13 + 4 + 3 =$; $13 \times 4 \times 3 =$; for subtraction or division, numbers must be placed so that the minuend or dividend is written first: $55 - 5$; $55 \div 5$).

The T step, "Tie down the sign," reminds students to check to be sure they are using the correct operation in the equation that they have set up. They can be taught to go back to the underlined sentence in the word/story problem and check for any keywords that they have highlighted. This also is an excellent step to provide students practice explaining (orally, in writing, or by drawing pictures) the operation/process they will use and why. Practicing helps students solidify their mathematical understanding. By completing the steps of FAST, students have a systematic framework for comprehending *and* making mathematical sense of the word/story problem. The following example illustrates how to implement each step of FAST.

Sam and Maria went to the music store to buy some of their favorite CDs.

Sam has (**3 CDs**) and Maria has (**4 CDs.**)

<u>How many CDs do they have altogether?</u>

1. Find what your are solving for: <u>student underlines the question</u>.

2. Ask yourself, what is the important information: student finds and circles the (number phrases)

3. Set up the equation: student sets up equation: 3 CDs __ 4 CDs =

4. Tie down the sign: 3 CDs + 4 CDs =

*When the equation is set up, the student uses DRAW FOR BASIC MATH to find the solution.

Once students have set up the appropriate equation, they can solve it to determine the solution to the word/story problem. If students have difficulty solving the equation, then they can use DRAW FOR BASIC MATH to solve it (see previous description of the strategy). DRAW FOR BASIC MATH provides students with a systematic process for solving basic equations involving the four operations ($+$, $-$, $\times$, $\div$) using whole numbers and fractions.

FASTDRAW FOR BASIC MATH[3]:
TO HELP ME SOLVE WORD/STORY
PROBLEMS USING THE FOUR OPERATIONS (+, −, x, ÷)

Find what you are solving for.
Ask yourself, what is the important information.
Set up the equation.
Tie down the sign.
Discover the sign.
Read the problem.
Answer, or draw and check.
Write the answer.

Find what you are solving for.

- Look for the question mark.

- Underline the information that tells you what you are solving for.

- Underline keywords twice.

Ask yourself what is the important information.

- Read each sentence.

- Find number phrases and circle them.

Set up the equation.

- Write the equation with the numbers in the correct order.

---

[3]From TEACHING STUDENTS WITH LEARNING PROBLEMS: 5/E by Mercer/Mercer, © 2001. Reprinted by permission of Pearson Education, Inc., Upper Saddle River, NJ.

Tie down the sign.

- Reread the underlined sentence.
- Check highlighted keywords and operation signs.
- Say aloud the operation sign and what it means (e.g., addition means I have to combine the numbers).
- Solve the problem if you can, or draw pictures to solve it using DRAW.

Discover the sign.

- Scan the problem and find the operation sign (+, −, x, ÷).
- Circle and say the name of the operation sign.
- Say what the sign means.

Read the problem.

- Read the whole problem.
- Say the problem aloud as you read it.

Answer, or draw tallies and/or circles and check your answer.

- Answer the problem if you know how to solve it.
- If you don't know how the solve the problem, then draw pictures to solve it.
- Check your answer.

Write the answer.

- Write down the answer to the problem.

STRATEGIES FOR PRE-ALGEBRA AND BEGINNING ALGEBRA CONCEPTS/SKILLS

What Are Strategies for Properties of Rational Numbers (Commutative, Associative, Distributive)?

Students with learning disabilities and ADHD often experience difficulties recognizing situations that represent various properties of rational numbers. Some students do not possess a solid understanding of number and number sense, and/or they don't conceptually understand the processes of addition, subtraction, multiplication, and division. These students need appropriate instruction that provides them with the conceptual understanding necessary to understand properties of rational numbers.

Other students have difficulty with this skill because they don't attend to cues that identify the properties. For students with learning disabilities and ADHD to be successful at working with properties of rational numbers, they need conceptual understanding (number sense of the four operations) and the ability to identify mathematical patterns that are unique to each property. The COMAS, ASSOC, and DIST strategies provide students with a systematic process for identifying important cues that help them determine the property that a particular mathematical statement represents. Each strategy incorporates several letters that are in the name of the property. Each letter represents a particular characteristic that is common to the mathematical property. Students use each step to successively check for characteristics of that property. If the mathematical statement/equation has all characteristics represented in the steps of the strategy, then the mathematical statement/equation represents the property that corresponds with the strategy.

Although the strategies are primarily written to help students identify mathematical statements already written, the strategies also can be used to guide students to write mathematical statements that represent each property. Teach students to use the steps of each strategy as cues for writing number statements that represent a particular property.

COMAS:
TO HELP ME USE THE COMMUTATIVE
PROPERTY TO CALCULATE OR SOLVE PROBLEMS

Common numbers or letters and operation sign.
Opposite position.
Mirror image.
Addition or multiplication?
Same total.

Common numbers or letters and common operation sign.

- Each side of the equation has the same numbers and operation signs.

$$2 + 3 = 3 + 2$$

  - Both sides have the number 2
  - Both sides have the number 3
  - Both sides have a + sign

Opposite position.

- The position of the numbers or letters on one side are in the opposite position on the other side.

$$2 + 3 = 3 + 2$$

  - The 2 is the first number on left side but is the second number on the right side.
  - The 3 is the second number on left side but is the first number on the right side.

Mirror image.

- The right side of the equation is the mirror image of the left side.

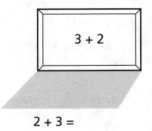

2 + 3 =

Addition or multiplication?

- The operation signs are either addition signs (+) or multiplication signs (x).

Same total.

- The total of each side is equal.

$$2 + 3 = 3 + 2$$

$$(= 5) \quad (= 5)$$

ASSOC:
TO HELP ME USE THE ASSOCIATIVE
PROPERTY TO CALCULATE OR SOLVE PROBLEMS

Are any numbers or letters grouped by parentheses?
See if the groupings change from one equation to the next.
Same numbers/letters, signs, and total?
One, two, three numbers/letters or more.
Can be all addition signs or all multiplication signs.

Are any numbers or letters grouped by parentheses?

- Numbers/letters in at least one equation are grouped by parentheses.

$$(4 + 7) + 3 = 14 \quad 4 + 7 + 3 = 14$$
$$3 \times 6 \times 8 = 144 \quad (3 \times 6) \times 8 = 144$$
$$(7 + 5) + 7 = 19 \quad 7 + (5 + 7) = 19$$

- In each set of equations, numbers are grouped by parentheses for at least one of the two equations.

See if the groupings change from one equation to the next.

- How numbers are grouped for each equation is different.

$$(4 + 7) + 3 = 14 \quad 4 + 7 + 3 = 14$$

parentheses (group)   no parentheses (no group)

$$3 \times 6 \times 8 = 144 \quad (3 \times 6) \times 8 = 144$$

no parentheses (no group)   parentheses (group)

$$(7 + 5) + 8 = 20 \quad 7 + (5 + 8) = 20$$

7 + 5 grouped   5 + 8 grouped

Same numbers/letters, signs, and total?

- Equations must have the same numbers or letters.
- Equations must have the same operation signs.
- Equations have the same total.

One, two, *THREE* numbers/letters or more.

- Equations must have three numbers or more.

Can be *all* addition signs or *all* multiplication signs.

- Each equation must have only addition signs or only multiplication signs.

DIST:
TO HELP ME USE THE DISTRIBUTIVE PROPERTY
TO CALCULATE OR SOLVE PROBLEMS

Does one side include parentheses?
Identify that the other side has more numbers and no
    parentheses.
See the "double number."
Total is the same.

Does one side of the equals sign include parentheses?

- Left side *or* right side of equals sign has parentheses.

$$5(3 + 4) = 5 \times 3 + 5 \times 4$$

parentheses on left side

$$5 \times 3 + 5 \times 4 = 5(3 + 4)$$

parentheses on right side

Identify that the other side has more numbers and no parentheses.

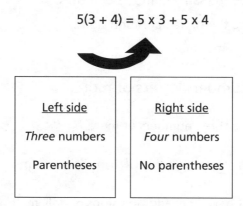

$$5(3 + 4) = 5 \times 3 + 5 \times 4$$

Left side	Right side
Three numbers	*Four* numbers
Parentheses	No parentheses

See the "double number."

- Number outside parentheses will be written twice on other side.

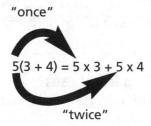

"once"

$$5(3 + 4) = 5 \times 3 + 5 \times 4$$

"twice"

Total is the same.

- Both sides equal the same total.

What Are Strategies for Order of Operations?

Order of operations is an important concept because it allows students to successfully solve problems that involve multiple operations. This skill is an important prerequisite for successfully managing algebra I courses. Students with learning disabilities and ADHD may understand how to apply each operation in a problem such as $34 + 62 \times 3 \div 4 - 2 =$ ___; however, they often have difficulty performing operations in the appropriate order. Several potential reasons students have difficulty with order of operations include nonunderstanding of the properties of rational numbers (i.e., commutative, associative, distributive), memory deficits, and attention problems. Understanding properties of rational numbers provides students with a conceptual framework to recognize why performing certain operations before others can be problematic. This understanding helps students "check" the reasonableness of their solution. Memory deficits make it difficult for students to retrieve from memory which operation should be completed first. Attention problems can result in distractibility whereby students do not accurately process operation signs. Because students with learning disabilities and ADHD may not closely attend to every operation sign, they may perform operations "out of order" (because they "missed" an operation and computed based on what they actually attended to), they may perform the wrong operations (because they misinterpreted a sign due to their distractibility), or they may not include a specific operation as they problem solve (because they missed an operation sign due to distractibility).

The ORDER strategy is used to assist students who are *initially* learning to solve multioperation problems that require understanding of the order of operations (Allsopp, 2001). ORDER provides students with a step-by-step process for solving problems involving multiple operations. The O step, "Observe the problem," cues students to read the problem and look for multiple operation signs. This is an important step because it cues students to attend to whether there are multiple operations.

The R step, "Read the signs," reminds students to look at each sign and identify the operation it represents. Students can be taught to circle the signs as they do this and say aloud what each sign represents. Circling the signs and saying aloud what they represent provide students multisensory cueing. This "self-cueing" prompts students to attend to the important cues. Encouraging students to do this can be helpful initially and can be faded as students become more successful at recognizing each and every operation represented in future problems.

The D step, "Decide which operation to do first," reminds students that operations must be performed in a particular order, thereby prompting them to *think* before impulsively performing operations in the order they are written (a common but inefficient strategy used by many students with learning disabilities and ADHD). The E step, "Execute the rules of order," provides students with a systematic process for deciding which operations should be performed first. The *rule of order,* captured in the phrase, "Many Dogs Are Smelly!" helps students remember which operation should be solved first. The first letter in each word of the phrase, "Many Dogs Are Smelly!" stands for one of the basic math operations (multiplication and division come before addition and subtraction). The phrase "Pew Eee!" could be added in front of "Many Dogs Are Smelly!" later on as students begin working with problems that involve parentheses and exponents.

You are strongly encouraged to provide students with plenty of opportunities to practice problems without parentheses and exponents before teaching order of operations with parentheses and exponents. The additional symbols involved with parentheses and exponents, as well as the concepts the symbols represent, make determining order of operations even more problematic because they increase the potential for distractibility and confusion. It is also important that students understand the concepts represented by parentheses and exponents before including them in order of operations. A picture cue can

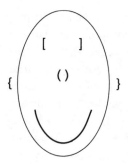

Figure 12.6. Picture cue for order of operations.

be added when students begin working with multioperation problems that include parentheses, brackets, and braces (see Figure 12.6). Students use this picture cue at the E step of the ORDER strategy. The picture cue denotes the order for solving operations within parentheses, braces, and brackets. Parentheses (nose of the face) are first, braces (eyes of the face) are second, and brackets (ears of the face) are last.

The R step, "Relax, you're done!" reminds students to reinforce themselves for a job well done. Teaching students to provide themselves with positive reinforcement is a wonderful strategy for all students.

ORDER:
TO HELP ME SOLVE
PROBLEMS INVOLVING ORDER OF OPERATIONS

Observe the problem.
Read the signs.
Decide which operations to do first.
Execute the rules of order.
Relax, you're done!

Observe the problem.

- Look for multiple operation signs, symbols, and numbers.

Read the signs (identify operations).

- Identify the operations represented by the signs (+, –, x, ÷).
- Say each operation aloud.

Decide which operation to do first.

- Remember the rules of order:
Many Dogs Are Smelly! (multiplication, division, addition, subtraction).
Pew Eee! Many Dogs Are Smelly! (parentheses come before exponents,
then multiplication, division, addition, subtraction).

Execute the rules of order

- Many Dogs Are Smelly! (for equations that *do not* have parentheses and
exponents).
- Pew Eee! Many Dogs Are Smelly! (for equations that *do* have parentheses
and exponents).

Relax, you're done!

- Tell yourself that you did a good job!

What Are Strategies for Adding Positive and Negative Integers?

Working with positive and negative integers can be problematic for students
with learning disabilities and ADHD for several reasons. The abstract nature
of the concept *negative* may make it difficult for students to obtain a solid conceptual understanding of negative numbers. When adding positive and negative integers, students benefit from being able to estimate the reasonableness
of their solutions. Without possessing a solid understanding of "positive" and
"negative" and how positive and negative numbers relate, students may lack
the ability to estimate.

Providing students with concrete experiences representing positive and
negative integers can enhance their conceptual understanding of how positive
and negative numbers relate to each other. For example, color-code counting
chips so that light-colored chips represent positive numbers and dark-colored
chips represent negative numbers. Students can add positive and negative integers by representing each with the appropriate number of colored chips. Students match chips so that the same number of light-colored and dark-colored
chips are grouped in pairs. The remaining chips represent the solution (e.g., two
leftover light-colored chips represent a *positive 2;* four leftover dark-colored chips
represent a *negative 4;* if there are no chips left over, then the solution is 0).

$$-8 + 4 = -4$$

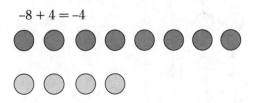

Table 12.3. Adding positive and negative integers cue sheet

Problem	What to do	Sign of sum
Positive + positive	Add	+
Negative + negative	Add	–
Positive + negative or Negative + positive	Larger number – smaller number	Sign of larger number

Due to attention problems, students may not attend to mathematical symbols that signal whether integers are positive or negative. If students do not attend to mathematical symbols, then they will not be successful when adding positive and negative integers. Using visual and kinesthetic cueing makes mathematical symbols more easily discernable to students with attention problems. Color-coding - and + symbols can be helpful. Teaching students to circle each symbol while saying it aloud also can be a helpful cueing strategy.

The ADD strategy provides students with a systematic process for adding positive and negative integers (Allsopp, 2001). The A step, "Ask yourself, 'Is this an addition problem?'" reminds students to check to determine whether the problem involves addition. Students can be taught to point to the operation sign and say silently whether it is an addition sign.

The first D step, "Decide what signs are given for each number," reminds students to look for mathematical symbols that identify integers as positive or negative. Students can be taught to circle negative integers and, if appropriate, write a + sign on the top left side of a positive integer (students may or may not need this additional cueing). Some students will benefit from pointing to each circled sign and saying each integer aloud (e.g., *positive 24; negative 13*).

The second D step, "Determine the problem, what to do, and the sign of the sum," provides students with a process for solving the problem. At the concrete and representational levels, students use their concrete materials or drawings to complete this step. At the abstract level, the Adding Positive and Negative Integers Cue Sheet provides students with a visual guide for making this problem-solving decision (see Table 12.3).

The ADD strategy can be taught at all three levels of understanding. At the concrete level, discrete materials that are color-coded to signify positive and negative integers can be used. At the representational level, students can be taught to represent positive and negative integers with simple drawings. The same procedure for solving the problem at the concrete level can be used.

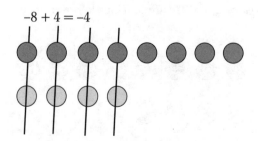

$$-8 + 4 = -4$$

When students have mastered adding positive and negative integers at the concrete and representational levels, the Adding Positive and Negative Integers Cue Sheet can be included as an aid to determining solutions without the use of concrete materials or drawings (abstract level of understanding).

ADD:
TO HELP ME ADD POSITIVE AND NEGATIVE INTEGERS

Ask yourself, "Is this an addition problem?"
Decide what signs are given for each number.
Determine the problem, what to do, and the sign of the sum.

Ask yourself, "Is this an addition problem?"

- Read the problem.
- Look for an addition sign.

Decide what signs are given for each number.

- Check for positive and negative signs and circle negative integers.

Determine the problem, what to do, and the sign of the sum.

- Use the Adding Positive and Negative Integers Cue Sheet.

How To Implement the ADD Strategy

9 + –6   = ___   1. **A:** student looks for addition sign.

9 + (–6)   = ___   2. **D:** student determines the sign for each integer
                          and circles the negative integer.

9 + –6   = _3_   3. **D:** student decides three things: 1) whether the
                          problem adds a positive and a negative integer

or two negative integers; 2) whether to subtract the absolute values of the integers (if they are positive and negative) or add their absolute values (if both are negative integers); and 3) the student determines what sign the sum takes (negative if integers are negative or the sign of the integer that has the greatest absolute value). Table 12.3 illustrates a cue sheet students can refer to when making these decisions.

What Are Strategies for Determining Square Root?

Students may not be able to recall basic multiplication facts, making it difficult to recall fact "doubles" and their products (e.g., 4 x 4 = 16; 8 x 8 = 64). Second, students may not understand the relationship of products to their factors (e.g., that the number 16 has different sets of factors, one of which, 4 x 4, represents its square root). Third, students may have difficulty obtaining a meaningful understanding of square root because of the abstract nature of the concept.

The ROOT-IT strategy provides students with a systematic process for determining square root and for establishing a meaningful understanding of square root (Allsopp, 2001). The ROOT-IT strategy can be used to determine the square root of a number at the concrete, representational (drawing), and abstract levels of understanding. The strategy will be most helpful to your students if first taught at the concrete and representational levels before moving to the abstract level.

The R step, "Read the number inside the square root sign," cues students to first read (and process) the number for which they will determine the square root. Students can be taught to identify the square root symbol during this step as well. Relating the square root symbol to something visually meaningful can be helpful (e.g., a checkmark $\sqrt{}$ with a roof $\sqrt{}$).

The O step, "Organize the number in groups, starting with groups of two," provides students with a starting point for examining factors as the potential square root. At the concrete level, students represent groups with discrete counting objects (e.g., counting chips, beans, pennies) At the representational level, students can draw tallies or dots to represent groups. At the abstract level, students simply "think" or say aloud, "two groups of two" or "2 times 2." Figure 12.7 illustrates this process using concrete objects or drawings.

The second O step, "Observe the groups and ask, 'Does it add up?'" guides students to add the total represented by the groups. At the concrete and representational levels, students simply count the number of objects or pictures. At the abstract level, students determine the product by recalling the appropriate multiplication fact or computing the product using paper and pencil. Once students have determined the total or product, they compare it to the number inside the square root sign. If the total and the number inside the square root

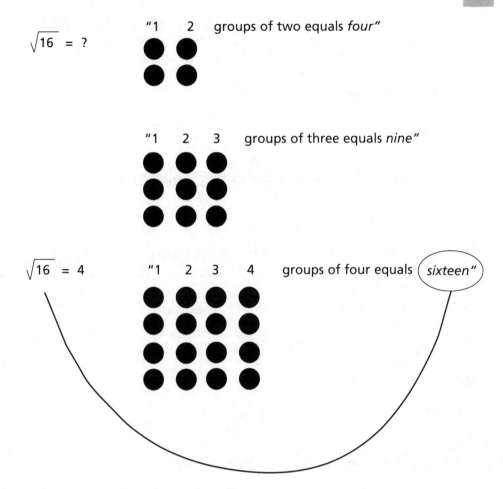

Figure 12.7.   Example of using concrete objects or drawings to determine square root.

sign are the same, then students know the solution is the number of groups (the number of objects or drawings in each group also represents the square root).

The T step, "Tie down the answer, or continue grouping," cues students to write the solution, if appropriate, or continue examining groups by proceeding to the next set of groups (e.g., three groups of three, four groups of four, five groups of five). The I and T steps provide students with a process for checking their answers. The I step, "Identify the square root by circling/counting the total number of groups," cues students to count the number of groups and check to see that the number of groups is the same as the solution. The T step, "Test the answer by counting," guides students to check the total of all groups as well as to check to be sure that the number of objects or drawings in each group is the same as the number of groups (e.g., when there are three groups, there are three objects/drawings in each group).

When students have verified their answer, they can be confident their solution is correct. By experiencing this process at the concrete and representational levels, students are provided with appropriate experiences that make the concept of square root more meaningful/tangible. These experiences also provide students with a tangible way to learn abstract factors by *seeing* them. The process taught by the ROOT-IT strategy also provides students with a systematic way to determine square roots when their memory for facts fails them.

ROOT-IT:
TO HELP ME DETERMINE SQUARE ROOTS

Read the number inside the square root sign.
Organize the number into groups, starting with two groups of two.
Observe the groups and ask, "Does it add up?"
Tie down the answer, or continue grouping.
Identify the square root by circling/counting the total number of groups.
Test the answer by counting.

Read the number inside the square root sign.

$$\sqrt{16} \quad \text{"sixteen"}$$

Organize the number into groups, starting with two groups of two.

- Draw dots or tallies.
- Start with two groups of two dots or tallies in each group.

1   2   groups of two

Observe the groups and ask, "Does it add up?"

- Multiply the number of groups by the number of dots or tallies in each group (or add the total number of dots or tallies).

- Compare the total to the number inside the square root sign.

$\sqrt{16} = ?$

"1　2　groups of two equals *four*" (four does not equal sixteen)

Tie down the answer, or continue grouping.

- If the total of dots or tallies equals the number inside the square root sign, then move to the next step.
- If not, continue grouping dots and tallies (three groups of four, four groups of four, etc.).
- Stop grouping when the total number of dots or tallies equals the number inside the square root sign.

Identify the square root by circling/counting the total number of groups.

- When the total equals the number inside the square root sign, count the total number of groups.
- The total number of groups is the "square root" (see Figure 12.8).

Test the answer by counting.

- Check your answer by counting all of the dots and tallies.
- Check to see if the total does equal the number inside the square root sign.

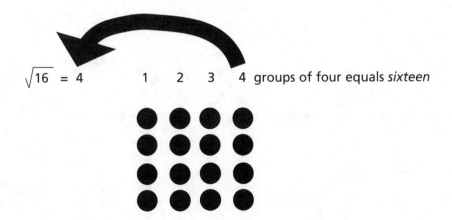

$\sqrt{16} = 4$　　1　2　3　4 groups of four equals *sixteen*

Figure 12.8. Totaling the number of groups is the same as the "square root."

WHAT ARE STRATEGIES FOR
ONE-VARIABLE ALGEBRA EQUATIONS?

When confronted with one-variable algebra equations, students with learning disabilities and ADHD often fail to relate their prior experiences with unknowns or variables (e.g., $4 \times a = 12$; $24 + 7 = a$; $a - 3 = 9$). The letters that represent

$4x + 2x = 12$

1. Represent the variable "x" with circles. By combining like terms, there are six "x's."

$6x = 12$

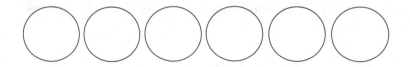

2. The total, "12," is represented with twelve tallies or dots.

3. The total, "12," is divided equally among the circles.

$x = \dfrac{12}{6}$

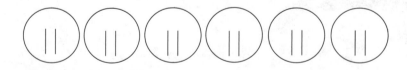

4. The solution is the number of tallies represented in one circle–the variable 'x."

$x = 2$

Figure 12.9. Drawing solutions to one-variable algebra equations.

variables in one-variable algebra problems are intimidating to the students because they either don't remember doing basic computation problems with letters (in elementary school), or they believe the letters mean something different because this is *algebra!* Students also may have difficulty recalling basic facts, a necessary prerequisite skill for solving these type of equations efficiently. In addition, the multiple steps involved in solving algebra equations can be a barrier for students with learning disabilities and ADHD. Students sometimes have trouble recalling all the steps required for solving one-variable algebra equations, making success difficult.

When teaching students how to solve this type of equation, it is helpful to explicitly relate their prior experiences with unknowns or variables to variables contained in one-variable algebra equations. An excellent way to link their prior knowledge of unknowns or variables to one-variable algebra equations is to have students solve several basic equations involving unknowns (e.g., 4 x a = 12; a − 3 = 9). Then, demonstrate how to solve them. Emphasize to students that the number they replaced the letter for is the unknown or variable. Use one equation as an example and solve it using concrete objects. Continuing with concrete objects, change the value of one number in the equation and show students how the unknown or variable changes as well.

The DRAW strategy for solving one-variable algebra equations provides students with a process for developing both a conceptual and a procedural understanding of this beginning algebra skill (Allsopp, 1997, 1999, 2001; Mercer, 1994). Particular steps of the DRAW strategy will assist students in overcoming the barriers mentioned previously. The DRAW strategy is primarily used to solve one-variable algebra equations at the representational and abstract levels of understanding. However, like the DRAW strategy for basic computation of whole numbers and fractions, the DRAW strategy for one-variable algebra equations can be used as this skill is first taught at the concrete level of understanding. This mnemonic will be familiar to students who have used DRAW to solve basic addition, subtraction, multiplication, and division problems. However, *the steps are different,* so guide students through the process for solving one-variable algebra equations.

The D step, "Discover the variable and the operations," cues students to examine the equation closely, especially noting the variable. Some students will benefit from circling the variable.

$$\left(4a\right) + \left(2a\right) + 9 - 3 = 30$$

The R step, "Read the equation and combine like terms," tells students to read the entire equation aloud and combine like terms. Reading the equation aloud or to themselves in a low voice provides students auditory cueing and it makes it more likely they will attend to all the components of the equation. Students are taught to combine common variables as well as integers.

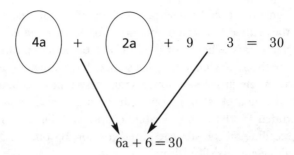

The A step, "Answer the equation, or draw and check," is where students either solve the equation at the abstract level (by recalling facts and "balancing" the equation to isolate the variable), or they use concrete objects or drawings to solve for the variable. Students should also be taught to check their solutions during this step. This is an important step for students with learning disabilities and ADHD because of their potential learning characteristics of impulsivity and attention problems/distractibility. Figure 12.9 illustrates how to draw solutions to one-variable algebra equations. At the concrete level, plates can be used instead of drawing circles, and appropriate concrete materials can be used to represent integers (counting objects for whole numbers, fraction pieces for fractions). The W step, "Write the answer for the variable and check the equation," reminds students to write the solution once they have checked to verify that it is accurate. Using a drawing of a "balance" or "see-saw" can be a meaningful cue as you teach students about balancing the two sides of an algebra equation (see Figure 12.10).

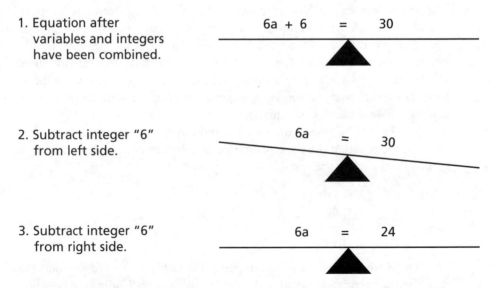

Figure 12.10. Drawing of a "balance" or "see-saw" to be used to teach students about balancing the two sides of an algebra equation.

DRAW FOR ALGEBRA:
TO HELP ME SOLVE
ONE-VARIABLE ALGEBRA EQUATIONS

Discover the variable and operations.
Read the equation and combine like terms.
Answer equation, or draw and check.
Write the answer for the variable.

Discover the variable and operations.

- Scan the equation and look for operation signs (+, −, x, ÷).
- Circle the operation signs.

Read the equation and combine like terms on each side of the equation.

- Read the whole equation out loud.
- Look for like terms.
- Combine like terms.

Answer the equation, or draw and check.

- If you know the answer or if you can solve the equation without drawing, then write the answer.
- If you don't know the answer or how to solve the equation without drawing, then draw the answer.

Write the answer for the variable and check the equation.

- Write the number that represents the answer.
- Substitute your answer for the letter in the original equation.
- Work the problem and see if the left side equals the right side.

What Are Strategies for Solving Algebra Word/Story Problems?

The section about strategies for solving word/story problems involving addition, subtraction, multiplication, and division of whole numbers and fractions discusses reasons why word/story problem solving can be difficult for students with learning disabilities and ADHD. Similar to the FASTDRAW FOR BASIC MATH strategy for solving word/story problems involving the four operations (whole numbers and fractions), the FASTDRAW FOR ALGEBRA strategy for solving algebra word/story problems (Allsopp, 1997, 1999, 2001; Mercer, 1994) provides students with a systematic process for finding the important information in the text of the word/story problem and setting up and solving an equation to solve the problem. Although the two strategies are similar in terms of purpose, the individual steps are different based on the difference in the mathematics skills they pertain to. However, students who are familiar with the FASTDRAW FOR BASIC MATH strategy for solving word/story problems involving the four operations have a useful foundation for using the FASTDRAW FOR ALGEBRA strategy to solve algebra word/story problems. FAST

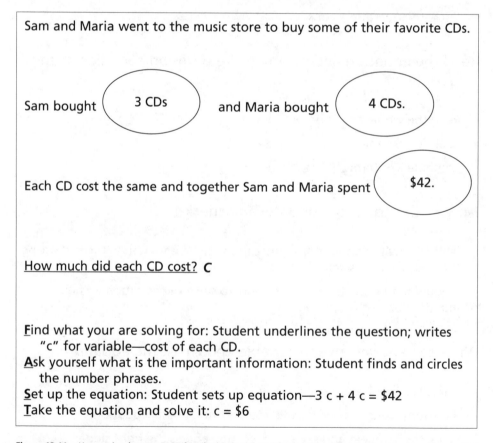

Sam and Maria went to the music store to buy some of their favorite CDs.

Sam bought (3 CDs) and Maria bought (4 CDs.)

Each CD cost the same and together Sam and Maria spent ($42.)

How much did each CD cost? _C_

<u>F</u>ind what your are solving for: Student underlines the question; writes "c" for variable—cost of each CD.
<u>A</u>sk yourself what is the important information: Student finds and circles the number phrases.
<u>S</u>et up the equation: Student sets up equation—3 c + 4 c = $42
<u>T</u>ake the equation and solve it: c = $6

Figure 12.11. How to implement FAST for algebra word problems. When the equation is set up, the student can use DRAW to find the solution, if needed.

provides students with a strategy for finding the important information in an algebra word/story problem and setting up an equation. DRAW FOR ALGEBRA, described previously, can then be used to solve the algebra equation. Figure 12.11 illustrates how to implement each step of FASTDRAW FOR ALGEBRA described in the following paragraphs.

The F step, "Find what you are solving for," cues students to search for the sentence or phrase that describes what problem needs to be solved. Similar to the previous FASTDRAW FOR ALGEBRA strategy, students can be taught to look for a question mark or a keyword that signals the problem to be solved. Students can be taught to circle the question mark (or keyword) and then underline the corresponding sentence or phrase. Students are then taught to identify the variable in the sentence or phrase and choose a letter that represents the variable (e.g., the letter c would be appropriate for the variable representing the cost of a CD). The letter representing the variable is then written after the sentence or phrase.

The A step, "Ask yourself, 'What information is given?'" cues students to read through the word/story problem and look for information that will be helpful for solving the problem identified in the previous step. Students can be taught to look for particular words or phrases that indicate important information in algebra situations (e.g., number phrases). A helpful strategy for doing this is to read each sentence and then ask yourself, "Was there a number phrase (or other relevant keyword/phrase)?" Students circle the important information they find. Modeling this step is important because students with learning disabilities and ADHD often do not implement systematic strategies because of attention problems and impulsivity. Also, some students do not feel equipped to find information in a word/story problem because of reading difficulties or because they don't know what to look for. In many cases, they simply guess or never read the entire text. When they learn an effective strategy for finding important information in word/story problems, then they are more likely to complete this step.

The S step, "Set up the equation," cues students to take the important information found in the word/story problem and use it to set up an appropriate equation for solving the algebra problem. Students need multiple models from you in order to set up equations accurately. Providing students with cues as they initially learn this skill can be effective instructionally. We have found it helpful to provide blanks as well as phrases beneath the blanks to describe what important information goes in them. Once students become successful using this level of cueing, then the phrases can be removed. With practice, students master setting up equations with just the blanks. Later, the blanks can be removed and students are successfully setting up equations without any cues. Figure 12.12 illustrates this cueing process.

Once the equation is set up, then step T, "Take the equation and solve it," cues students to solve the equation. DRAW is available if students need cueing for solving the equation they have set up.

Stage 1–High level of cueing:

$$\underline{\qquad} + \underline{\qquad} = \underline{\qquad}$$

Cost of   Cost of   Total cost
Sam's CDs Maria's CDs

Stage 2–Medium level of cueing:

$$\underline{\qquad} + \underline{\qquad} = \underline{\qquad}$$

Stage 3–No cueing

Figure 12.12.   Cueing ideas for setting up algebra equations. Cueing examples are from word/story problem in Figure 12.11. The cues depicted represent the equation 3c + 4c = $42.

FASTDRAW FOR ALGEBRA:
TO HELP ME SOLVE ALGEBRA WORD/STORY PROBLEMS

Find what you are solving for.
Ask yourself, "What information is given?"
Set up the equation.
Take the equation and solve it.
Discover the variable and the operations.
Read the equation and combine like terms.
Answer the equation, or draw and check.
Write the answer for the variable and check the equation.

Find what you are solving for.

- Look for the question mark.
- Underline the information that tells you what you are solving for.
- Name the variable (what you are solving for) with a letter and write it after the question mark.

Ask yourself, "What information is given?"

- Read each sentence.
- Find the number phrases and circle them.

Set up the equation.

- Write the equation with the variable and the numbers in the correct order.

Take the equation and solve it.

- Solve the equation and write the answer.
- If you can't solve the equation, then use DRAW to solve it.

Discover the variable and the operations.

- Scan the equation and look for the operation signs (+, −, x, ÷).
- Circle the operation signs (+, −, x, ÷).

Read the equation and combine like terms on each side of the equation.

- Read the whole equation out loud.
- Look for like terms.
- Combine like terms.

Answer the equation, or draw and check.

- If you know the answer or if you can solve the equation without drawing, then write the answer.
- If you don't know the answer or how to solve the equation without drawing, then draw the answer.

Write the answer for the variable and check the equation.

- Write the number that represents the answer.
- Substitute your answer for the letter in the original equation.
- Work the problem and see if the left side equals the right side.

ABOUT THE FOLLOWING CASE STUDY

This particular case study is more expansive than the case studies presented in other chapters. We believe that a more in-depth case study is needed for the area of mathematics because of its content-specific nature and because it typically receives less emphasis in the literature compared to other areas of learning. Why strategies were taught in response to the student's learning needs and the particular demands of the targeted mathematics course are emphasized.

The case study is organized into sections to make reading easier. The case study concludes with a section that summarizes successes and problems. Tips/solutions to the problems encountered are provided to stimulate your thinking about how to deal with situations in which the strategies and your instruction were not as successful as you'd like. It is recommended that you review the strategy(ies) highlighted in this case study before reading. The case study will be more meaningful if you have a basic understanding of these strategy(ies).

CASE STUDY AT A GLANCE

Student: Michelle
Grade: 10
Disability: Learning disabilities (reading and mathematics)
Learning characteristics: Memory retrieval problems, impulsivity, attention problems (distractibility), passive learning
Resource teacher: Mr. Kim
Course: Algebra I
Skill/concept: One-variable algebra word/story problems and equations
Strategies: FASTDRAW FOR ALGEBRA, DRAW FOR ALGEBRA
Background: Did not pass algebra I competency as ninth grader; taking 2-year algebra I option this year; has difficulty activating prior mathematics knowledge due to memory problems and distractibility; results in impulsive responses when doing mathematics; reading fluency problems affect comprehension of word/story problems; has strong verbal communication skills

MICHELLE, A STUDENT WITH MATHEMATICS DIFFICULTIES

About Michelle

Michelle is a tenth-grade student who is currently taking algebra I. Michelle was identified with learning disabilities in the third grade. Michelle has been receiving resource services for reading and math since that time. Although Michelle has greatly improved her reading decoding skills over the years, she is not a fluent reader. Her difficulty with fluency often affects her reading comprehension. Michelle also has struggled in mathematics through the years. Although she has passed her mathematics courses before high school, Michelle has demonstrated problems recalling basic mathematics knowledge (e.g., multiplication facts) when she needed to apply it in later grades, particularly seventh and eighth grades. Michelle's IQ score is well within the average range (full scale score = 106), and she communicates very well verbally. Although Michelle has not been identified with ADHD, she does demonstrate significant distractibility. In particular, her distractibility tends to be most pronounced when she is working independently (e.g., solving mathematics problems, reading text). Michelle also can be impulsive at times. Her impulsivity tends to be greatest when she is confronted with schoolwork that involves concepts she has not mastered. At times, her impulsiveness becomes a barrier because it prevents her from using her prior knowledge about a topic or concept to problem solve (passive learning). Memory retrieval problems also make it difficult for Michelle to use her prior knowledge because it often takes her an extended period of time to retrieve the piece of information needed.

How Michelle's Learning Characteristics Have Impacted Her Performance in Algebra I

Michelle can cognitively grasp the concepts presented in her algebra I course. However, her distractibility, impulsiveness, memory problems, and reading fluency difficulties are significant barriers to her learning efficiently in a typical algebra I course. Michelle's memory retrieval problems seem to be the most significant barrier because they prevent her from actively using the mathematics she has previously learned in an efficient way. This situation frustrates Michelle, which in turn only fuels her impulsivity and distractibility. For example, Michelle may initially understand a concept being presented in class, but as she tries to implement what she learned during independent practice in class or for homework, she often has trouble recalling what she learned during instruction. In addition, her difficulty with recalling basic mathematics knowledge and skills such as addition, subtraction, multiplication, and division facts makes problem solving even more difficult. Michelle's reading fluency affects her when solving word/story problems. She does not always understand what problem has been presented in the word/story problem, causing her to reread the word/story problem over and over. This laborious process leads to frustration and a tendency to rush through problems without applying a systematic strategy for solving them. Because this is the beginning of the year, Michelle is just starting the course. She is anxious because this is her second try at passing algebra I, and she knows she must pass it in order to receive a standard diploma. Her resource teacher is equally concerned. If she cannot help Michelle develop some effective mathematics strategies, then Michelle will not pass her algebra I competency. She does not want to see the algebra I competency become Michelle's barrier to achieving a standard diploma.

What Strategies Were Selected and Why

Michelle's resource teacher, Mr. Kim, discusses the situation with Michelle and together they choose to concentrate on strategies that will help Michelle solve one-variable word/story problems and equations. This makes sense to Michelle because she remembers from last year that the difficulty she had solving for variables only led to greater difficulty in the course as the year continued. Michelle reviews the mathematics strategies with her teacher as her teacher points out the purpose and characteristics of each strategy. Together, they decide that learning to use the FASTDRAW and DRAW FOR ALGEBRA strategies for solving one-variable algebra word/story problems and equations will be most helpful at this point in the course. In the back of his mind, Michelle's resource teacher concludes that the best way he can assist Michelle with her algebra I course is to teach her strategies that allow her to conceptually understand and perform those pre-algebra and beginning algebra skills necessary for success in algebra I. Several characteristics of the FASTDRAW and DRAW FOR ALGEBRA strategies fit Michelle and her learning characteristics because they provide her with a systematic process for solving basic algebra word/story problems and equations. Imbedded in the strategies are techniques (e.g., drawing pictures to complete division facts, drawing pictures to represent variables in a meaningful way, picking out important information from text in a word/story problem) that will help Michelle perform basic skills essential for success. These include basic skills that she consistently has difficulty with due to memory problems, reading fluency difficulties, impulsivity, and distractibility.

How the Selected Strategies Were Taught to Meet Michelle's Learning Characteristics and Course Demands

Mr. Kim uses the Active Learner Approach to teach the FASTDRAW and DRAW FOR ALGEBRA strategies to Michelle (see Chapter 5 for a detailed description of the Active Learner Approach). Mr. Kim emphasizes several areas as he and Michelle work together. One area of emphasis is ensuring that Michelle clearly understands the purpose of the strategies and how they incorporate mathematics skills Michelle has already been exposed to. Mr. Kim uses LIP (link to prior knowledge/experiences, identify learning objective, provide rationale for learning skill) as a way to introduce each strategy. Mr. Kim believes that Michelle is most in need of explicit links between the strategies and how they incorporate skills and knowledge that she is already familiar with. He did this by showing how FASTDRAW and DRAW can be used to solve basic computation word/story problems and equations. Michelle quickly sees how these strategies "work" with concepts she understands. She also realizes that the strategy steps really replicate the steps she would normally use to solve such problems. It is also encouraging to Michelle to see how simple pictures such as tallies and circles can be used to solve mathematics problems. Mr. Kim emphasizes what a great general problem-solving strategy drawing pictures is and how he often uses this strategy when trying to solve problems he has difficulty with.

As Mr. Kim models the strategies, he first teaches them using concrete materials. Because he knows Michelle loves music, Mr. Kim brings in some CD cases as a way to represent variables. Michelle brings in some bottle tops from her favorite soft drink to use as concrete representations of whole numbers. Michelle really likes the fact that Mr. Kim tries to make the concrete materials meaningful to her and didn't just pull out elementary level manipulatives like the counting bears she remembers using in first and second grade. He makes a cue sheet and poster that has the steps of the strategies. As he models each step with the CD cases and bottle tops, he prompts Michelle to say the steps in her own words and to describe what he is doing as he models. Mr. Kim thinks this will be helpful to Michelle because her verbal communication skills are strong. Interestingly, Michelle begins to understand what solving for a variable really means because she can physically see and move them (CD cases)! Another interesting realization occurs to both Mr. Kim and Michelle as they work with the concrete materials. As Michelle "divides" the bottle caps among the CD cases to determine what the variable (one CD case) equals, she remembers what division actually means. She tells Mr. Kim that she once knew this but had forgotten it. Division had just been a procedure to her—sometimes a frustrating one—for as long as she could remember. Mr. Kim has never really thought about this situation but certainly can relate to it because he admits to himself that he never really thinks about what division actually means when he divides. Michelle practices using concrete materials for a couple of days to solve multiple word/story problems and equations. She and Mr. Kim play a board game in which each has to solve a problem written on a card in order to move the number of spaces determined by a roll of a pair of dice. Extra spaces can be moved if one player can catch the other performing a step of the strategy incorrectly or missing a step completely. Michelle's confidence grows as her understanding of solving problems with variables increases. Soon, Michelle is able to solve five out of five problems correctly using each strategy. This is evidence to Mr. Kim that Michelle is ready to move to the representational level.

At the representational level, Mr. Kim emphasizes the drawing process (step A of DRAW) because Michelle is becoming proficient in remembering what to do with the other steps from her concrete experiences. Mr. Kim draws squares to represent variables and dots to represent whole numbers. Michelle likes the fact that she can solve mathematics problems by drawing squares and dots. It makes sense to her that the drawings are simplistic representations of the concrete materials they used previously (squares for CD cases and dots for bottle caps). Michelle continues to have access to the strategy cue sheets as she practices drawing solutions. Mr. Kim emphasizes the F and A steps of FASTDRAW at this level of instruction because of Michelle's reading problems. He believes she will greatly benefit from learning how to pick out the problem to be solved and the important information from the text of the word/story problem. Michelle continues to practice drawing solutions to problems using FASTDRAW and DRAW for several days. When she is able to solve eight out of eight problems in a given amount of time, Mr. Kim knows she is ready to move to the abstract level.

At the abstract level, Mr. Kim models using FASTDRAW and DRAW without drawing pictures. He continues to encourage Michelle to describe what he is doing and why as he models. Michelle seems to really benefit from using language to describe what she understands. In fact, Mr. Kim thinks this was one of the most helpful instructional accommodations for Michelle. Michelle develops a strategy notebook in which she keeps the FASTDRAW and DRAW strategies. She organizes them in a section titled *Math* and makes a tab that reads, "one-variable algebra problems." Michelle continues to practice using the strategies independently and in game formats with Mr. Kim. One additional activity Mr. Kim includes is a 5-minute period of time in which he and Michelle write algebra word/story problems together. They will decide what type of problem they want to solve and then each take turns developing a sentence until the word problem illustrates the chosen problem. As she gets better at writing word/story problems, Michelle finds it easier and easier to find the important information in word/story problems she is solving.

Results

Michelle demonstrates that she conceptually understands what variables are and how to solve for them in one-variable algebra word/story problems and equations. She demonstrates this by using both concrete materials and drawing pictures to solve these types of problems. Michelle also is able to describe what each step "means" as Mr. Kim models the strategies at each level of understanding. Michelle's confidence with these problems seems to be greatly enhanced, particularly given the fact that these strategies represent skills she has not been successful with in the past. She significantly improves her ability to comprehend word/story problems and to pick out important information to use for solving word/story problems. Unfortunately, Michelle continues to be inconsistent at dividing whole numbers when solving algebra equations at the abstract level. Her memory retrieval for division facts continues to be problematic. Mr. Kim encourages her to draw solutions when she "gets stuck." He also suggests that she use a calculator when needed as long as her algebra teacher agrees it is okay. Sometimes, Michelle does not use her strategy notebook when solving problems in her algebra class because other students do not have one and she doesn't want to "stick out." This leads to her forgetting a step resulting in incorrect solutions. To help Michelle, her algebra teacher posts a small poster with the strategies on them. She spends a few minutes describing the strategies and invites all students to use them. She is careful not to single Michelle out in any way.

How Michelle Benefited from Mr. Kim's Instruction

Conceptual Understanding   Mr. Kim's emphasis on linking the strategies to Michelle's prior knowledge about basic computation provided Michelle with a "learning anchor" to which she could attach new knowledge.

Michelle benefited from a C-R-A sequence of instruction. Having concrete representations of variables and whole numbers provided Michelle with a tangible way to understand solving one-variable algebra problems. Encouraging Michelle to use her strong verbal communication abilities as a way to describe her understanding added to her conceptual understanding.

Finding Important Information in Word/Story Problems   The systematic process taught in the F and A steps provided Michelle an easy-to-follow procedure. Before, her reading problems and impulsivity made this skill difficult.

By writing word/story problems together in a supported fashion, Mr. Kim provided Michelle with an effective way to strengthen her understanding of the form(s) these word problems take. This made finding the important information easier.

Confidence   Michelle's newfound conceptual understanding of skills she previously had difficulty with demonstrated to her that she indeed could learn algebra.

Mr. Kim's technique of ensuring that Michelle had mastered the strategy at each level of understanding before moving to the next demonstrated that Michelle was not moving too fast through the levels of understanding. Students with learning disabilities and ADHD often are moved too quickly to the abstract level before they have become proficient at the concrete and representational levels. This results in nonunderstanding of the concept behind the particular mathematics procedure, enhancing students' feelings of inadequacy in mathematics.

Advanced Thinking

- Why do students with learning disabilities and ADHD need to learn advanced thinking skills?

- What are the different subskills of advanced thinking?

- What is special about teaching advanced thinking with the Active Learner Approach?

- What are strategies for sequencing skills?

- What are strategies for determining compare-and-contrast relationships?

- What are strategies for determining categories?

- What are strategies for determining cause-and-effect relationships?

- What are strategies for teaching problem solving skills?

WHY DO STUDENTS WITH LEARNING DISABILITIES AND ADHD NEED TO LEARN ADVANCED THINKING SKILLS?

In the past, when students with disabilities were placed in special education classes, limited demands for advanced thinking skills were made on them. The special education curriculum in these classes focused on remedial and/or functional areas of learning. The remedial curriculum was directed at developing academic skills not mastered at age-appropriate levels by the students, whereas the functional curriculum emphasized skills necessary for everyday life and the workplace. In the past, students with disabilities, especially at the middle and secondary levels, were provided with a remedial/functional special education curriculum. Currently, they are given a general education curriculum with grade expectations that are the same for all students. This movement has been precipitated by the Individuals with Disabilities Education Act (IDEA) Amendments of 1997 (PL 105-17) requirements for participation in the general education curriculum and high-stakes testing (see Chapter 2).

At the secondary level, the general education curriculum requires students to master advanced thinking skills to master the content. For example, the Virginia Standards of Learning (1998) requires students to understand cause-and-effect relationships (e.g., the end-of-course world history test item that requires understanding of the cause of the decline in the Aztec population between 1500 and 1600, the end-of course biology test item that requires projecting the effect of harvesting mussels on the food chain of phytoplankton–zooplankton–mussels–starfish).

To successfully master the general education curriculum at the secondary level, students must have advanced thinking skills, such as sequencing, comparing and contrasting, categorizing, determining cause and effect, and problem solving. At the elementary and middle school levels in general education, there is some emphasis on developing a foundation for these advanced thinking skills, but instruction on them is most prominent at the secondary level.

To meet the demands for advanced thinking skills, students must develop the corresponding cognitive abilities. These advanced cognitive skills, also called *higher-order processing*, may be more difficult for students with learning disabilities than lower-order processing (Vaughn, Gersten, & Chard, 2000). Many students with learning disabilities have not developed these to the degree that their peers without disabilities have. This is, in part, because some students were not exposed to the general education curriculum at the elementary and middle school levels to the same degree as students without disabilities. This may be because students with disabilities are often pulled out of general education classes to receive remedial instruction. The decision to focus on either remedial instruction or the general education curriculum has negative consequences whatever choice is taken. If the general education curriculum is provided over remedial instruction at the elementary and middle school levels, then students with disabilities will fall farther behind in their academic skills. If the remedial curriculum is provided over the general education curriculum, then students

with disabilities will miss instruction in foundational skills for advanced thinking and background knowledge in the subject matter areas. The resolution of
the debate as to which curriculum to provide must be made on an individual
basis by the student's individualized education program (IEP) team, with recognition that the negative consequences of each choice must be fully explored and
evaluated by the team.

Another factor that negatively impacts students with disabilities meeting
the demands for advanced thinking skills at the secondary level is related to the
nature of their disabilities. Some students have weak advanced cognitive skills
(see Chapter 2). The degree to which these students can meet the requirements
for advanced thinking is not known because there is little research in this area.
Furthermore, the interaction between impairments in advanced cognitive areas
and lack of participation at early levels of the curriculum is not known. The
extent to which students with disabilities in cognitive functioning will be able
to meet the demands for advanced thinking skills of the general education curriculum is not known. To complicate matters, there are no accommodations or
modifications that can be used to have students use advanced thinking skills
without the corresponding cognitive processes unless the curriculum is watered
down, which is not the purpose of having students participate in the general
education curriculum. By watering down the curriculum, students with disabilities would not have to use advanced cognitive processes. Instead, they
could use lower-level cognitive processes. For example, if students with disabilities in forming categories had good memorization abilities, then they would be
taught to memorize the categories in their biology classes, rather than understand the basis for forming categories. With this approach, students might be
able to do adequately on tests, but they would not master the understanding
that is necessary to retain the information and have it available for use in building additional knowledge.

Current emphasis on higher-order process training is a manifestation of
the first approach to intervention in the field of learning disabilities emphasized
by Kirk and others (Minskoff, 1998). Over the years, there has been a trend
away from process training, but the resurgence of interest in strategy training
of students and focus on cognitive processing reflects a return to the basic approach that dominated the field of learning disabilities in the 1960s.

WHAT ARE THE DIFFERENT
SUBSKILLS OF ADVANCED THINKING?

Although a number of advanced thinking subskills exist, only those areas most
involved in secondary general education curriculum demands have been included in the Active Learner Approach strategies. Understanding the problem-
solving process and how to apply it is necessary for mastery of all academic
content. The challenge of understanding the general education secondary curriculum involves organizing the vast amount of information that is presented in
each subject matter area. Ways of organizing information involve the thinking

processes of sequencing, comparing and contrasting, determining cause and effect, and categorizing.

These five areas are related to analysis of textual structure that is often done in the field of reading comprehension (Vacca & Vacca, 2002). When reading expository text, skilled readers logically analyze the relationship among ideas. Five usual patterns of text structure are usually analyzed in reading texts: description, sequence, comparison and contrast, cause and effect, and problem solving (Vacca & Vacca, 2002). Bos and Vaughn (2002) expanded these to include argument and persuasion. We have used the last four for training advanced thinking skills but have substituted categorization for description because categorization is important in subject matter areas such as science and social studies. We have also expanded this model of textual structure from just reading material to studying and analyzing material that is absorbed through reading or lecture. The following five subskills (and the corresponding Active Learner Student Questionnaire items found in Appendix A) are taught with the Active Learner Approach.

- Sequencing: "I have difficulty organizing information sequentially."

- Comparing and contrasting: "I have difficulty comparing and contrasting ideas."

- Categorization: "I have difficulty understanding how information is organized into categories."

- Cause-and-effect relationships: "I have difficulty determining cause-and-effect relationships."

- Problem solving: "I have difficulty with problem solving."

WHAT IS SPECIAL ABOUT TEACHING ADVANCED THINKING WITH THE ACTIVE LEARNER APPROACH?

There are two essential elements in the Active Learner Approach to teaching advanced thinking skills—making thinking *explicit* and making thinking *visible*. These two elements have been identified as necessary for teaching thinking skills to students without disabilities (Beyer, 1997). Making thinking explicit is accomplished through think-alouds and verbalizing by the teacher and students as they process information. Because thinking is a silent mental activity it is hard to teach. By thinking aloud and reflecting on the content, the steps involved in analyzing information become apparent and explicit. With this approach, a reflective cognitive style can be developed by the students. This makes it possible for the teacher to model the steps in thinking and the students to attempt to use them following the teacher's model.

Thinking is made visible by using graphic representations of the relationships of the ideas. The graphic representation visually demonstrates the means for organizing the information. In the strategies described next, suggestions for use of graphic organizers to visually demonstrate the relationships are provided. The software program, *Inspiration* (1998), is recommended as an electronic means of using graphic organizers to visibly demonstrate relationships.

WHAT ARE STRATEGIES FOR SEQUENCING SKILLS?

Subject matter content at the secondary level is so complex and involves so much information that it is necessary to organize it in order to understand and recall it. Students must learn to impose different ways of organizing information, and one of the ways is to sequence information based on spatial factors, time, order of importance, or steps in a process. They must understand the importance of spatial organization for subjects such as geography and time sequencing for understanding history. Order of importance and steps in a process are significant for organizing information for the sciences. The 1st STOP strategy is used to guide students in analyzing these four types of sequential aspects of information in various subject matter areas.

The first step of the 1st STOP strategy has students analyze ways information can be sequenced–space, time, order of importance, and process. They are to identify which type of sequence is involved in the content that they are studying. Then, they are to pick the appropriate step corresponding to the material. For example, if the sequence involves spatial information, then they would use Step 2 of the strategy; if the sequence involves time factors, then they would use Step 3, and so forth. They are taught to use visualization and self-talk to help them learn all types of sequential information.

The second step of the 1st STOP strategy helps students analyze information that can be represented spatially (e.g., time zones, position of planets around the sun). The strategies used to recall spatially arranged information involve using visual imagery to recall how the information looked when originally seen, using meaningful associations, color coding and other visual cues, and creation of mnemonics.

The third step of the 1st STOP strategy helps students learn to sequence information using time factors. Strategies to help students understand and recall these sequences involve constructing time lines and making meaningful associations.

The fourth step of the 1st STOP strategy helps students to sequence information based on evaluation of the importance of the items. Self-talk of the meaningful relationship of the items is an important strategy for learning such sequential information. The final step of 1st STOP helps students sequence information using the steps in a process (e.g., digestion of food). Graphic organizers showing the steps in the sequence and self-talk involving meaningful analysis of the steps are important strategies to use for such sequential information.

1ST STOP:
TO HELP ME ORGANIZE INFORMATION SEQUENTIALLY

1st decide on sequence to use.
Spatial sequences.
Time sequences.
Order of importance.
Process sequences.

When studying information that can be organized sequentially, decide if the information can be arranged by putting it in a spatial order, putting it in a time order, ranking items by their importance, or ordering steps in doing a process. Then, use the step that corresponds to the type of organization you selected. For all types of sequences, use two techniques to help you organize the information. First, use visualization in which you try to picture the sequence in your mind's eye. Second, use self-talk in which you read the items in the sequences and explain to yourself *why* they are in this order.

1st decide on the sequence to use.

- Look over the information you are studying, and ask yourself if this information can be organized on the basis of space, time, order of importance, or process sequence (how things work).

- After you have decided which of the four types of sequences is involved, go to that step.

Spatial sequences.

- Spatial sequences involve analysis of how things look (e.g., the location of the planets from the sun, the four time zones in the continental United States, the relationship between weather and distance from the equator).

- To help understand and recall spatial sequences, try to visualize in your mind's eye how the information looked when you saw it. When studying, look at the spatial sequence, then shut your eyes and try to visualize it. For example, when studying the four time zones, look at the map with the time zones, then shut your eyes and picture the map in your mind's eye. It might also be helpful to draw a simple picture to show the information.

- You should also use self-talk to identify meaningful associations between the items in the sequences (e.g., *"The East Coast is on the right of a map, and the West Coast is on the left. I know that New York is in the eastern time zone and that is later than the time in the rest of the country. I know that Chicago is in the middle of the country and that it is in the central time zone. Then, the Rocky Mountains are in the mountain time zone. California, which is on the West Coast, is on the Pacific Ocean and that is in the Pacific time zone. If you start with the eastern time zone, then each of these time zones is 1 hour later than the next one. If it's 10 P.M. in New York, it's 9 P.M. in Chicago, 8 P.M. in the Rocky Mountains, and 7 P.M. in California.")*

- Another helpful strategy for recalling and understanding spatial sequences is to use color or other visual cues.

    - Example: *"I am going to color each of the countries nearest the equator red to show that they are hot because of their location."*

- Use of mnemonics may also help with recalling and understanding spatial sequences.

    - Example: To recall the names of the planets in order from the sun, Mercury, Venus, Earth, Mars, Jupiter, Saturn, Uranus, Neptune, and Pluto, use the sentence, *My very eager mother just set up new pickles.*

Time sequences.

- To help understand time sequences, use a time line or a visual organizer.

- Draw a line and write important dates on one side and corresponding events on the other side. Or, you can make a time line or visual organizer with just the events in order. Numbering the events may help you remember the order.

    - For example, for a time line on the events surrounding Pearl Harbor, write *December 7, 1941* and *Japan's surprise attack on Pearl Harbor,* then *December 8, 1941* and *United States declares war on Japan*, and then *December 11, 1941* and *United States declares war on Germany and Italy.*

- As you write each event on the time line, say the date, the events, and explain the relationship between each of the events on the time line. This will keep you from just trying to memorize without understanding the basis for the items in the sequence.

Order of importance.

- Sequences with order of importance involve analyzing concepts and rating them from the most important to the least important.

- To create sequences of items that are ranked by importance, make a list and number the items; 1 will be the most important, and each item will be less important than the one before.

- Rewrite your list in the correct order.

- Read the list aloud and explain to yourself why the first item is most important, the second less important, and so forth.
    - For example, to recall the names of the presidents in terms of their
      importance, make the following list: 1) George Washington, 2) Abra-
      ham Lincoln, 3) Thomas Jefferson, and 4) Franklin Roosevelt. Use self-
      talk to describe why this ranking has been made
    - Example: *"George Washington is ranked first because he was able to
      bring the country together at the time of independence. Without
      him, the country may not have been successful in breaking away from
      England. Abraham Lincoln was ranked second in importance because
      he was able to bring us through the Civil War and prevent the coun-
      try from breaking into two separate countries. Thomas Jefferson was
      important because he doubled the size of the country by buying the
      Louisiana Purchase. Franklin Roosevelt was important because he got
      us through the Depression and World War II."*

Process sequences.

- Analyze the steps in a process and write them in order as you verbally
  describe each step to yourself. Make sure that you describe the relationships of the steps to each other.
- Show the relationships by using arrows, numbers, or lines.
    - For example, to recall the steps in the digestive process, make a list
      like the following and say what happens at each step.

    1. Mouth: digestion of food begins

        ↓

    2. Esophagus: food passes to stomach

        ↓

    3. Stomach: digestion continues

        ↓

    4. Gall bladder: emulsion

        ↓

    5. Small intestine: digestion and absorption of nutrients

        ↓

    6. Large intestine: digestion and absorption of water and minerals

        ↓

7. Rectum: undigested food

8. Anus: exit for undigested food

WHAT ARE STRATEGIES FOR DETERMINING COMPARE-AND-CONTRAST RELATIONSHIPS?

One of the major ways of organizing information is by identifying similarities and differences between ideas. Graphic organizers should be the major means of teaching compare-and-contrast relationships. When comparing two items, the Venn diagram is a good way to visually represent the overlap in items representing similarities and the nonoverlapping areas as differences. Lists can be constructed when comparing more than two items. These lists should contain items written on the horizontal axis and the qualities to be analyzed written on the vertical axis. If an item has this quality, a checkmark is made in the appropriate column. Describing the relationships between the items as the graphic representations are drawn provides think-alouds.

The LID strategy is designed to assist students to organize information on the basis of comparing and contrasting. The first step in this strategy has the students make a list of the items to be compared. The second step has them systematically identify the similarities and differences between the items. The third step has them create a graphic representation of the items being compared.

LID:
TO HELP ME COMPARE AND CONTRAST IDEAS

List the items to be compared.
Identify the similarities and differences.
Draw a graphic representation of the relationship.

This strategy is helpful for studying ideas that have to be compared based on their similarities and differences. Making such comparisons is necessary for most, if not all, academic subjects. It is important to write down or draw the relationships because it is easier to understand relationships when they are shown visually.

List the items.

- Make a list of the items to be compared.

- Write these items at the top of a column.

- For example, if for your science class you were comparing the three fresh-water ecosystems, then you would have three columns—one for rivers and streams, another for ponds and lakes, and another for wetlands.

Identify the similarities and differences.

- Use a systematic approach to identify factors for comparing each of the items. These factors should be based on your readings and lecture notes.

- When making lists, write one factor on each line of the page. Then, go across the columns and ask yourself if this factor applies to the item in a particular column. If it does, then put a check in the column. If it does not, then leave the column blank.

- Analyze the columns. If there is a check going across all the columns, then this factor is a shared similarity of all the items. If there is a check going across some of the columns, then the factor is shared by those items listed at the top of the columns. Those items without checks differ. Likewise, if items do not have checks, then they share the similarity.

- After you have constructed the listings, verbally describe the similarities and differences among the items to yourself.

- For the example of the rivers and streams, ponds and lakes, and wetlands, they all are similar on the first factor, which is freshwater ecosystem. The second factor (they flow in and out of each other) applies to rivers and streams and ponds and lakes but not to wetlands, so rivers and streams and ponds and lakes are similar on this factor, but wetlands differ. The third fac-tor (may be temporary) applies only to wetlands, so rivers and streams and ponds and lakes are similar on this factor, but wetlands differ.

Draw a graphic representation of the relationship of the items

- If you are comparing two items, then draw a Venn diagram with two par-tially overlapping circles. Write the similarities of the two items in the over-lapping part of the circles and write the differences in the parts of the circle that do not overlap.

- Color-coding when writing similarities and differences may also be helpful. You may want to write factors that are similar in one color and factors that differ in another.

WHAT ARE STRATEGIES FOR DETERMINING CATEGORIES?

Organizing information into abstract categories is an efficient way of handling large amounts of data. Categorization is extremely important to most subject matter areas at the high school level but most important to the field of science. What makes the categories difficult to understand at this level is the abstract criteria used to classify items in a category. Concrete criteria, such as appearance, are the basis for categorization at earlier levels; however, the criteria become more abstract with higher-level academic content. Students must understand the criterion used to organize the information into categories if they are to grasp the meaning of the content. Use of graphic organizers showing commonalities of categories as well as interrelationship between subcategories aids the students in understanding abstract categories.

The CANDY strategy is used to assist students in organizing information into categories. The first step in this strategy has the students write the title of the category. Then, they are to identify the attribute (or attributes) that makes all members of this category alike. The third step has them name the major members of the category. Then, they are to identify different subcategories under each category. The last step has them draw a graphic representation to show the interrelationship of the category and the subcategories.

CANDY:
TO HELP ME UNDERSTAND
HOW INFORMATION IS ORGANIZED INTO CATEGORIES

Category title.
Attribute of all category members.
Name all category members.
Differentiate category members.
You can draw the categories.

This strategy is useful when studying abstract school content, especially science and social studies content in which categories are frequently used (e.g., types of rocks, clouds, governments). This strategy helps you organize large amounts of complex information and shows the interrelationships between the information. It shows you why items are placed in categories and also how the items in a particular category differ. This strategy helps you think using a top-down approach. You start at the top with the category and then go down to think about the specific members that are in the category. CANDY helps you understand how information is organized so that you don't have to just memorize it.

Category title.

- Write the title of the category that you are studying (e.g., types of rocks, types of governments).
  - For example, if you are studying different categories of clouds, you might have to classify clouds on the basis of their altitude (e.g., high clouds, middle clouds, low clouds). You would write *high clouds* as the title of the first category.

Attribute of all category members.

- Ask yourself why the members are grouped together in the category. *"What do all the members in the category have in common?"*
- Write down the factor that all the members of the category share.
  - For example, for the category of high clouds, you would write that these are clouds that have bases above 18,000 feet and are composed of ice crystals.

Name all category members.

- Use self-talk and say the different members that belong in the category.
- Then, write down all the members of the category. For example, for the category of high clouds, you would write:
  - Cirrus
  - Cirrocumulus
  - Cirrostratus

Differentiate the category members.

- Ask yourself how each of the members in the category differs from each other. *"What is different about this member from the other members in the category?"*
- Write a description of each category showing what is common to all members in the category and what is unique about each member.
  - For example, for the category members of high clouds, you would write:
    - Cirrus: high clouds that have wispy, thin, curled-up ends
    - Cirrocumulus: high clouds that are patchy or wavelike

- Cirrostratus: high clouds that are thin, allowing the sun and moon to shine through

You can draw the categories.

- Make a graphic representation of the category title and members that belong in the category. Put the title of the category in a circle in the middle, and write the attribute that is common to all members of the category. Then, draw smaller circles with the names of the category members, and write what is special about them.

- Use the graphic representation to help you study. Try not to memorize but, instead, try to see the interrelationship of the members of the category.

WHAT ARE STRATEGIES FOR DETERMINING CAUSE-AND-EFFECT RELATIONSHIPS?

Cause-and-effect relationships are basic to understanding all subject matter content. Understanding such relationships involves seeing two aspects of the relationship—the cause that enables something to occur and the effect that is the event that occurs. Students need to look at this type of relationship as an equation in which both sides must be balanced. Use visual cues to demonstrate this relationship, whenever possible.

The IFF 2 strategy is designed to help students analyze cause-and-effect relationships. To begin, three steps are used to identify the cause of a given event. Then, these same three steps are used to identify effects of a given cause. The first step has the students identify an event; then, find the probable cause of the event and find all other possible causes. This series of steps is repeated to identify the effects of a given cause. Initially, the students identify an event; then, find the probable effect of this event and find all other possible effects.

IFF 2:
TO HELP ME DETERMINE CAUSE-AND-EFFECT RELATIONSHIPS

Identify an event.
Find one cause.
Find other causes.
Identify an event.
Find one effect.
Find other effects.

This strategy has two parts, one to help determine the cause or causes of events and the other to determine the effect or effects of events. When analyzing cause and effect relationships, you need to think back and forth. If you are looking for a cause or causes of an event, then you need to think back. If you are looking for an effect or effects of an event, then you need to think forward. Both require you to start with an event and then reason backward or forward from the event. The three steps in the first part of this strategy are the same as the last three steps. They differ in that the first three steps look at causation and the last three steps look at effects or results.

Identify an event.

- Clearly identify the event for which you want to find the cause or causes.

- Write this down so that you are clear about the starting point of your thinking process.

Find one cause.

- Some events have only one cause. Ask yourself if this event fits this category.

- Use self-talk or visual aids to clearly demonstrate to yourself the nature of the cause-and-effect relationship. One way to show causation is to write the event and then draw an arrow to the left of the event and write the cause. This will show that you are reasoning backward to find the cause of the event.

  - For example, if you are studying the causes of avalanches and landslides, then you will find that there is one cause (i.e., substances that overcome friction between the snow or rocks and the underlying ground that holds the snow or rocks in place on a slope). You might explain this to yourself by saying, *"Substances such as water, ice, and sand overcome friction by making the underlying surface slippery and providing a cushion that snow or rock can move over. This movement is called an avalanche or landslide."* You also might try to visualize in your mind's eye the actions that take place with an avalanche or landslide. You might picture rocks on a slope and water under the rocks carrying them downhill.

Find other causes.

- Some events have more than one cause. Ask yourself if this event fits this category.

- Use self-talk or visual aids to clearly demonstrate to yourself the nature of the cause-and-effect relationship. Think about why all the causes are necessary and why one or a few might not fully explain the event. One way to show multiple causation is to write the event and then to the left of the event make a list of all the possible causes of the event. Draw an arrow

from the event back to each of the causes listed. This will show that you are
reasoning backward to find multiple causes.

- For example, if you are studying the Salem witch trials, then you may
  have learned that there are four major reasons for the trials: the Puritan lifestyle, a strong belief in the devil and witchcraft, the divisions
  within the Salem village, and expectations for children. You might
  explain this to yourself by saying, *"There are four reasons for the
  Salem witch trials. First, the Puritan lifestyle had a rigid moral code
  that made anyone who did not follow the code suspicious. Second,
  the people viewed the devil as equal to God and believed that witches
  were possessed by the devil. Third, there were strong economic and
  social differences between the people of Salem and the poorer people who were accused of witchcraft. Fourth, children were expected
  to behave as adults. The two girls who made the accusations of witchcraft were viewed as little adults."*

Identify an event.

- Clearly identify the event for which you want to find the effect or effects.

- Write this down so that you are clear about the starting point of your
  thinking process.

Find one effect.

- Some events have only one effect. Ask yourself if this event fits this category.

- Use self-talk or visual aids to clearly demonstrate to yourself the nature of
  the cause and effect relationship. One way to show effect is to write the
  event and then draw an arrow to the right of the event and write the
  effect. This will show that you are reasoning forward to project the effect
  of the event.

  - For example, if you are studying the effects of drinking and driving,
    then you find that alcohol affects the nervous system by slowing it
    down, and this eventually results in decreased ability to drive. You
    might explain this to yourself by saying, *"The effect of alcohol on a
    person's ability to drive is like a sedative and slows down the nervous
    system."*

Find other effects.

- Some events have multiple effects. Ask yourself if this event fits into this
  category.

- Use self-talk or visual aids to clearly demonstrate to yourself the nature of
  the cause and effect relationship. Think about why all the effects are likely
  and why one or a few might not be sufficient to explain the relationship.
  One way to show multiple effects is to write the event and then to the right

of this make a list of all the possible effects of the event. Draw an arrow from the event forward to each of the effects listed. This will show that you are reasoning forward to project multiple effects.

- For example, if you are studying the inner body effects of smoking, then you may have learned that there are six effects: shortness of breath, coughing, dizziness, increased rate of cancer, increased rate of heart disease, and increase rate of lung problems. You might explain this to yourself by saying, *"There are six effects of smoking on the inner body. These are shortness of breath, coughing, dizziness, more cancer, more heart disease, and more lung problems."*

WHAT ARE STRATEGIES FOR TEACHING PROBLEM-SOLVING SKILLS?

The importance of problem-solving skills has long been recognized in special education. The sequence taught in most problem-solving approaches has the following steps:

- Identify the problem.
- Project all possible solutions to the problem.
- Evaluate the consequences of the various solutions.
- Select the one that seems to have the potential to work best.
- Put the solution into action.
- Evaluate whether the solution used solved the problem.

This problem-solving sequence has been used as the basis for strategies for many years. Minskoff used this sequence as the basis for training social skills in the workplace (1994), and Bos and Vaughn (2002) used it to develop problem-solving skills applied to social situations. Deshler, Ellis, and Lenz (1996) used this sequence to develop strategies for various academic purposes. Beyer (1997) recommended this sequence for teaching thinking to students without disabilities.

The SOLVED strategy is designed to teach students to apply the problem-solving steps across all academic content areas. They are to use this to solve problems (e.g., how to achieve adequate oil supply without destroying the environment) or understand how others solved problems (e.g., how Truman solved the problem of ending the war with the Japanese by dropping the atom bomb). Each of the six steps in this strategy encompasses complex thinking skills and needs to involve different graphic organizers. Because of the complexity of each of the steps, it is important to provide explicit modeling.

The first step of SOLVED has the students set out the problem, which requires comprehension of all aspects of the problem. Many students do not clearly identify the problem, so they become lost in subsequent steps. They should write down the problem to be sure that they have correctly identified it.

The second step has them outline all possible solutions to the problem by brainstorming. At this stage, they must be taught to try to produce as many solutions as possible and not censure any. Students with disabilities may require a lot of guidance at this step because they may not be divergent thinkers who readily produce ideas based on varying relationships. Rather, they may be convergent thinkers who see things in conventional ways. Students should make a web of all the projected solutions with the problem represented as a circle in the center of the web. The next step has the students list the consequences of the various solutions they have projected. This requires the students to make logical connections between each of the solutions and the consequences that will most likely result from putting them into action. Have the students create graphic organizers using a cause-and-effect format for each solution for which the consequences are projected. This will help them with the next step in which they rank the solutions on the basis of how well they will achieve the result of solving the problem with minimal or no negative consequences. Next, they are to execute actions that put the top-ranked solution into practice. In some cases, they will describe actions that would have to be put into effect to implement the solution. Finally, they are to evaluate whether the solution worked. If it does not, they have to return to earlier steps in the problem-solving model and choose the next highest-ranked projected solution and determine if that would effectively solve the problem.

SOLVED:
TO HELP ME WITH PROBLEM SOLVING

Set out the problem.
Outline all possible solutions.
List the consequences.
View the rankings.
Execute the solution.
Did it work?

This strategy is designed to help you understand the process of problem solving. You can apply it to solving your own problems or understanding how others have solved problems. For each step, use self-talk to verbalize the thinking required. Also, use graphic organizers to help you represent the relationship between the ideas at each of the steps.

Set out the problem.

- Identify the problem to be solved.
- Say it in your own words. Then, write it down so you are sure that you understand it.
  - For example, if the problem is how to solve the gasoline crisis, then write: *What are all the ways that the gasoline shortage can be solved?*

Outline all possible solutions.

- Brainstorm all of the ways that the problem might be solved.
- Don't reject any solution at this step.
- Construct a graphic organizer with the problem written in a circle in the center and all the possible solutions written in circles that come out of the center circle.
  - For example, for the gasoline shortage, the following solutions might be projected:
    - Conservation
    - Alternate fuels
    - Electric cars
    - Unlimited exploration of oil in the United States
    - Unlimited exploration throughout the world
    - More fuel-efficient cars
    - More public transportation

List the consequences of each of the solutions that were outlined.

- Think of what will be the likely effect of each solution. Think of the solution as a cause and the consequence as the effect.
- Create a graphic organizer for each solution in which the solution is written in the center circle and the consequences for it are written in circles that project from the center circle.
  - For example, for the consequences of unlimited exploration of oil in the United States, the following consequences might be projected:
    - Might result in ecological problems
    - Might not be limitless reserves of oil

View the rankings.

- On the basis of the consequences you projected, rank the solutions in terms of what will work with the fewest negative consequences.

- View the rankings and select the highest-ranked solution (or solutions) as the choice to be put into action. There may be no one best solution but several solutions that have to be considered together.

- For the previous example, you might rank the possible solutions in the following order based on the ease with which they could be put into effect and with the least resistance from the public.

    - More fuel-efficient cars

    - More public transportation

    - Conservation

    - Alternate fuels

    - Electric cars

    - Unlimited exploration of oil in the United States

    - Unlimited exploration in the world

Execute the solution.

- The highest-ranked solution (or solutions) should be put into action. Think of all the things that would have to be done to make the solution work. Make a list of these.

- To execute the previous example, the list of actions that would have to be taken might include getting car manufacturers to increase fuel efficiency, getting governments to allocate more money for public transportation, getting the public to change its opinion toward use of public transportation, and so forth.

Did it work?

- If you put the solution into action, then evaluate it to see if it worked. If it did not, then go back and view the other possible solutions and consider which should be tried.

- If it is not possible to put the solution into action, as in the previous example, then list questions that need to be answered to determine if the solutions worked. For example, you might ask:

    - Do people use more public transportation if more options are provided?

- Would auto manufacturers willingly increase fuel efficiency?
- Who would pay for production of alternate forms of fuel?

- In some cases, you will need to go back and start the problem-solving process again to search for the best solutions to the problem.

SUSAN, A STUDENT WITH ADVANCED THINKING SKILLS DIFFICULTIES

Susan is a high school sophomore who was diagnosed with a learning disability in math when she was in second grade. She has received resource services for her learning disability and has made substantial progress in her math skills and, most recently, received a C in her algebra II class. This semester, Susan's major problem is difficulty understanding material in her biology class. She has an excellent memory and has been able to do adequately on tests; however, the amount of information that she has to learn has increased greatly. Susan has difficulty with advanced thinking skills, especially categorizing, and does not grasp the basis for placing items in categories. She is having difficulty understanding the many categories of her biology class and is doing poorly on tests. She tries to memorize the content without understanding it. Mr. Singer, Susan's special education resource teacher, and Susan discuss the use of the CANDY strategy as an aid for helping her understand biology concepts. Mr. Singer models how to use this strategy to graphically represent the classification of animals into kingdom, phylum, class, order, family, genus, species, and variety. Mr. Singer has to provide a lot of structure to assist Susan in identifying the important attributes of categories. He also reinforces Susan with candy whenever she uses the strategy appropriately. As the semester progresses, she is able to identify attributes when guided by Mr. Singer; however, she is not able to move to the independent practice stage. In addition, Susan is unable to generalize use of this strategy to other classes, especially her economics class. For example, she does not understand the basis for the categories of primary, secondary, and tertiary economies.

Although Susan's grades improve in her biology tests, she continues to struggle with understanding the concepts. Mr. Singer decides to continue instruction on CANDY for a second semester in hope of moving Susan to the independent practice stage. He also will provide guided practice with categories that Susan has to learn for her economics class. Susan agrees with Mr. Singer about the need for her to continue using the CANDY strategy. She continues to demonstrate motivation to learn to independently categorize information in her classes.

References

Allsopp, D.H. (1997). Using classwide peer tutoring to teach beginning algebra problem solving skills in heterogeneous classrooms. *Remedial and Special Education, 16*(6), 367–379.

Allsopp, D.H. (1999). Using modeling manipulatives, and mnemonics with eighth-grade math students. *Teaching Exceptional Children, 32*(2), 74–81.

Allsopp, D.H. (2001). *Building algebra skills series: Effective teaching strategies for students experiencing difficulty learning pre-algebra and beginning algebra skills*. Tampa, FL: Biggest Dog Learning Systems.

American Education Research Association. (2000). *AERA position statement concerning high-stakes testing in preK-12 education*. Retrieved September 13, 2000, from http://www.aera.net/about/policy/stakes.htm.

Association on Higher Education and Disability (AHEAD). (1996, July). Guidelines for documentation of a specific learning disability. *Alert, 10*–12.

Bender, W.N. (1998). *Learning disabilities: Characteristics, identification and teaching strategies*. Needham Heights, MA: Allyn & Bacon.

Bernard, C. (1990). *Teaching mathematics in the elementary school: Childhood education mathematics games, activities and laboratory materials*. Unpublished manuscript, University of Florida, Gainesville.

Beyer, B.K. (1997). *Improving student thinking: A comprehensive approach*. Needham Heights, MA: Allyn & Bacon.

Bos, C.S., & Vaughn, S. (2002). *Strategies for teaching students with learning and behavior problems* (5th ed.). Needham Heights, MA: Allyn & Bacon.

Bosman, A.T., & Van Orden, G.C. (1997). Why spelling is more difficult than reading. In C.A. Perfetti, L. Rieben, & M. Fayol (Eds.), *Learning to spell: Research, theory, and practice across languages* (p. 21–47). Mahwah, NJ: Lawrence Erlbaum Associates.

Brown, J.I., Fischo, V.V., & Hanna, G. (1993). *Nelson Denny Reading Test*. Itasca, IL: Riverside Publishing Company.

Bryan, J.H., Sonnefeld, L.J., & Grabowski, B. (1983). The relationship between fear of failure and learning disabilities. *Learning Disability Quarterly, 6,* 217–222.

Carnine, D. (1999). Bridging the research-to-practice gap. *Exceptional Children, 63,* 513–520.

Chall, J. (1983). *Stages of reading development*. New York: McGraw-Hill.

Chan, L.K. (1991). Promoting strategy generalization through self-instructional training in students with reading disabilities. *Journal of Learning Disabilities, 24,* 427–433.

Davis, S.J. (1990). Applying content study skills in co-listed reading classrooms. *Journal of Reading,* 277–281.

Deshler, D.D., Ellis, E.S., & Lenz, B.K. (1996). *Teaching adolescents with learning disabilities: Strategies and methods* (2nd ed.). Denver: Love Publishing.

Devine, T.G. (1981). *Teaching study skills: A guide for teachers*. Needham Heights, MA: Allyn & Bacon.

Disability Rights Advocates. (2001). *Do no harm: High stakes testing and students with learning disabilities*. Oakland, CA: Author.

Duke, N.K., & Pearson, P.D. *Effective practices in reading comprehension*. Retrieved December 22, 2001, from http://ed-web3.educ.msu.edu/pearson/pdpaper/Duke/ndpdp.html.

Englert, C.S., Raphael, T.E., Anderson, L.M., Anthony, H.M., & Stevens, D.D. (1991). Making strategies and self-talk visible: Writing instruction in regular and special education. *American Educational Research Journal, 23,* 337–372.

Foorman, B., Fletcher, J., & Francis, D. (n.d.). *A scientific approach to reading instruction*. Retrieved December 22, 2001, from http://www.ldonline.com/ld_indepth/reading/cars.html.

Glidden, H. (1999). *Making standards matter.* Washington, DC: American Federation of Teachers.

Grant, R. (1993). Strategic training for using text headings to improve students' processing of content. *Journal of Reading, 36,* 482–488.

Hallahan, D., Kauffman, J.M., & Lloyd, J.W. (1999). *Introduction to learning disabilities* (2nd ed.). Needham Heights, MA: Allyn & Bacon.

Harris, K.R., & Graham, S. (1992). *Helping young writers master the craft: Strategy instruction and self-regulation in the writing process.* Cambridge, MA: Brookline Books.

Harris, K.R., & Graham, S. (1996). *Making the writing process work: Strategies for composition and self-regulation.* Cambridge, MA: Brookline Books.

Henderson, C. (Ed.). (1998). *Profile of 1996 college freshmen with disabilities.* Washington, DC: HEATH Resource Center, American Council on Education.

Heubert, J.P., & Hauser, R.M. (1999). *High stakes: Testing for tracking, promotion, and graduation.* Washington, DC: National Academy Press.

Hughes, C.A., Ruhl, K.L., Deshler, D.D., & Schumaker, J.B. (1993). Test-taking strategy for students with emotional and behavior disorders. *Journal of Emotional and Behavior Disorders, 1,* 189–198.

Individuals with Disabilities Education Act (IDEA) Amendments of 1997, PL 105-17, 20 U.S.C. §§ 1400 *et seq.*

Individuals with Disabilities Education Act of 1990, PL 101-476, 20 U.S.C. §§ 1400 *et seq.*

Inspiration. (1998). *Classroom ideas using Inspiration for teachers by teachers.* Portland, OR: Inspiration Software, Inc.

King-Sears, M.E., Mercer, C.D., & Sindelar, P.T. (1992). Toward independence with keyword mnemonics: A strategy for science vocabulary instruction. *Remedial and Special Education, 13,* 22–33.

Kohn, A. (2001). Fighting the tests: A practical guide to rescuing our school. *Phi Delta Kappan, 82*(5), 348–357.

Kucan, L., & Beck, I.L. (1997). Thinking aloud and reading comprehension research: Inquiry, instruction, and social interaction. *Review of Educational Research, 67,* 271–299.

Lenz, B.K., Ellis, E.S., & Scanlon, D. (1996). *Teaching strategies to adolescents and adults with learning disabilities.* Austin, TX: PRO-ED.

Lerner, J.W. (2000). *Learning disabilities: Theories, diagnosis and teaching strategies* (8th ed.). Boston: Houghton Mifflin.

Leslie, L., & Caldwell, J. (2001). *Qualitative Reading Inventory–3.* New York: Addison Wesley Longman.

Liedtke, W. (1983, November). Diagnosis in mathematics: The advantages of an interview. *Arithmetic Teachers,* 181–184.

Lyon, G.R. (1999). *Keys to success: A national summit on research in learning disabilities.* Retrieved December 22, 2001, from http://www.ldonline.org/ld_indepth/reading/ncld_summit99.html.

Lyon, G.R., Alexander, D., & Yaffee, S. (1997). Programs, promise, and research in learning disabilities. *Learning Disabilities: A Multidisciplinary Journal, 8,* 1–6.

Manset, G., & Washburn, S.J. (2000). Equity through accountability? Mandating minimum competency exit examinations for secondary students with learning disabilities. *Learning Disabilities Research & Practice, 15*(3), 160–167.

Mastropieri, M.A., & Scruggs, T.E. (2000). *The inclusive classroom: Strategies for effective instruction.* Upper Saddle River, NJ: Prentice Hall.

Mastropieri, M.A., Scruggs, T.E., Bakken, J.P., & Whedon, C. (1996). Reading comprehension: A synthesis of research in learning disabilities. In T.E. Scruggs & M.A. Mastropieri (Eds.), *Advances in learning and behavioral disabilities* (pp. 201–227). Greenwich, CT: JAI Press.

Mather, N., & Goldstein, S. (2001). *Learning disabilities and challenging behaviors: A guide to intervention and classroom management.* Baltimore: Paul H. Brookes Publishing Co.

McConnell, L.M., McLaughlin, M.J., & Morison, P. (Eds.). (1997). *Educating one and all: Students with disabilities and standards-based reform.* Washington, DC: National Academy Press.

McLesky, J., Henry, D., & Axelrod, M.I. (1999). Inclusion of students with learning disabilities: An examination of data from reports to Congress. *Exceptional Children, 66*(1), 55–66.

Meichenbaum, D., & Beimiller, A. (1998). *Nurturing independent learners: Helping students take charge of their learning.* Cambridge, MA: Brookline Books.

Mercer, C.D. (1994). *Solving division equations: An algebra program for students with learning problems.* Unpublished manuscript, University of Florida, Gainesville.

Mercer, C.D., Jordan, L., Allsopp, D.H., & Mercer, A.R. (1996). Learning disabilities and definitions and criteria used by state education departments. *Learning Disabilities Quarterly, 19,* 217–232.

Mercer, C.D., Jordan, L., & Miller, S.P. (1996). Constructivistic math instruction for diverse learners. *Learning Disabilities Research & Practice, 11,* 147–156.

Mercer, C.D., Lane, H.B., Jordan, L., Allsopp, D.H., & Eisele, M.R. (1996). Empowering teachers and students with instructional choices in inclusive settings. *Remedial and Special Education, 17,* 226–236.

Mercer, C.D., & Mercer, A.R. (2001). *Teaching students with learning problems* (6th ed.). Upper Saddle River, NJ: Merrill/Prentice Hall.

Miller, S.P., & Mercer, C.D. (1997). Educational aspects of mathematics disabilities. *Journal of Learning Disabilities, 30*(1), 47–56.

Minskoff, E.H. (1994). *Workplace Social Skills Training Manual.* Fishersville, VA: Woodrow Wilson Rehabilitation Center.

Minskoff, E.H. (1998). Sam Kirk: The man who made special education special. *Learning Disabilities Research & Practice, 13*(1), 15–21.

Minskoff, E.H., & DeMoss, S. (1994). Workplace social skills and individuals with learning disabilities. *Journal of Vocational Rehabilitation, 4*(2), 113–121.

Minskoff, E.H., Minskoff, J.G., & Allsopp, D. (2001). *A systematic model for curriculum-based assessment and intervention for postsecondary students with mild disabilities* (Final Report). Harrisonburg, VA: James Madison University, Department of Special Education.

National Council of Teachers of Mathematics. (2000). *Principles and standards.* Retrieved December 10, 2001, from http://www.nctm.org/standards.

Ohanian, S. (1999). *One size fits few: The folly of educational standards.* Portsmouth, NH: Heinemann.

Pauk, W. (1997). *How to study in college (6th ed.).* Boston: Houghton Mifflin.

Rettig, M.D., & Canady, R.L. (1998). High failure rates in required mathematics courses: Can a modified block schedule be part of the cure? *NASSP Bulletin, 82*(596), 56–65.

Richeck, M., Caldwell, J., Jennings, J., & Lerner, J. (1996). *Reading problems: Assessment and teaching strategies.* Upper Saddle River, NJ: Prentice Hall.

Rivera, D.P., & Smith, D.D. (1997). *Teaching students with learning and behavior problems* (3rd ed.). Needham Heights, MA: Allyn & Bacon.

Ruzic, R. (n.d.). *Lessons for everyone: How students with reading-related learning disabilities survive and excel in college courses with heavy reading requirements.* Paper presented at American Educational Research Association, Seattle, April, 2001. Retrieved December 20, 2001, from http://www.cast.org/udl/index.cfm?i-1540.

Sabornie, E.J., & deBettencourt, L.U. (1997). *Teaching students with mild disabilities at the secondary level.* Upper Saddle River, NJ: Prentice Hall.

Santos, K.E., & Rettig, M.D. (1999). Going on the block: Meeting the needs of students with disabilities in high school with block scheduling. *Teaching Exceptional Children, 31*(3), 54–59.

Schumaker, J.B., Denton, P., & Deshler, D.D. (1984). *The learning strategies curriculum: The paraphrasing strategy.* Lawrence: Institute for Research on Learning Disabilities, University of Kansas.

Sexton, M., Harris, K.R., & Graham, S. (1998). Self-regulated strategy development and the writing process: Effects on essay writing and attributes. *Exceptional Children, 64*(3), 295–311.

Stanovich, K.E. (1986). Matthew effects in reading: Some consequences of individual differences in the acquisition of literacy. *Reading Research Quarterly, 21,* 360–406.

Strichart, S.S., Mangrum, C.T., & Iannuzzi, P. (1998). *Teaching study skills and strategies to students with learning disabilities, Attention Deficit Disorder, and special needs* (2nd ed.). Needham Heights, MA: Allyn & Bacon.

Swanson, H.L. (1999). Instructional components that predict treatment outcomes for students with learning disabilities: Support for a combined strategy and direct instruction model. *Learning Disabilities Research and Practice, 14*(3), 129–140.

Swanson, S., & Howell, C. (1996). Test anxiety in adolescents with learning disabilities and behavior disorders. *Exceptional Children, 62*(5), 389–398.

Tarver, S.G., Hallahan, D.P., Kaufman, J.M., & Ball, D.W. (1976). Verbal rehearsal and selective attention in children with learning disabilities: A developmental lag. *Journal of Experimental Child Psychology, 22,* 375–385.

Thurlow, M.L., Elliott, J.I., & Ysseldyke, J.E. (1998). *Testing students with disabilities: Practical strategies for complying with district and state requirements.* Thousand Oaks, CA: Corwin Press.

Torgesen, J.K. (1982). The learning disabled child as an inactive learner: Educational implications. *Topics in Learning and Learning Disabilities, 2*(1), 45–52.

Vacca, R.T., & Vacca, J.L. (2002). *Content area reading: Literacy and learning across the curriculum.* Needham Heights, MA: Allyn & Bacon.

Vaughn, S., Bos, C.S., & Schumm, J.S. (1997). *Teaching mainstreamed, diverse, and at-risk students in the general education classroom.* Needham Heights, MA: Allyn & Bacon.

Vaughn, S., Gersten, R., & Chard, D.J. (2000). The underlying message in LD intervention research: Findings from research syntheses. *Exceptional Children, 67*(1), 99–114.

Virginia Department of Education. (1997). *Guidelines for participation in the Standards of Learning Assessment.* Richmond: Author.

Virginia Standards of Learning Assessments. (1998). *Sample items for end-of-course tests.* Richmond: Commonwealth of Virginia Department of Education.

Wagner, M. (1991). *Dropouts with disabilities: What do we know? What can we do?* Menlo Park, CA: SRI International.

Woodcock, R.W., McGraw, K.S., & Mather, N. (2001). *Woodcock-Johnson III: Tests of achievement.* Itasca, IL: Riverside Publishing.

Appendix A

Active Learner
Student Questionnaire

Active Learner Student Questionnaire

Name: _____ Date: _____

The purpose of this questionnaire is to help you to understand your learning strengths and areas of difficulty so that you can work on improving those areas in which you have difficulties.

Read each statement and then write:
Y for **yes** if it always applies to you
S for **sometimes** if it applies to you sometimes
N for **no** if it never applies to you

ORGANIZATION

Time management

_____ I don't use a planner or calendar.

_____ I don't keep track of tests and assignments.

_____ I have trouble getting to class.

_____ I have difficulty setting goals.

Materials management

_____ I don't keep a separate notebook for each class.

_____ I forget to bring things I need to class.

_____ I forget to bring home things that I need for studying or for homework.

TEST TAKING

_____ I get extremely nervous when I take a test.

_____ I have difficulty completing tests on time.

_____ I don't read directions or questions carefully.

_____ I have difficulty understanding multiple-choice questions.

_____ I have difficulty with true/false tests.

_____ I have difficulty with essay tests.

_____ During a test, I have difficulty remembering what I studied.

Academic Success Strategies for Adolescents with Learning Disabilities and ADHD
by Esther Minskoff and David Allsopp
©2003 Paul H. Brookes Publishing Co.

STUDY SKILLS

_____ I find it hard to start studying.

_____ I can't stay focused when I study.

_____ I'm easily distracted by things that happen around me when I study.

_____ I have difficulty studying from my notes.

_____ I have difficulty studying from books.

_____ I don't know how to organize information from books and notes.

_____ I have difficulty remembering information for tests.

NOTETAKING

_____ I can't write down everything the teacher says because the teacher talks too fast.

_____ The notes that I take are disorganized and hard to understand.

_____ I have trouble taking notes from a taped lecture.

_____ The notes I take when I read don't help me.

_____ I have difficulty taking notes because I get distracted.

READING

Vocabulary

_____ I have difficulty understanding difficult words that I read.

_____ I forget vocabulary words I learn.

Comprehension

_____ I have difficulty getting the overall ideas when I read material for my classes.

_____ I have difficulty understanding the main idea when I read.

_____ I have difficulty understanding the details when I read.

_____ I have difficulty understanding stories that I read.

_____ I read slowly.

_____ I have difficulty understanding what I read from the computer screen.

_____ I don't usually use aids to help me read.

Academic Success Strategies for Adolescents with Learning Disabilities and ADHD
by Esther Minskoff and David Allsopp
©2003 Paul H. Brookes Publishing Co.

WRITING

Mechanics

_____ I have difficulty spelling.

_____ I have difficulty using correct capitalization.

_____ I have difficulty using commas correctly.

_____ I have difficulty using colons and semicolons correctly.

_____ I have difficulty writing good sentences.

_____ I have difficulty proofreading for spelling, punctuation, capitalization, and sentences.

Composition

_____ I have difficulty writing paragraphs.

_____ I have difficulty finding the words to say what I mean.

_____ I have difficulty organizing my ideas when I write stories.

_____ I have difficulty organizing my ideas when I write research papers and essays.

_____ I have difficulty writing introductions and conclusions.

_____ I have difficulty finding information when I write research papers and essays.

_____ I have difficulty keeping to the topic.

_____ I have difficulty proofreading to see if my writing makes sense.

MATHEMATICS

Foundational math skills

_____ I have difficulty calculating answers to problems with whole numbers or fractions (addition, subtraction, multiplication, division).

_____ I have difficulty deciding the place value of digits in a number (e.g., that the 7 in the number 33,700 means seven hundreds).

_____ I have difficulty determining greater than, less than, and equal to when comparing numbers.

_____ I have difficulty solving word or story problems with whole numbers or fractions.

Academic Success Strategies for Adolescents with Learning Disabilities and ADHD
by Esther Minskoff and David Allsopp
©2003 Paul H. Brookes Publishing Co.

Pre-algebra and beginning algebra

_____ I have difficulty using the commutative property, 25 + 49 = 49 + 25, to help me calculate or solve problems.

_____ I have difficulty using the associative property, (2 x 45) x 12 = 2 x (45 x 12), to help me calculate or solve problems.

_____ I have difficulty using the distributive property, 8(7 + 6) = 8 x 7 + 8 x 6, to help me calculate or solve problems.

_____ I have difficulty solving problems using order of operations (e.g., problems that have more than one operation sign: 3 + 5 x 6 – 2 ÷ 5).

_____ I have difficulty adding positive and negative numbers.

_____ I have difficulty determining square roots of numbers.

_____ I have difficulty solving one-variable algebra equations.

_____ I have difficulty solving algebra word or story problems.

ADVANCED THINKING

_____ I have difficulty organizing information sequentially.

_____ I have difficulty comparing and contrasting ideas.

_____ I have difficulty understanding how information is organized into categories.

_____ I have difficulty determining cause-and-effect relationships.

_____ I have difficulty with problem solving.

Academic Success Strategies for Adolescents with Learning Disabilities and ADHD
by Esther Minskoff and David Allsopp
©2003 Paul H. Brookes Publishing Co.

Active Learner
Teacher Questionnaire

Active Learner Teacher Questionnaire

Student's name: _____ Date: _____

Teacher's name: _____

The purpose of this questionnaire is to help you identify the learning strengths and areas of difficulty for a particular student so that you can use strategies to help the student improve those areas of difficulty.

Read each statement and then write:
Y for **yes** if it always applies to the student
S for **sometimes** if it applies sometimes
N for **no** if it never applies to the student
DK for **don't know.**

ORGANIZATION

Time management

_____ Doesn't use a planner or calendar

_____ Doesn't keep track of tests and assignments

_____ Has trouble getting to class

_____ Has difficulty setting goals

Materials management

_____ Doesn't keep a separate notebook for each class

_____ Forgets to bring things needed to class

_____ Forgets to bring home things needed for studying or for homework

TEST TAKING

_____ Gets extremely nervous when taking a test

_____ Has difficulty completing tests on time

_____ Doesn't read directions or questions carefully

_____ Has difficulty understanding multiple-choice questions

_____ Has difficulty with true/false tests

_____ Has difficulty with essay tests

_____ During a test, has difficulty remembering what he or she studied

Academic Success Strategies for Adolescents with Learning Disabilities and ADHD
by Esther Minskoff and David Allsopp
©2003 Paul H. Brookes Publishing Co.

STUDY SKILLS

_____ Finds it hard to start studying

_____ Can't stay focused when studying

_____ Easily distracted by things that happen when he or she studies

_____ Has difficulty studying from notes

_____ Has difficulty studying from books

_____ Doesn't know how to organize information from books and notes

_____ Has difficulty remembering information for tests

NOTETAKING

_____ Doesn't write down everything you say

_____ Notes are disorganized and hard to understand

_____ Has trouble taking notes from a taped lecture

_____ Notes from reading material are poor

_____ Has difficulty taking notes because he or she gets distracted

READING

Vocabulary

_____ Has difficulty understanding difficult words that he or she reads

_____ Forgets vocabulary words that were learned

Comprehension

_____ Has difficulty getting the overall ideas from reading material for classes

_____ Has difficulty understanding the main idea from reading material

_____ Has difficulty understanding the details from reading material

_____ Has difficulty understanding stories that he or she reads

_____ Reads slowly

_____ Has difficulty understanding what he or she reads from the computer screen

_____ Doesn't usually use aids to help with reading

Academic Success Strategies for Adolescents with Learning Disabilities and ADHD
by Esther Minskoff and David Allsopp
©2003 Paul H. Brookes Publishing Co.

WRITING

Mechanics

_____ Has difficulty with spelling

_____ Has difficulty using correct capitalization

_____ Has difficulty using commas correctly

_____ Has difficulty using colons and semicolons correctly

_____ Has difficulty writing good sentences

_____ Has difficulty proofreading for spelling, punctuation, capitalization, and sentences

Composition

_____ Has difficulty writing paragraphs

_____ Has difficulty finding the words to say what he or she means

_____ Has difficulty organizing ideas when writing stories

_____ Has difficulty organizing ideas when writing research papers and essays

_____ Has difficulty writing introductions and conclusions

_____ Has difficulty finding information when writing research papers and essays

_____ Has difficulty keeping to the topic

_____ Has difficulty proofreading to see if his or her writing makes sense

MATHEMATICS

Foundational math skills

_____ Has difficulty calculating answers to problems with whole number operations or fractions (addition, subtraction, multiplication, division)

_____ Has difficulty deciding the place value of digits in a number (e.g., that the 7 in the number 33,700 means seven hundreds)

_____ Has difficulty determining greater than, less than, and equal to when comparing numbers

_____ Has difficulty solving word or story problems with whole numbers or fractions

Academic Success Strategies for Adolescents with Learning Disabilities and ADHD
by Esther Minskoff and David Allsopp
©2003 Paul H. Brookes Publishing Co.

Pre-algebra and beginning algebra

_____ Has difficulty using the commutative property, 25 + 49 = 49 + 25, to help calculate or solve problems

_____ Has difficulty using the associative property, (2 x 45) x 12 = 2 x (45 x 12), to help calculate or solve problems

_____ Has difficulty using the distributive property, 8(7 + 6) = 8 x 7 + 8 x 6, to help calculate or solve problems

_____ Has difficulty solving problems using order of operations (e.g., problems that have more than one operation sign: 3 + 5 x 6 − 2 ÷ 5)

_____ Has difficulty adding positive and negative numbers

_____ Has difficulty determining square roots of numbers

_____ Has difficulty solving one-variable algebra equations

_____ Has difficulty solving algebra word or story problems

ADVANCED THINKING

_____ Has difficulty organizing information sequentially

_____ Has difficulty comparing and contrasting ideas

_____ Has difficulty understanding how information is organized into categories

_____ Has difficulty determining cause-and-effect relationships

_____ Has difficulty with problem solving

Academic Success Strategies for Adolescents with Learning Disabilities and ADHD
by Esther Minskoff and David Allsopp
©2003 Paul H. Brookes Publishing Co.

Appendix C

Active Learner Approach Questionnaire Items and Corresponding Strategies

ORGANIZATION

Time Management

I don't use a planner or a calendar.	Planners
I don't keep track of tests and assignments.	3C
I have trouble getting to class.	LIST
I have difficulty setting goals.	TAP-D

Materials Management

I don't keep a separate notebook for each class.	BAND
I forget to bring things I need to class.	CLASH
I forget to bring home things that I need for studying or for homework.	ADAPT

TEST TAKING

I get extremely nervous when I take a test.	BRAVE
I have difficulty completing tests on time.	FLEAS
I don't read directions or questions carefully.	RAINS
I have difficulty understanding multiple-choice questions.	CRAM
I have difficulty with true/false tests.	SQUID
I have difficulty with essay tests.	RULE-WE
During a test, I have difficulty remembering what I studied.	SPORT

STUDY SKILLS

I find it hard to start studying.	CHECK
I can't stay focused when I study.	S2 TOP
I'm easily distracted by things that happen around me when I study.	PATS
I have difficulty studying from my notes.	R 3 HI
I have difficulty studying from books.	CON AIR
I don't know how to organize information from books and notes.	WORRY
I have difficulty remembering information for tests.	BREAK

NOTETAKING

I can't write down everything the teacher says because the teacher talks too fast.	I SWAM

The notes that I take are disorganized and hard to understand.	CORNELL METHOD
I have trouble taking notes from a taped lecture.	PP 123
The notes I take when I read don't help me.	SCROL
I have difficulty taking notes because I get distracted.	TASSEL

READING

Vocabulary

I have difficulty understanding difficult words that I read.	So We Go C
I forget vocabulary words I learn.	IF IT FITS

Comprehension

I have difficulty getting the overall ideas when I read material for my classes.	BCDE
I have difficulty understanding the main idea when I read.	RAP-Q
I have difficulty understanding the details when I read.	Ask 5 W's & 1 H & Answer
I have difficulty understanding stories that I read.	SPORE
I read slowly.	WARF
I have difficulty understanding what I read from the computer screen.	RUD PC
I don't usually use aids to help me read.	PASTE

WRITING

Mechanics

I have difficulty spelling.	We See Dark Light
I have difficulty using correct capitalization.	PACKED
I have difficulty using commas correctly.	AS I WAIT
I have difficulty using colons and semicolons correctly.	LSLT
I have difficulty writing good sentences.	CC-CIA
I have difficulty proofreading for spelling, punctuation, capitalization, and sentences.	SCOPE

Composition

I have difficulty writing paragraphs.	IBC
I have difficulty finding the words to say what I mean.	SAT
I have difficulty organizing my ideas when I write stories.	SPORE
I have difficulty organizing my ideas when I write research papers and essays.	POWER
I have difficulty writing introductions and conclusions.	OSWALD
I have difficulty finding information when I write research papers and essays.	TB NAIL
I have difficulty keeping to the topic.	TREE
I have difficulty proofreading to see if my writing makes sense.	FAST

MATHEMATICS

Foundational Math Skills

I have difficulty calculating answers to problems with whole numbers or fractions (addition, subtraction, multiplication, division).	DRAW FOR BASIC MATH
I have difficulty deciding the place value of digits in a number (e.g., that the 7 in the number 33,700 means seven hundreds).	FIND
I have difficulty determining greater than, less than, and equal to when comparing numbers.	SPIES
I have difficulty solving word or story problems with whole numbers or fractions.	FASTDRAW FOR BASIC MATH

Pre-algebra and Beginning Algebra

I have difficulty using the commutative property, $25 + 49 = 49 + 25$, to help me calculate or solve problems.	COMAS
I have difficulty using the associative property, $(2 \times 45) \times 12 = 2 \times (45 \times 12)$, to help me calculate or solve problems.	ASSOC
I have difficulty using the distributive property, $8(7 + 6) = 8 \times 7 + 8 \times 6$, to help me calculate or solve problems.	DIST

I have difficulty solving problems using order of operations (e.g., problems that have more than one operations sign: $3 + 5 \times 6 - 2 \div 5$).	ORDER
I have difficulty adding positive and negative numbers.	ADD
I have difficulty determining square roots of numbers.	ROOT-IT
I have difficulty solving one-variable algebra equations.	DRAW FOR ALGEBRA
I have difficulty solving algebra word or story problems.	FASTDRAW FOR ALGEBRA

ADVANCED THINKING

I have difficulty organizing information sequentially.	1st STOP
I have difficulty comparing and contrasting ideas.	LID
I have difficulty understanding how information is organized into categories.	CANDY
I have difficulty determining cause-and-effect relationships.	IFF 2
I have difficulty problem solving.	SOLVED

Student–Teacher
Agreement to Use the
Active Learner Approach

Student–Teacher Agreement
to Use the Active Learner Approach

The Active Learner Approach can provide useful tools for helping students achieve success in their classes. It takes the commitment and hard work of both students and teachers for the Active Learner Approach to work. This agreement emphasizes the importance of students and teachers working as a team! Your signature affirms your willingness to do everything you can to make this team effort a success.

Student

I understand how learning strategies can help me achieve success with my classes. I also understand that in order for learning strategies to be helpful to me, I need to work hard and take an active role in my learning. I will take learning strategies seriously, including listening while my teacher teaches each strategy, asking questions when I have them, enthusiastically participating in all learning activities, and completing all assignments. I understand my teacher will also work hard to ensure that the learning experiences provided me match my learning needs, including doing his or her best to help me select the best strategies for me, teaching each strategy in an effective way, and assisting me as I use strategies to meet the demands of my classes.

_____   _____

Student signature   Date

Teacher

I understand that I play a very important part in helping my student master learning strategies. I have ensured that my student understands the purpose of learning strategies and how learning strategies can be a useful tool for academic success. I have also provided my student a general overview of the process we will use for learning strategy instruction. I will do my best to help my student select strategies that meet his or her particular learning needs and to work with his or her classroom teachers to ensure that the strategy matches specific course demands. I also will carefully plan and teach each strategy in ways that are beneficial to my student. I know that my student should be an active participant in this teaching/learning process, and I agree to ask for feedback as we work together to teach and learn each strategy.

_____   _____

Teacher signature   Date

Academic Success Strategies for Adolescents with Learning Disabilities and ADHD
by Esther Minskoff and David Allsopp
©2003 Paul H. Brookes Publishing Co.

Index